VALUES AND ETHICS IN M

FOUNDATIONS OF MENTAL HEALTH PRACTICE

The Foundations of Mental Health Practice series offers a fresh approach to the field of mental health by exploring key areas and issues in mental health from a social, psychological and a biological perspective. Taking a multidisciplinary approach, the series is aimed at students and practitioners across the people professions, including student nurses, social workers, occupational therapists, psychiatrists, counsellors and psychologists.

Series editors:

Thurstine Basset worked as a community worker and social worker before becoming involved in mental health training and education in the 1980s. He is Director of Basset Consultancy Ltd and has experience of working with a number of universities, statutory and voluntary mental health organisations, service user and carer groups. He has published widely across the fields of mental health training and education. In collaboration with Theo Stickley, he is a co-editor of *Learning about Mental Health Practice* (2008). He is also an editor of the *Journal of Mental Health Training, Education and Practice*.

Theo Stickley is Associate Professor of Mental Health Nursing at the University of Nottingham. He has authored and edited many books and journal articles about mental health. Each represents his interest in promoting a fair, just and genuinely caring way in which to think about and deliver mental health care. His area of research is promoting mental health through participatory arts and he advocates a creative approach to care delivery.

Available now:

Working with Dual Diagnosis: A Psychosocial Perspective by Darren Hill, William J. Penson and Divine Charura
From Psychiatric Patient to Citizen Revisited by Liz Sayce
Models of Mental Health by Gavin Davidson, Jim Campbell, Ciaran Shannon and Ciaran Mulholland
Values and Ethics in Mental Health: An Exploration for Practice by Alastair Morgan, Anne Felton, Bill (K.W.M.) Fulford, Jayasree Kalathil and Gemma Stacey

VALUES AND ETHICS IN MENTAL HEALTH

An Exploration for Practice

ALASTAIR MORGAN
ANNE FELTON
BILL (K.W.M.) FULFORD
JAYASREE KALATHIL
AND
GEMMA STACEY

First published 2016 by
PALGRAVE

Palgrave in the UK is an imprint of Macmillan Publishers Limited, registered in England, company number 785998, of 4 Crinan Street, London, N1 9XW.

Palgrave Macmillan in the US is a division of St Martin's Press LLC, 175 Fifth Avenue, New York, NY 10010.

Palgrave is a global imprint of the above companies and is represented throughout the world.

Palgrave® and Macmillan® are registered trademarks in the United States, the United Kingdom, Europe and other countries.

ISBN 978–1–137–38258–0

This book is printed on paper suitable for recycling and made from fully managed and sustained forest sources. Logging, pulping and manufacturing processes are expected to conform to the environmental regulations of the country of origin.

A catalogue record for this book is available from the British Library.

A catalog record for this book is available from the Library of Congress.

Library of Congress Cataloging-in-Publication Data

Felton, Anne.
  Values and ethics in mental health : an exploration for practice / Anne Felton and [four others].
    pages cm
  Summary: "This book equips readers with a sound understanding of the value-base of mental health care and provides them with the skills and knowledge to demystify complex values in decision-making in order to reach outcomes which are focused on the needs of service users. Engaging case examples and exercises link theory and practice throughout" — Provided by publisher.
    ISBN 978–1–137–38258–0 (paperback)
  1. Psychiatric ethics.   2. Mental health services—Moral and ethical aspects.
    RC455.2.E8F45 2015
    174.2'9689—dc23

2015023903

Printed in China

Contents

List of Boxes, Figures and Tables

BOXES

FIGURES

TABLES

Acknowledgements

The authors and publishers would like to thank the Sainsbury Centre for Mental Health and the authors for Exercise 3.1, based on Woodbridge and Fulford, *"Whose Values?" A Workbook for Values-based Practice in Mental Health Care* (2004); Cambridge University Press and the authors for Sally Coombs' story, based on "Recovery in Schizophrenia: A Values Wake-up Call" in Fulford et al. *Essential Values-based Practice* (2012); The New Economics Foundation for Figure 5.1 from Slay and Stephens, *Co-production in Mental Health: A Literature Review* (2013); Wiley Publishers, Kim Woodbridge-Dodd and the editors for Figure 3.1 from Fulford and Woodridge, "Practising Ethically: Values-Based Practice and Ethics – Working Together to Support Person-centred and Multidisciplinary Mental Health Care" in Stickley and Basset, *Learning about Mental Health Practice* (2008).

The National Institute for Mental Health England no longer exists but we are grateful to Antony Sheehan as the Chief Executive at the time for his initiative in setting up the NIMHE Values Project Group. We are grateful also to Piers Allott as the Chair of the Group and to all the Group members for their contributions to developing the NIMHE Values Framework (see Box 4.1).

The 3 Keys programme was funded by the UK's Department of Health. We are grateful to all those involved in the project group (as listed in the 3 Keys report) and in the consultation. We are grateful also to members of the Bristol Group working on the pilot implementation project: Yvonne Anderson, Lu Duhig, Bill Fulford, Julie Hankin, Joanna Hicks, Justine Keeble, Martin Hember, Sylvia Matthews, Michael O'Neill and Richard Shaw.

We would like to thank the members of the Critical Values Based Practice Network, based in Nottingham, for invaluable discussions and support that have contributed towards the ideas expressed in this book; and also Dr R. Srivatsan (Anveshi Research Centre for Women's Studies, Hyderabad, India) and Dr Shubha Ranganathan (Department of Liberal Arts, IIT, Hyderabad, India) for comments on earlier drafts of Chapter 6.

Notes on Contributors

Alastair Morgan is a Senior Lecturer in the School of Nursing, Midwifery and Social Work at the University of Manchester. He is a critical theorist with a particular interest in the first generation of the Frankfurt School. Alastair has published widely on topics in critical theory, psychiatry and ethical issues in mental health practice. He is the editor of a collection entitled *Being Human: Reflections on Mental Distress in Society*, published by PCCS Books in 2008. He is the author of *Adorno's Concept of Life*, published by Bloomsbury in 2007.

Anne Felton is an Assistant Professor in Mental Health at the School of Health Sciences, University of Nottingham. She led the development and delivery of a series of modules on person-centred nursing care for an undergraduate nursing course. Anne has been involved in a number of projects working in partnership with service users to enable their participation in nurse education. Her research interests include risk, recovery, social inclusion and shared decision making. Anne has published in the field of therapeutic risk taking, social inclusion and service user involvement in education. She has undertaken a PhD exploring tensions in mental health practice relating to supporting choice and enforcing control.

Bill (K.W.M.) Fulford is a Fellow of St Catherine's College and Member of the Philosophy Faculty, University of Oxford, and Emeritus Professor of Philosophy and Mental Health, University of Warwick Medical School. His previous posts include Honorary Consultant Psychiatrist, University of Oxford, and Special Adviser for Values-Based Practice in the Department of Health, UK. He is Director of the recently launched Collaborating Centre for Values-based Practice at St Catherine's College. His *Essential Values-based Practice* (2012), co-authored with Ed Peile, is the launch volume for a new series from Cambridge University Press on values-based medicine.

Jayasree Kalathil has a background in critical humanities and cultural studies, and runs Survivor Research, a virtual collective of mental health user/survivor researchers and activists. She has published book chapters, reports and papers on representations and narratives of madness, especially in relation to race, gender, recovery, peer support and human rights. A children's book exploring madness, *The Sackclothman*, was published in 2009 and translated into two languages. Jayasree was a co-chair of the Social Perspectives Network and edited *Open Mind* magazine (2010–12). She is currently co-editing a special issue of *Philosophy, Psychiatry & Psychology* on user/survivor research and co-production, and a book on racialisation, human rights and mental health.

Gemma Stacey qualified as a mental health nurse in 2004 after completing the undergraduate Master of Nursing programme at the University of Nottingham. She went on to work for the Nottinghamshire Healthcare Trust in a range of recovery oriented community servicers. In 2006, Gemma began a part-time research post at the University of Nottingham which involved managing an action research project exploring service user involvement in the assessment of student nurses in practice (SUSA). She has gone on to implement and evaluate a range of educational initiatives centred on lived experience. This complements Gemma's doctoral research interest in the socialisation of student nurses and the educational factors which influence the development, maintenance and expression of person-centred values. She is the leader of the Critical Values Based Practice Network, which conducts research into this area and had an explicit focus on the perception and influence of power and hierarchy amongst professional groups. Gemma is currently employed as an Assistant Professor in Mental Health in the School of Health Sciences at the University of Nottingham, where she is the Deputy Lead for Graduate Entry Nursing.

List of Abbreviations

BPD	Borderline Personality Disorder
DALY	Disability Adjusted Life Year
DSM-5	Diagnostic and Statistical Manual of Mental Disorders (5th edn)
GCMH	Grand Challenges in Global Mental Health
ISL	Inquiry into the Schizophrenia Label
MCA	Mental Capacity Act
mhGAP	Mental Health Gap Action Programme
NHS	National Health Service
NICE	National Institute for Health and Care Excellence
NIMH	National Institute of Mental Health
NIMHE	National Institute for Mental Health England
NOS	National Occupational Standards for Mental Health
NSUN	National Service User Network
QALY	Quality Adjusted Life Year
RCT	randomised controlled trial
STR	support, time and recovery
UNCRPD	UN Convention on the Rights of Persons with Disabilities
VBP	values-based practice
WRAP	Wellness and Recovery Action Planning

1 | Ethics and values in mental health practice

Chapter Summary

This chapter will:

- Introduce the importance of ethical thinking and ethical questions for mental health practice.
- Show the need for values and values-based practice as a complement to ethical thinking.
- Emphasise the plurality and diversity of values, and the aim of balanced decision making where values are in conflict.
- Discuss the context of power, in which both ethics and values operate.
- Raise the question of what it means to put people who use services at the centre of values-based practice.
- Raise issues about narratives and how they are presented in this book.

Ethics in mental health practice

Any person involved in the mental health system, either as a practitioner or as a recipient of care and support (although the two are not mutually exclusive), immediately realises that mental health care raises significant and important ethical questions and dilemmas. Working in mental health care and psychiatry raises questions that are central components of ethical and philosophical deliberation. Radden writes that:

> "Conceptions of rationality, personhood and autonomy, the preeminent philo-sophical ideas and ideals grounding modern-day liberal and humanistic societies such as ours, also frame our understanding of mental disorder and rationales for its social, clinical and legal treatment" (Radden, 2004: 3).

Questions of what it means to reason, what it means to be a person and how we can determine our own lives are raised acutely when we work with or experience states of mental distress. Jamison (2011) has written of how experiencing mental distress inevitably raises larger questions of identity, meaning and one's place in society. These questions of meaning cannot be separated from the experience of distress itself as this experience is intrinsically bound up with identity, personhood and our position in society.

Ethical questions in mental health care, though, relate not only to questions of identity, meaning and culture, but also to how people who experience mental distress are treated and how we can justify that treatment. Mental health care remains the one area of health care where people can be treated against their will, even if they have capacity to understand the treatment (Department of Health, 2008). What right do mental health practitioners have to enforce treatment, label distress in medical terms and determine how people live their lives, often on the basis of imprecise formulations of risk and dangerousness (Szmukler and Holloway, 2000)? These questions are vital, inescapable and not open to easy answers.

One central way of trying to respond to these dilemmas is by taking a traditional biomedical approach. This approach emphasises the necessity of familiarising the reader with ethical theories and then offering a framework or guide for thinking through ethical dilemmas (such as the principlist approach offered by Beauchamp (1999) and Beauchamp and Childress (2012)). This approach to mental health ethics is vitally important and we begin our book in this relatively familiar territory by exploring four approaches to ethical theory: deontology, consequentialism, virtue ethics and narrative ethics. We then consider the four principles of biomedical ethics and their application in mental health contexts. However, it rapidly becomes clear that a pure approach focussing on ethics alone is not sufficient for equipping the modern mental health practitioner to work in the complex arena of twenty-first-century mental health care.

Our book is labelled as an exploration for mental health practice, as we focus on exploring key dilemmas and skills for working with values and ethics in everyday practice. We are not claiming to present an exhaustive survey of all of the issues that are concerned with ethics and professionalism in mental health care. There are many texts which approach the topic of ethics in mental health practice with different lenses and perspectives (for example, Dickenson and Fulford (2000), Banks and Gallagher (2009), Bloch et al. (2009), Barker (2011), Sadler et al. (2015)).

The distinctive contribution that this volume provides is a focus on the integration of working with ethics and values, and an approach to working with contested values, alongside an emphasis on recovery-focussed and compassionate care. The focus on ethics needs to be supplemented with a consideration of how ethical principles fit into the wider context of values, and how awareness of values can lead the practitioner to a more informed and inclusive mental health practice. Therefore, we also emphasise a skills-based approach to developing practitioners who are competent at working with a variety of values and negotiating conflicts in an inclusive manner.

However, working with values and ethics is not sufficient. Any considered analysis of the issues of working ethically and in a values-based manner has to take account of the context of power in mental health practice. All mental health policy acknowledges the need to put the recipient of services at the heart of any health care. The current mantra in UK health services is "no decision about me without me" (Coulter and Collins, 2011). However, there is little detailed consideration of how this can happen, given a context in which there remain significant inequalities of power and in which the voice of service users is often not heard and occasionally is silenced. Integral to this volume is an emphasis on narratives, the concept of recovery, and the question of diversity and minority voices. We cannot consider a truly values-based ethical practice without negotiating the inequalities of power that exist within mental health care and in wider society.

Throughout this volume we use the terms "service user", "survivor" and "person experiencing distress/mental health problems" to refer to actual people with lived experience of mental distress. There can be no one language that is universally acceptable to this group of people and each term has its own usefulness and problems. We have, however, used terms that have come from the mental health user/survivor movement and avoided terms that represent purely medical ways of thinking about mental distress (Kalathil and Perry, 2014).

Why values?

As we have already noted, this book opens in the relatively familiar territory of ethics for mental health practice, but by the end of Chapter 2, it is clear that ethical decision making needs to be embedded within the wider context of values. With the broadening of horizons to include values within ethical thinking, there is an emphasis on three key elements to values which are central to mental health practice. We set these out briefly here and return to them in more detail in Chapters 3 and 4.

First, there is an emphasis on the plurality of values. Values are various and multiple; they incorporate ethical principles but are wider than ethics, even including the importance of aesthetic questions, as we emphasise in this volume. The variety of values means that we cannot necessarily, and even should not, try to prescribe correct or appropriate values beyond broad frameworks of shared values (such as the four principles, discussed in Chapters 2 and 3). Working with values means the ability to negotiate this plurality, and being aware of the multiplicity of values is a key skill in values-based practice. This emphasis on plurality means that the idea of a correct answer to dilemmas or conflicts over values is a "category mistake". We cannot attempt to resolve all conflicts over values but, instead, learn to work sensitively with the variety of values and how to make balanced judgements in individual situations.

The diversity of values leads us to a second key point: conflicts over values are the norm, rather than the exception. This is particularly the case in mental health care, but is more the case than we often think in the rest of health care. Furthermore, we cannot look to something called "evidence" to solve these issues of values in practice. Indeed, we suggest that scientific advances in mental health care actually increase choices, rather than giving definitive solutions and, therefore, might increase the scope for values to come into play, as our choices are determined by our values.

Stating that values-in-conflict is the norm is not a pessimistic statement. Reflecting on the diversity of values might inevitably lead us to the idea that conflict will arise. However, a central skill for values-based practice is working with conflicting values, without suppressing them. We emphasise here the important concept of "dissensus" as a way of acknowledging the diversity of values without suppressing different perspectives. This emphasis on plurality and conflict should not obscure the possibility of shared values. Indeed, although conflicts in values are the norm, if we develop the skills to raise awareness of fundamental values, we can often uncover a shared framework for our values that enables us to build collaborative care.

This emphasis on awareness brings us to the third key addition that the move towards values brings to ethical debates and practice in mental health care. Values are pervasive but often pushed into the background. Indeed, we often only become aware of them when something goes wrong or breaks down (what is known as the "squeaky wheel" principle in Values Based Practice (VBP); see Chapter 4, see also Fulford et al. (2012)). Throughout this book, we explore the principles and practice of making values explicit, which initially is often concerned with bringing one's own values and those of others into the open. Awareness of values is the key skill to working in an inclusive and collaborative manner.

Power and diversity

Supplementing ethical theories and the principles approach with an awareness of values and the skills needed to work with diversity should enable us, in an ideal world, to work towards inclusive mental health practice. However, we do not work or live in an ideal world. Significantly, we work in an environment marked by differentials of power which impact negatively on those of us who receive mental health services. It is easy to pay "lip service" to the necessity of inclusion, but those in receipt of mental health services still often feel disempowered and excluded from the key decisions that are taken about their care (NICE, 2012). The emphasis on recovery principles and social inclusion in recent mental health care internationally has contributed to attempts to transform mental health services into more user-oriented care. These developments have been driven by service users themselves organising politically and therapeutically (Campbell, 2009). However, as we consider in Chapters 8 and 9, even the act of diagnosis in mental health care is an act replete with problems of power, labelling and discrimination.

Any approach to ethics and values in mental health practice has to take account of the key issue of power and how the voices of service users have largely been ignored in the history of psychiatry. We consider this history of silencing of personal narratives in detail in Chapter 6. We need to take account of the manner in which notions of madness have often intersected with notions of race and gender to oppress and discriminate against subjugated groups in society. Throughout this book, we return to the issues of power, and discrimination against minority and subjugated groups in order to take full account of the challenges of inclusive practice. Awareness of values needs to be supplemented with an awareness of power relationships and what we can do to try to introduce more participatory decision making at the heart of mental health care. This is the basis of recovery practice as we describe in the final chapters of the book.

Our narrative in writing this book

Writing this book was a challenge. As co-authors, we all differ in our values, experience and background. This is particularly the case when it comes to our experience of mental health practice and care, either as practitioners, academics, or those who have lived experience of mental distress. In many ways, writing the book was an experiential form of learning what it means to be aware of different values and different voices.

An instructive example of this learning relates to the structure of the book. As part of the structure, the reader will regularly be directed to reflective examples and "case studies" aimed at developing skills for thinking through "real life" scenarios.

However, we questioned ourselves about the writing of these reflective examples. For some of us, the writing of "case studies" and examples had become "second nature". We were used to producing these narratives to aid with education, and did not consider the ethics of (re)presenting another person's narrative, of having the audacity to write a fictional story as if it were "real life". For others, however, the routine appropriation and re-interpretation of our narratives in the form of medical notes, case studies and "data" was a real issue tied to questions of agency, voice and self-determination. This was especially true for those of us who had engaged with psychiatry and mental health care as "service users". In a fascinating article, Costa et al. (2012) have written of the way that snippets of service users' lives have been "colonised" and presented as "truths" for the education of mental health professionals. They call for the "recovery" of their stories and control over their own narratives. In Chapter 6, we foreground this key issue of how power operates in creating knowledge about mental distress and the role of survivor narratives in this.

In presenting "real life" examples in this book, we have used both extracts from personal narratives and autobiographies, as well as traditional case studies. We have tried to make this clear in the text. Case studies are usually based on one or more "real life" practice examples but have been fictionalised in characterisation and context. In that sense, they are both real and imaginary, and the hope is that we will encourage debate and critical practice about real dilemmas in mental health care. Extracts from personal narratives and autobiographies have been appropriately referenced and, where relevant (especially in the case of online narratives), permission to use these extracts has been sought from authors. In both cases, however, there is always the danger of the "narrative" being turned into a "specimen" for examination. Indeed, there is a long history of this kind of clinical display of cases in psychiatry (Hustvedt, 2011).

The philosopher Judith Butler has written eloquently about the processes involved in giving an account of oneself (Butler, 2005). She writes that any account that a person gives of themselves always takes place in a context. I am giving an account to someone, or some institution or discipline, and this produces a problem of power – particularly a problem of what is allowed to be said within that context. A narrative is also a form of address, a way of giving account or being held to account within power relations. This understanding is further complicated when other people's "narratives" are presented for academic purposes, and we ask you to reflect on this intrinsic issue with the case studies you use as you progress through the book.

The structure of the book

Having acknowledged these intrinsic difficulties, this book is inherently one that calls for active reading. We often ask you to write as you read, and to engage in exercises and activities. The book opens (Chapter 2) by outlining ethical theories for mental health practice. Each of the ethical theories discussed, however, faces the problem of content: how do ethical theories provide answers to the complex dilemmas posed in mental health practice?

Chapter 3 thus extends Chapter 2 into the wider world of values showing how, besides ethics, we need a complete tool kit of ways of working with values in health care. Chapter 4 then introduces one of these tools in more detail, values-based practice. Being primarily skills-based, one strength of values-based practice is that it is, literally, a practice – it supports balanced decision making between conflicting values in individual clinical situations. An important limitation of values-based practice, however, is that it does not address issues of power. Hence, Chapter 5 introduces concepts of power and their importance across a range of issues in mental health. Chapters 6 and 7 explore values and power in relation to two key areas: personal narratives of madness and distress, and their role in psychiatric scholarship (Chapter 6); and issues of autonomy and coercion (Chapter 7). An often neglected yet crucial area of operation of values and power in mental health is the whole question of how (and by whom) a mental health issue is understood. Chapters 8 and 9 tackle this issue head on, looking first at some of the theoretical debates about mental distress, values and labelling (Chapter 8); and then at recent work on and exemplars of values-based assessment in practice (Chapter 9). In Chapter 10, we draw together the ethics-plus-values theme of the book around "recovery". This, in turn, leads on in Chapter 11 to the centrality in mental health care of the identity of unique individual persons.

Working with ethics and values in mental health practice is a process of self-exploration before it is a process of therapeutic working. We hope that the book provides you with the skills and resources with which to negotiate the dilemmas inherent in mental health care, and the opportunity to fashion new and more inclusive responses to these dilemmas.

REFERENCES

Banks, S. and Gallagher, A. (2009) *Ethics in Professional Life: Virtues for Health*. Basingstoke: Palgrave Macmillan.

Barker, P. (ed.) (2011) *Mental Health Ethics: The Human Context*. London: Routledge.

Beauchamp, T. (1999) "The Philosophical Basis of Psychiatric Ethics", in Bloch, S., Chodoff, P. and Green, S. (eds) *Psychiatric Ethics*. Oxford: Oxford University Press.

Beauchamp, T. and Childress, J. (2012) *Principles of Biomedical Ethics*. Oxford: Oxford University Press.

Bloch, S. and Green, S.A. (eds) (2009) *Psychiatric Ethics* (4th edn). Oxford: Oxford University Press.

Butler, J. (2005) *Giving an Account of Oneself*. New York: Fordham University Press.

Campbell, P. (2009) "The Service User/Survivor Movement", in Reynolds, J., Muston, R., Heller, T., Leach, J., McCormick, M., Wallcraft, J. and Walsh, M. (eds) *Mental Health Still Matters*. Palgrave: Milton Keynes.

Costa, L., Voronka, J., Landry, D., Reid, J., McFarlane, B., Reville, D. and Church, K. (2012) "Recovering our stories: A small act of resistance", *Studies in Social Justice*, 6(1): 85–101.

Coulter, A. and Collins, A. (2011) *Making Shared Decision Making a Reality. No Decision About Me, Without Me*. London: Kings Fund.

Department of Health (2008) *Mental Health Act 1983 Code of Practice – 2008 Revision*. London: TSO.

Dickenson, D. and Fulford, K.W.M. (2000) *In Two Minds: A Casebook of Psychiatric Ethics*. Oxford: Oxford University Press.

Fulford, K.W.M., Peile, E. and Carroll, H. (2012) *Essential Values-based Practice: Clinical Stories Linking Science with People*. Cambridge: Cambridge University Press.

Hustvedt, A. (2011) *Medical Muses: Hysteria in Nineteenth-Century Paris*. London: Blooomsbury.

Jamison, K. (2011) *An Unquiet Mind. A Memoir of Moods and Madness*. Surrey: Picador.

Kalathil, J. and Perry, E. (2014) "Speaking about ourselves", *Mental Health Today*, May–June: 21.

NICE (National Institute for Health Care Excellence) (2012) *Service User Experience in Adult Mental Health – NICE Guidance on Improving the Experience of Care for People using Adult NHS Mental Health Services*. British Psychological Society and Royal College of Psychiatrists, National Collaborating Centre for Mental Health.

Radden, J. (ed.) (2004) *The Philosophy of Psychiatry. A Companion*. Oxford: Oxford University Press.

Sadler, J.Z., van Staden, W. and Fulford, K.W.M. (eds) (2015) *The Oxford Handbook of Psychiatric Ethics*. Oxford: Oxford University Press.

Szmukler, G. and Holloway, F. (2000) "Reform of the Mental Health Act. Health or safety?", *British Journal of Psychiatry*, 177: 196–200.

FOUNDATIONS OF
MENTAL
HEALTH
PRACTICE

2 | Ethics: Theories, contexts and questions

Chapter Summary

This chapter will:

- Introduce the reader to definitions of ethics and moral philosophy and consider the centrality of ethical questions to mental health practice.
- Outline four core theoretical approaches for mental health practice – deontology, consequentialism, virtue ethics and the ethics of care.
- These four theoretical approaches are each related to practical examples of mental health care and practice.
- Outline the four principles of biomedical ethics – autonomy, beneficence, non-maleficence and justice.
- Offer case examples and exercises to deepen and enhance learning and reflection.

Definitions of morality and ethics

Ethics is the inquiry into how we should live. As Singer (1994) writes, ethics raises a series of key questions for the individual. How do I know whether my actions are right or wrong? How do I know whether the goals that I seek in my life are good or bad? What is the relationship between my life as an individual and my life as a member of a larger community? Is there such a thing as a good life, or a good society? Are there a set of principles that can guide my practice to produce good intentions or outcomes?

As these questions indicate, ethics is simultaneously both extremely abstract and urgently practical (Adorno, 2000). This can cause frustration in the student of ethical thinking. We come to ethics because we want answers and guidance on how to act, and we come away with confusion and more questions. In his lectures on moral philosophy, the German philosopher T.W. Adorno introduces his first lecture by telling his students that he will not be providing any easy answers by using a metaphor of "stones and bread":

> "So if I am going to throw stones at your head, if you will allow the expression, it will be better if I say so at the outset than for me to leave you under the illusion that I will be distributing bread" (Adorno, 2000: 2)

This is perhaps not the easiest way of engaging your audience! However, there is a truth contained in this warning. Ethics holds out the promise of a set of straightforward answers to key questions of life but anyone who has studied ethics, in even a minor way, knows that simple answers to the questions we posed earlier are hard to find.

In many ways, this is as it should be, as the situations we face in mental health practice are complex and challenging. How do we balance our respect for the individual person with our responsibility to the wider community? What right do I have to coerce people to take their medication? What does it mean to be a good mental health worker? There are no straightforward answers to these questions, and there may be a legitimately diverse set of responses to them. As Alasdair MacIntyre has written, this may lead us to the conclusion that these ethical conflicts are "interminable and unsettlable" (MacIntyre, 1982: 210). We may throw our hands in the air and claim that if there are no answers, then there is no point asking the questions. Whether we like it or not, anyone working in mental health care faces ethical choices and decisions on a daily basis, and the purpose of thinking about ethics is to be clear about our choices and take responsibility for the decisions we make.

When discussing issues of ethics in mental health care, confusion arises through the use of the terms "morality" and "ethics". Why do we have these two terms, and what do they mean? Are they just different terms for the same thing, or are they related but distinct?

Moral philosophy is broadly concerned with a discussion of the fundamental justification of conceptions of right and wrong. Raphael describes it as the inquiry into "norms or values, about ideas of right and wrong, good and bad, what should and what should not be done" (Raphael, 1981: 8). This inquiry is not initially concerned with creating a set of principles to guide action, but aims to uncover and explore different fundamental justifications for actions. Moral philosophy so defined is in contrast to ethics, which is concerned with delineating a system of values and principles to guide action (Barker, 2011).

A second distinction can be drawn by arguing that morality more commonly refers to the collective norms of a society and culture, whereas ethics is concerned with individual action.

Beauchamp (1999: 25) defines morality as concerned with "shared social conventions about right and wrong that form a stable communal consensus", although we might argue that this confuses morality with notions of custom and habit. In contrast, when we think of codes of ethics, we think of precepts that apply to and guide individual action.

These distinctions are useful but can be confusing as the terms "morality" and "ethics" are often used synonymously in the literature or interchangeably (Raphael, 1981). In this book, by ethics we mean both the inquiry into the foundations of moral action and the practical application of such ideas. As befits a book concerned with practical ethics, we will focus on the practical application of ethical theories, but that does not mean there are always straightforward answers.

Four theoretical approaches to ethics

In the next section of the chapter, we will outline four theoretical approaches to ethics that can guide mental health practice. In each case, we will provide a possible example of legal and practical approaches that apply to each of these theories. The first two theories to be discussed are deontology and consequentialism. These theories are both act-based; they assess the morality of actions. The third theory we will briefly explore is virtue ethics, which is broadly character-based; it assesses the morality of character, rather than action. The fourth theory we will examine is the ethics of care, which assesses morality based on the quality of relationships, rather than actions or character alone. All of these theories have important implications for mental health practice.

Deontology

Deontological theories assess the morality of actions based on the motivation for action. When we try to assess the moral worth of an action, we ask the person why they chose to act in a particular way, and we assess the worth of the action based on this motivation. However, not all motivation is legitimate, but only motivations that accord with a duty to act in a good way. Therefore, these moral theories are usually termed "duty-based" theories (Beauchamp, 1999). When assessing the morality of an action, we need to assess whether that action was in accordance with a morally good motivation.

The most important philosopher to lay out a notion of duty-based moral theory was the German philosopher Immanuel Kant (1724–1804). Kant's term for a morally good motivation is a "good will", and he advocates a rigorous moral approach where there is nothing that can be called good "without qualification, except a good will" (Kant, 1985: 395). The problem for deontology is how to give an account of such a "good will". What are its components, and how does it direct me to act?

Kant's characteristic response to such a question is to inquire into the core conditions for the possibility of moral action. What are the core characteristics of any action that would count as moral regardless of social context or individual desires (O'Neill, 1994)? Therefore, deontology is an abstract approach, which attempts to provide a universal underpinning for all moral actions. Kant provides this universal underpinning for all moral actions through a statement which he terms the "categorical imperative" (Kant, 1985). The categorical imperative states that every moral action must be "universalisable". This means that, if I act in a particular situation, then my action can only be assessed as morally good if I would expect everyone else to act in the same way if a similar situation were to arise. This seems a very "bare" ethical principle, one that does not give a great deal of content to the ethical decision, but Kant tries to reformulate this core imperative in different ways (O'Neill, 1994).

An important reformulation of the categorical imperative is that we should always treat other people as "ends rather than means" (Kant, 1985). By this, Kant means that each person has the autonomy to decide their own future, that this needs to be respected and that we cannot override this autonomy of choice and treat someone as a means to a larger goal by ignoring their right to have control over their own life.

Example: Deontology and the Mental Capacity Act

The Mental Capacity Act (2005) legally follows a deontological framework. Its core principle is that people are presumed to have the capacity to act as autonomous people capable of making their own decisions. When working with any individual, we must respect their right to make decisions for themselves, including the right to make an "unwise decision" (MCA, 2005). Although we may think that it is in someone's best interests to act in a particular way, we cannot override their right to make decisions about their own life unless they lack the capacity to make those decisions. The universal rule that is applied in this case is that you have the right to make your own choices and decisions in life. We will be referring in more detail to ethical issues concerning the Mental Capacity Act in Chapter 7.

This causes issues in mental health care and practice as the Mental Health Act (1983/2007) allows us to interfere with a person's right to make choices about their life if we feel they are putting themselves at risk or other people at risk due to their mental illness. The Act does not take a purely rights-based approach but balances rights of individuals with possible consequences and outcomes to try and achieve an overall good, which might involve overriding a person's immediate wishes.

The question of risk is often framed in neutral terms but the evaluation of risk involves ethical questions and values-based judgements that we will consider throughout the book.

Criticisms of deontology   The core problem for deontological theories is how to give content to such an abstract set of principles. We may think it is an important moral insight to try to make our actions as universal as possible and to treat people with respect for their autonomy but, often, deontology cannot solve issues of ethical conflict.

Reflective exercise 2.1

- What do you do when duties conflict? A person you are working with discloses to you that they have been involved in some compulsive shoplifting, and asks you to help them but keep this information confidential. Should you follow a duty of confidentiality, or a duty of reporting a crime to the police? It is difficult to decide between duties by following a deontological approach.

- What if following a rule produces undesirable consequences? One common deontological rule is that you should always tell the truth. However, sometimes telling the truth can cause distressing or unwanted consequences. You are working with a person who is an in-patient on an acute psychiatric ward under Section 3 of the Mental Health Act. You are aware that the psychiatric team are considering withdrawing the person's right to accompanied leave due to his increased mental distress. The person is talking to you about how much they are looking forward to their leave the next day. Do you tell them the truth about the current situation?

Consequentialism and utilitarianism

In contrast to deontological theories, consequentialist theories judge the morality of actions based on the consequences or outcomes of those actions. Therefore, an action is good if it has good consequences. The key task for consequentialist theories is to determine the nature of good outcomes (Thornton, 2007). The classical answer to the question of what constitutes a good outcome is given by the ethical theory known as "utilitarianism". The classical utilitarian philosophy was expressed by the English philosopher Jeremy Bentham (1748–1832), who argued that any action that increases overall happiness in society is a good action. He defined happiness purely as the experience of pleasure and the avoidance of pain. Bentham writes that "pleasures, then, and the avoidance of pain are the ends which the legislator has in view" (Bentham, 2007: 2). Classical utilitarians believe that we can measure pleasures and that we can calculate the total sum of pleasures in society, and that public policy should be geared towards the increase in total pleasures within societies.

Classical utilitarianism: A modern example – Happiness and wellbeing   In recent years, there has been a global movement to focus on happiness and wellbeing as a measure of population health, rather than simply focussing on financial measures (Cromby, 2011). This focus stems from a classically utilitarian position that the measure of a good society is a happy society and that the measure of happiness equates in a straightforward manner with asking people whether they feel good about their lives (Shaw and Taplin, 2007). In the UK, the Office for National Statistics now publishes regular reports documenting the happiness of the regions of the UK (Office for National Statistics, 2013) and public policy is guided by a focus on happiness and wellbeing. This approach stems from the work of the economist Richard Layard who is classically utilitarian in his approach, arguing that "it makes sense to define the good society as the happy society" (2011: 6).

Criticisms of consequentialist theories   There are many critiques of consequentialist theories. First, there is the question of how to define happiness. Classical utilitarianism equates happiness with pleasure. If someone feels happy, then it does not matter how they acquired their happiness, or what kind of happiness it is. We should not judge different kinds of pleasure. This sounds like a non-judgemental, egalitarian approach to moral theory. However, we could imagine a society in which people were given drugs to be happy and, for many of us, this artificial happiness compromises the notion of being happy. This is exactly the thought experiment carried out in Huxley's novel *Brave New World*, where the population are prescribed a drug called soma to keep them happy (Huxley, 2007). Some have questioned the over-prescription of anti-depressant medication as a form of artificial happiness (Kramer, 1997; Moncrieff, 2008). The worry about types of pleasure led the philosopher John Stuart Mill to criticise earlier utilitarians for relying too much on the idea that all pleasures are equal. Mill famously wrote that it was better to be "Socrates dissatisfied than a pig satisfied", arguing that utilitarians needed to pay attention to the quality of pleasures as well as to the amount of pleasures in society (Mill, 2004).

Many people have criticised the possibility of measuring and calculating experiences such as happiness (McMahon, 2006; Bruckner, 2010). When we come to try and give content to a notion of happiness, it can be much more complex and nuanced than we may first think. The economist Amartya Sen has argued that we should not focus narrowly on a notion of happiness but, instead, focus on human capabilities (Sen, 2001). The capabilities approach prioritises an awareness of the social conditions that enable people to live full lives according to their capabilities and choices, and thus draws attention to the social context within which a fulfilled life can thrive, rather than the individualist approach of traditional utilitarian theories (Sen, 2001).

Finally, prioritising overall population happiness can mean that individual rights are downplayed, as consequentialist theories may attempt to maximise happiness at large and ignore minority interests and rights. Consequentialist theories presume a neutral, value-free background, and ignore issues of power and how minority groups may be oppressed and discriminated against within society.

Reflective exercise 2.2

In his book *What Money Can't Buy* (2012), the American political philosopher Michael Sandel outlines a series of examples from daily life which raise ethical questions. Many of the examples revolve around consequentialist theories where cash incentives are given to people to maximise overall population happiness. Think about these examples and whether you think they are right or wrong, and why.

- Giving cash incentives for women who have an addiction to drugs to be sterilised.
- Giving people cash incentives to lose weight.
- Giving children cash incentives to improve their school grades.
- For more discussion on these issues, see the series of podcasts available at: http://www.bbc.co.uk/podcasts/series/r4sandel

---

Virtue ethics

Virtue ethics has its origins in Ancient Greek philosophy, particularly the work of Aristotle (Beauchamp, 1999; Thornton, 2007). Rather than focussing on the morality of actions, Aristotle's philosophy focuses on the morality of a character, and what it means to be a flourishing human being and a good citizen in society. The goal of morality is what Aristotle terms *eudaimonia* (Aristotle, 2009). This word is often translated as "happiness", but Aristotle means something far more encompassing and it is more accurate to term this a kind of flourishing. This is not only an individual flourishing, but is also a flourishing as part of a wider community. We cannot cultivate virtues only for ourselves, but we live a virtuous life by actively partaking in a wider society. In virtue ethics, moral questions take on a larger character than in act-based theories such as consequentialism and deontology (Allmark, 2013). Virtue theorists ask the following three questions:

- What makes a good character?
- What makes a good citizen?
- What makes a good society?

These questions are interrelated and interdependent – it is difficult to answer one question without inquiring into the others, as a virtuous character can only be expressed as a citizen within a good society.

Example: Virtue and the six "Cs" of compassionate care

One element of virtue ethics that is emphasised in current health care practice is the development of particular character traits or personality traits that can add up to a virtuous character (Plant and Narayanasamy, 2013). For example, the current strategy for nursing in England entitled *Compassion in Practice* follows a virtue-based approach (Department of Health, 2012). The document lays out six "Cs" which are six modern day nursing virtues: care, compassion, competence, communication, courage and commitment. A good nurse will be a nurse who, in her daily life, is skilful at expressing these virtuous acts. The problem with this approach can be that it ignores the wider culture of the "good" society. The virtues of a good practitioner are embedded within the virtues of a good society, so these virtues must mesh with, or be expressed through a wider culture. The Francis report (2013) into the breakdown in care at a Mid-Staffordshire hospital pointed to one serious problem with care being the issue of an institutional culture that was focussed on the business of the system, rather than the interests of patients. Therefore, before they can truly flourish, the six "Cs" as virtues need to be placed within a larger culture of the National Health Service (NHS) and of society more widely. There is evidence to suggest that the creation of individual virtues is a complicated process in health care, because students are often socialised into negative patterns of behaviour even before qualifying (Stacey et al., 2011; Curtis et al., 2012). Furthermore, this institutional culture is also reflected within a larger society where there is a problem with attitudes to ageing and to elder abuse (O'Keefe et al., 2007).

This focus on individual virtues ignores wider institutional structures that embed negative attitudes within society. In 1998, David "Rocky" Bennett died while being restrained in a mental health facility in the UK. The inquiry into his death concluded that a range of discriminatory judgements and responses to Bennett resulted in his eventual death (Norfolk, Suffolk and Cambridgeshire Strategic Health Authority, 2003). Singh (2007) has listed these failures as inadequate diagnoses, incoherent treatment, lack of consultation with family members and an inability to respond adequately to issues of racist abuse in in-patient facilities. Institutional racism provides a set of in-built attitudes and facilitates a "thoughtless" response that results from stereotyping and institutionalised forms of responding to minority ethnic groups (Macpherson, 1999). Singh (2007) writes of a catalogue of cases of psychiatric care in which this institutional racism is prevalent.

Critiques of virtue ethics   Virtue ethics can therefore be criticised for being too formal, and for ignoring particularities of context (Holland, 2010). It can be viewed as a constraining and limiting approach to ethics, as a true virtue ethics approach is based on the idea that there is a goal for human life as a whole, and a virtuous life is lived towards that "end". However, the issue is that people may have very different goals for their lives, so it is not straightforward to live always as part of a virtuous society. When asked what it means to live a morally good life, the philosopher Hegel wrote:

> "When a father inquired about the best method of educating his son in ethical conduct a Pythagorean replied: 'Make him a citizen of a state with good laws'."
> (Hegel, cited in Singer, 1994: 134).

This approach suggests that it is straightforward to be always in agreement with what the good society will look like and how to be a good, active member of such a society. The philosopher Alasdair MacIntyre (1982) has acknowledged that it is difficult in modern, secular societies to define an overall "good" for society which would embed the idea of a series of virtues for a good life. Nevertheless, in his book *After Virtue* he does outline a threefold approach for a modern conception of virtue which has been highly influential. MacIntyre (1982) suggests three core elements to modern virtue ethics.

- First, he argues for an account of the "goods" internal to a particular practice. In mental health care, we would try and articulate the set of virtues that are necessary for virtuous mental health practice. An example of this would be the capable practitioner framework that was developed by the Centre for Mental Health to try and articulate the capabilities needed for mental health practice (SCMH, 2001).
- Second, he argues for a notion of a "narrative unity" of a life. The virtues must, in some sense, fit into the narrative of a person's life as a whole – the virtues of mental health practice need to be integrated into the meaning of a person's identity.
- Third, the virtues must be embedded, in some sense, in the customs or moral traditions of a society. Pilgrim et al. (2010) examine the virtue of trust in health care and explore how trust is an implicit necessity for health care practice; they also observe that it needs to be embedded within societies, rather than simply treated as an individual attribute. It is this requirement of societal values that MacIntyre recognises is difficult in modern, pluralist societies. This can be a particular issue, as we have seen, when power differentials exist within society that impact on the kinds of "values" that hold sway and define the kind of society in which we live.

Exercise 2.1

As a mental health practitioner, you commence your career believing that it is important that the service user is the "expert on their experience" (Bird et al., 2011). You are working on an in-patient unit and you help someone to construct their own care plan, but the response to your work is that you are too "involved" with the person and that you need to maintain your professional distance.

You can access a video clip for this exercise at http://www.patientvoices.org.uk/ flv/0365pv384.htm, from the digital stories project developed at the University of Nottingham (Stacey and Hardy, 2011).

- How would you respond to the ward manager in this case?
- How easy do you think it would be to maintain your beliefs in practice?

Narrative ethics/ethics of care

The final theoretical framework is the notion of an ethics of care. This approach to ethics focuses on the attributes of ethical relationships. What are the qualities that exist within ethical relationships that are central to an ethical disposition (Noddings, 2012)? Ethical theorists emphasise qualities such as attentiveness, being with the person in distress and caring for the person. This work stems from feminist ethical theorists and, particularly, the ground-breaking work of the psychologist Carol Gilligan and her book *In a Different Voice* (2003). Gilligan argues in her book that traditional ethics, which focussed on abstract theorising about rights and outcomes, had a gendered aspect, as it represented elements of how masculinity had been constructed in Western societies. She argues that if we attend to girls and women's experiences of moral decision making, we arrive at a very different understanding of ethics, and particularly a different understanding of the idea of the self and of the idea of a moral action (Gilligan, 1986: 326).

We need to understand the self as related to others in terms of familial and personal commitments, rather than theorising an abstract, autonomous self, separate from all relationships. The moral self always exists in a situation, facing another person who is a particular individual with their own history and perspective (Blum, 1988). Moral decisions always spring from affective as well as cognitive motives, and we can only understand the right action within the context of a particular situation.

An ethics of care is often supplemented with a notion of narrative ethics. Kearney and Williams (1996: 29) emphasise the centrality of understanding stories as a way of providing "specific ways of imagining how the moral aspects of human behaviour may be linked with happiness/unhappiness". Narrative helps us to imagine particular lives and particular situations, and helps us to be concerned for "context sensitive" judgements in ethical life (Kearney and Williams, 1996). Wilks (2005) has written about how narrative approaches in social work practice provide a "powerful corrective" to more abstract ethical theorising (Wilks, 2005: 1252). Therefore, as Paulsen (2011) writes, a narrative ethicist focuses her attention on stories and meanings rather than on abstract theories of right and wrong.

Main features of ethics of care   The main features of an ethics of care are:

- a focus on relationships – a link here with the notion of relationship centred care in health care (Beach and Inui, 2006);
- the right action is understood only in its context – case-based reasoning, rather than principle-based reasoning (Beauchamp, 1999);
- prioritising the identity of the person, and understanding their identity;
- listening to the stories of the people for whom we care;

- emphasising the affective, rather than the cognitive, components of morality;
- focussing on the qualities of the caring relationship – such as caring, empathy, feeling with others and being sensitive to each other's feelings (Held, 2006).

❏ **Case example 2.1: Jasmine**

This case example invites you to reflect on how applying the different ethical principles to a particular situation does not necessarily result in clear cut answers. The case example is fictional and not based on any specific person, but nevertheless represents common dilemmas in current mental health practice.

Jasmine is a 39-year-old woman who has been admitted to a psychiatric ward under Section 3 of the Mental Health Act. She has a long history of admissions due to experiencing ideas that she has a special spiritual mission in life to communicate with nature by "living in the wild". When she becomes unwell, she leaves her accommodation and camps in parks and woods. She neglects her appearance and eats little, believing that "God will provide". She is offered anti-psychotic medication on the ward but she refuses this. Due to her lack of "insight" into her illness, the medical staff believe she needs medication and, although she is refusing medication, they choose to coerce her to take her medication. This approach is taken "in her own best interest" and to provide a better outcome for the future.

From a deontological perspective, she lacks the autonomy to make a decision because she is mentally unwell and experiencing delusional beliefs.

From a consequentialist perspective, we can act against her wishes, because the outcome will be better for her, even if currently she does not want medication.

From a virtue ethics perspective, we can focus on carrying out the forced injection in an ethical manner; as Armstrong (1999) writes, it is the manner in which the forced administration of medication takes place that affects the quality of experience. We can coerce the person, but in a virtuous way.

What difference would it make to focus on this case from the perspective of an ethics of care/narrative ethics?

- Can we listen to Jasmine's story and understand her perspectives?
- How could we attempt to understand her situation in relation to her context and her identity?
- How would you attempt to try and understand Jasmine's story from her perspective? What would be the key questions to ask here? Can we understand her identity and how she constructs the narrative of her life?
- What does being empathic and attentive to her needs mean here? Are there limits to an ethics of care when we are faced with the necessity of coercion?

Critiques of ethics of care/narrative ethics   An ethics of care has been criticised for a "disturbing lack of content" (Allmark, 1995: 20). It is too vague and unclear about how to act in particular situations and therefore cannot provide a moral guide to help us decide the right way to act. Allmark writes that the quality of caring is not ethically significant, as it is what we care about that is of ethical significance. He believes that the notion of "caring", per se, has no moral significance unless allied to a notion of what it is "good" to care about, so we may potentially "care" about the wrong things. Allmark argues that there could be a good torturer who is "sensitive" to a person's needs in order to be more skilled at torture. The torturer would use all the skills of caring to understand better how to produce an evil outcome. Therefore, the torturer becomes a highly skilled practitioner of torture through an understanding of the victim's needs, as he is then better able to deprive the victim of their needs. Allmark writes that you "need to be sensitive to people's needs in order to deprive them of them. What we care about is morally important, the fact that we care per se is not" (1995: 23).

However, if we attend to accounts of people who have been tortured, we hear that the process is one of dehumanising people; that in some manner the torturer must deny or suppress a common humanity or fellow feeling to be able to torture (Amery, 1980). Rather than using empathy as a tool to better hone a skill at torturing, the torturer must first deny a basic fellow feeling and turn the victim into something less than human. This suggests there is something morally significant about emotions such as empathy, and that they are not ethically neutral.

The idea of a narrative ethics has been criticised due to the question of what constitutes a narrative, and how this can be complicated in mental illness. Is it always easy to know your narrative or identity if you have an altered reality or a disturbed sense of your own identity (Thomas, 2008)? Therefore, we could argue that a person could be too mentally unwell at periods in their life to have a firm identity or story of their own life. However, such a critique has the danger of dismissing a person's experience. Thomas (2007) recommends that we have a more fluid and open notion of what it means to listen to or represent a narrative, rather than dismissing narrative completely. This is in accordance with notions of recovery that perceive identity as a fluid process that involves growth and incorporation of strange and unusual experiences into a developing, rather than fixed, narrative (SCIE, 2007).

There have recently been voices from within the survivor movement in mental health questioning the way in which survivor narratives are colonised, and taken out of context and used without respect for the initial formulation of a person's story. Costa et al. (2012) have written about a "disability tourism" in which narratives are displayed and used to support a variety of perspectives without regard to the context and situation in which a narrative is originally produced. Costa et al. (2012) write of a "consumption" of stories that fetishises a notion of "lived experience" without taking into account how narratives are produced within a social context and a mode of address; how a person is enabled to speak and permitted to speak. Controversially, however, the position held by Costa et al. has also been criticised for an inherent "value judgement" that prioritises narratives sharing the radical political agenda of the mainstream survivor movement above those tentatively telling their stories in more personally relevant ways (see Kalathil et al., 2013). These issues of personal narratives and the values, ethics and power relations that determine their worth or validity are discussed at length in Chapter 6.

The "four principles framework"

Beauchamp and Childress (2012) have proposed a series of principles that incorporate both duty-based and outcome-based ethics. These principles are a structure and guide for thinking, but they do not necessarily provide answers in each case – and, indeed, the principles may well conflict with each other in particular cases.

The first principle is *autonomy*: when a person has the capacity to make decisions, then they should be supported in the process and respected for their right to make decisions. Both duty-based and outcome-based theories respect autonomy, although outcome-based theories may override autonomy on occasions if the greater good requires. On paternalistic grounds, we might override someone's autonomy for the benefit of the wider community- or for the benefit of the person themselves (Breeze, 1998).

The second principle is *beneficence*: we should try in all instances to do the best for the people for whom we are caring. We have a duty to act for the best interests of the person with whom we are working. The principle of beneficence can support us when working as advocates for people to help them obtain the best care they need. However, it can also function as a way of acting in people's "best interests" against their expressed wishes, if we follow a paternalist approach (Roberts, 2004).

The third principle is *non-maleficence*: this incorporates the medical doctrine of, first, do no harm. We should always be wary of any action that causes harm to people. It is interesting that one of the key objectives in current strategy on mental health in the UK is to reduce avoidable harm caused to service users (Department of Health, 2011). The *No Health without Mental Health* strategy recognises that harm is often caused by services to service users, and aims to reduce avoidable harm caused by services (Department of Health, 2011). However, the question here is how to define "avoidable". For example, it is well evidenced that atypical antipsychotic medication causes weight gain and the possible development of type 2 diabetes (Lean and Pajonk, 2003). Following a strict principle of non-maleficence, this would mean that we would not prescribe this medication; however, we have to assess the risks and the benefits, so there is a conflict here between beneficence and non-maleficence.

The fourth principle is *justice*: all of our actions should be proportionate, and should provide equity of distribution and treatment in our care of individuals.

Exercise 2.2

Refer back to Case example 2.1 regarding Jasmine, and try and apply the four principles approach to Jasmine's case.

- Is it possible to respect all four principles when working with Jasmine?
- If not, which principle did you think had greater priority than the others and why?
- Did using the four principles approach help you more than using an ethics of care approach?

CONCLUSION

This chapter has introduced the reader to definitions of ethics and morality and considered the importance of ethics for mental health practice. The reader has been introduced to four core theoretical approaches to ethics in mental health care: deontology, consequentialism, virtue ethics and the ethics of care. Finally, the four principles of biomedical ethics have been outlined that bring together some of the core features of the different ethical theories.

Although this approach has been much criticised, it remains a widely used and provides a useful framework for thinking through ethical dilemmas in health care practice.

GLOSSARY OF KEY TERMS

Deontology – the theory that judges the morality of an action based on the motivation for the action.

Consequentialism – the theory that judges the morality of an action based on its outcome.

Utilitarianism – the theory that judges the morality of an action on the basis of whether it maximises pleasure and minimises pain.

Virtue ethics – ethical theories that focus on character virtues, and the virtues of living as a good citizen in a good society.

Ethics of care – ethical theories that focus on relationships, caring attributes, emotions and contexts as significant for moral theorising.

Narrative ethics – ethical theories that prioritise the meaning of narratives and reasoning about morality in relation to identities and stories.

FURTHER READING

Inside the ethics committee. Available at: http://www.bbc.co.uk/programmes/b007xbtd/episodes/guide

> This BBC radio programme often covers ethical issues in mental health care and is a good source for thinking practically about the principles outlined in this chapter.

All in the Mind. Available at: http://www.bbc.co.uk/programmes/b006qxx9

> This BBC radio programme covers mental health and psychology, and often considers ethical issues.

Michael Sandel – Public Philosopher. Available at: http://www.bbc.co.uk/podcasts/series/r4sandel

> A good series of programmes looking at practical ethical dilemmas from American philosopher Sandel.

REFERENCES

Adorno, T.W. (2000) *Problems of Moral Philosophy*, translated by Rodney Livingstone. Cambridge, UK: Polity Press.

Allmark, P. (1995) "Can there be an ethics of care?", *Journal of Medical Ethics*, 21(1): 19–24.

Allmark, P. (2013) "Virtue and austerity", *Nursing Philosophy*, 14(1): 45–52.

Amery, J. (1980) *At the Mind's Limits: Contemplations of a Survivor on Auschwitz and its Realities*, translated by Sidney Rosenfeld and Stella Rosenfeld. Bloomington and Indianapolis: Indiana University Press.

Aristotle (2009) *Nicomachean Ethics*, translated by David Ross. Oxford: Oxford University Press.

Armstrong, A. (1999) "Enforced medication and virtue ethics", *Journal of Psychiatric and Mental Health Nursing*, 6(4): 329–34.

Barker, P. (ed.) (2011) *Mental Health Ethics: The Human Context*. Oxon: Routledge.

Beach, M.C. and Inui, T. (2006) "Relationship-centered care. A constructive reframing", *Journal of General Internal Medicine*, 21(1 Suppl): S3–8.

Beauchamp, T. (1999) "The philosophical basis of psychiatric ethics", in Bloch, S., Chodoff, P. and Green, S. (eds) *Psychiatric Ethics*. Oxford: Oxford University Press.

Beauchamp, T. and Childress, J. (2012) *Principles of Biomedical Ethics*. Oxford: Oxford University Press.

Bentham, J. (2007) *An Introduction to the Principles of Morals and Legislation*. New York: Dover Publications.

Bird, V., Leamy, M., Le Boutillier, C., Williams, J. and Slade, M. (2011) *REFOCUS: Promoting Recovery in Community Mental Health Services*. London: Rethink.

Blum, L.A. (1988) "Gilligan and Kohlberg – implications for moral theory", *Ethics*, 98(3): 472–91.

Breeze, J. (1998) "Can paternalism be justified in mental health care?", *Journal of Advanced Nursing*, 28(2): 260–5.

Bruckner, P. (2010) *Perpetual Euphoria. On the Duty to be Happy*. Princeton: Princeton University Press.

Costa, L., Voronka, J., Landry, D., Reid, J., McFarlane, B., Reville, D. and Church, K. (2012) "Recovering our stories: A small act of resistance", *Studies in Social Justice*, 6(1): 85–101.

Cromby, J. (2011) "The greatest gift: Happiness, governance and psychology", *Social and Psychology Personality Compass*, 5(11): 840–52.

Curtis, K., Horton, K. and Smith, P. (2012) "Student nurse socialisation in compassionate practice: A grounded theory study", *Nurse Education Today*, 32(7): 790–5.

Department of Health (2011) *No Health without Mental Health: A Cross Government Mental Health Outcomes Strategy for People of All Ages*. Available at: https://www.gov.uk/government/uploads/system/uploads/attachment_data/file/213761/dh_124058.pdf (accessed 11 December 2013).

Department of Health (2012) *Compassion in Practice. Nursing, Midwifery and Care Staff: Our Vision and Strategy*. Available at: http://www.england.nhs.uk/wp-content/uploads/2012/12/compassion-in-practice.pdf (accessed 11 December 2013).

Francis, R. (2013) *Report of the Mid Staffordshire NHS Foundation Trust: Public Inquiry – Executive Summary*. London: TSO.

Gilligan, C. (1986) "Reply by Carol Gilligan", *Signs*, 11(2): 324–33.

Gilligan, C. (2003) *In a Different Voice: Psychological theory and Women's Development*. Cambridge, MA: Harvard University Press.

Held, V. (2006) *The Ethics of Care: Personal, Political and Global*. Oxford: Oxford University Press.

Holland, S. (2010) "Scepticism about the virtue ethics approach to nursing ethics", *Nursing Philosophy*, 11(3): 151–8.

Huxley, A. (2007) *Brave New World*. London: Vintage.

Kalathil J., Russo, J. and Shulkes, D. (2013) *Personal Narratives of Madness: Annotated Bibliography*. Available at: http://global.oup.com/booksites/content/9780199579563/narratives/ (accessed 29 May 2015).

Kant, I. (1985) *Foundations of the Metaphysics of Morals*, translated by Lewis White Beck (2nd edn). New York: Macmillan.

Kearney, R. and Williams, J. (1996) "Narrative and ethics", *Proceedings of the Aristotelian Society, Supplementary Papers*, 70: 47–61.

Kramer, P. (1997) *Listening to Prozac*. London: Penguin.

Layard, R. (2011) *Happiness: Lessons from a New Science* (2nd edn). London: Penguin.

Lean, M. and Pajonk, F.-G. (2003) "Patients on atypical anti-psychotic drugs. Another high-risk group for type 2 diabetes", *Diabetes Care*, 26(5): 1597–605.

MacIntyre, A. (1982) *After Virtue – A Study in Moral Theory*. London: Duckworth.

Macpherson, W. (1999) *The Stephen Lawrence Inquiry*. Available at: https://www.gov.uk/government/uploads/system/uploads/attachment_data/file/277111/4262.pdf (accessed 14 July 2015).

McMahon, D. (2006) *The Pursuit of Happiness. A History from the Greeks to the Present.* London: Penguin Books.

MCA (Mental Capacity Act) (2005) *Code of Practice.* London: TSO.

Mental Health Act (1983/2007) *Code of Practice.* London: TSO.

Mill, J.S. (2004) "Utilitarianism", in Mill, J.S. and Bentham, J. (2004) *Utilitarianism and Other Essays,* edited by Alan Ryan. London: Penguin.

Moncrieff, J. (2008) *The Myth of the Chemical Cure: A Critique of Psychiatric Drug Treatment.* Basingstoke: Palgrave Macmillan.

Noddings, N. (2012) "The language of care ethics", 40(4): 52–6.

Norfolk, Suffolk and Cambridgeshire Strategic Health Authority (2003) "Independent Inquiry into the Death of David Bennett". Norfolk, Suffolk and Cambridgeshire Strategic Health Authority.

O'Keefe, M., Hills, A., Doyle, M., McCreadie, C., Scholes, S., Constantine, R., Tinker, A., Manthorpe, J., Biggs, S. and Erens, B. (2007) *UK Study of Abuse and Neglect of Older People. Prevalence Survey Report.* King's College, London: National Centre for Social Research.

O'Neill, O. (1994) "Kantian Ethics", in Singer, P. (ed.) *A Companion to Ethics.* Oxford: Blackwell.

Office for National Statistics (2013) *Personal Well-being across the UK, 2012–13.* Available at: http://www.ons.gov.uk/ons/dcp171778_328486.pdf (accessed 10 December 2013).

Paulsen, J. (2011) "A narrative ethics of care", *Health Care Analysis,* 19(1): 28–40.

Pilgrim, D., Tomasini, F. and Vassilev, I. (2010) *Examining Trust in Health Care: A Multi-disciplinary Perspective.* Basingstoke: Palgrave Macmillan.

Plant, N. and Narayanasamy, A. (2013) "Ethical theories", in Stickley, T. and Wright, N. (eds) (2013) *Theories for Mental Health Nursing.* London: Sage.

Raphael, D.D. (1981) *Moral Philosophy.* Oxford: Oxford University Press.

Roberts, M. (2004) "Psychiatric Ethics: A critical introduction for mental health nurses", *Journal of Psychiatric and Mental Health Nursing,* 11(5): 583–8.

Sainsbury Centre for Mental Health (2001) *The Capable Practitioner – A Framework and List of the Practitioner Capabilities required to implement The National Service Framework for Mental Health.* Available at: http://www.centreformentalhealth.org.uk/pdfs/the_capable_practitioner.pdf (accessed 12 December 2013).

Sandel, M. (2012) *What Money Can't Buy: The Moral Limits of Markets.* London: Allen Lane.

Shaw, I. and Taplin, S. (2007) "Happiness and mental health policy: A sociological critique", *Journal of Mental Health,* 16(3): 359–73.

Sen, A. (2001) *Development as Freedom.* Oxford: Oxford University Press.

Singer, P. (ed.) (1994) *Ethics.* Oxford: Oxford University Press.

Singh, S. (2007) "Institutional racism in psychiatry: Lessons from inquiries", *Psychiatric Bulletin,* 31: 363–5.

SCIE (Social Care Institute for Excellence) (2007) *A Common Purpose: Recovery in Future Mental Health Services.* Available at: http://www.scie.org.uk/publications/positionpapers/pp08.pdf (accessed 29 May 2015).

Stacey, G. and Hardy, P. (2011) "Challenging the shock of reality through digital storytelling", *Nurse Education in Practice,* 11(2): 159–64.

Stacey, G., Johnston, K., Stickley, T. and Diamond, B. (2011) "How do nurses cope when values and practice conflict"?, *Nursing Times,* 107(5): 20–3.

Thomas, P. (2008) "Towards a critical perspective on 'narrative loss' in schizophrenia", in Morgan, A. (ed.) *Being Human. Reflections on Mental Distress in Society.* Ross-on-Wye: PCCS Books.

Thornton, T. (2007) *Essential Philosophy of Psychiatry.* Oxford: Oxford University Press.

Wilks, T. (2005) "Social work and narrative ethics", *British Journal of Social Work,* 35(8): 1249–64.

3 | Ethics and values: Developing a values toolkit

Chapter Summary

This chapter will:

- In Part I, discuss values.
- In Part II, discuss values in health care.

Part I Values:

- The variety of values.
- Foreground and background values.
- Shared values: Complex and conflicting.
- Values and clinical decision making.

Part II Values in health care:

- Values in the clinical encounter.
  - ◆ Person-*values*-centred practice.
  - ◆ Your values matter too.
- Ethics and clinical decision making.
- Introducing the values tool kit.

Building on the ideas about ethics we covered in Chapter 2, this chapter takes you through a number of brief exercises to explore the wider world of values. Part I of the chapter describes some of the main features of values that are important in health care. Part II then looks at how these features play out in practice in an episode from the story of a fictitious person whom we will call Sally Coombs, whose story is developed from several practice-based examples.

A key learning point from the chapter as a whole is that values include more than ethics. Ethical values are important in health care but so, too, are values of many other kinds. We will be looking at some of these other values in the first part of the chapter. Just as there are many different kinds of values in health care, so there is a variety of tools to help us work more effectively with them in our day-to-day practice. Again, the different kinds of ethics covered in Chapter 2 are important in the tool kit. But we need other tools as well. We will be introducing some of these other tools in the second part of the chapter and looking at one of them – values-based practice – in more detail in Chapter 4.

Part I – Values

The word "value" is very much part of everyday language, with values popping up everywhere you look. So, it might seem that a natural starting point for thinking about values in mental health would be to ask what this commonly-used word "values" really means.

Well, be warned: philosophers have been thinking about this question for two thousand years. If you want to read more about the philosophy of values, there are some suggestions in the Further Reading section at the end of this chapter. For now, though, we want to start in the "here and now" with a question about what values mean *to you*.

Exercise 3.1

This exercise is in two parts.

- First, write down three words (or very short phrases) that mean values to you.

Don't spend too long thinking about this. It is not a test that you can get right or wrong. The idea is to work quickly just writing down the first three words that come into your head. So, think of this as a kind of word association exercise.

- Second, compare what you have written down with others in your group; or if you are working on your own compare your list with the lists of words shown in Table 3.1

Note: it is really important to write down your own three words before comparing your list with others. Don't do the exercise just "in your head". Set your words down on paper, or use a computer; then, when you have *written or typed your own three words*, see how they compare with the words others have come up with.

LIST 1	LIST 2	LIST 3
☐ Core beliefs	☐ Concepts that govern ethics	☐ What you believe in
☐ Your perspective on the world	☐ Right and wrong	☐ Self-esteem
☐ Principles – cultural, individual	☐ Belief systems	☐ Principles
☐ Justice	☐ Ideals and priorities	☐ Integrity
☐ Anything that is valued	☐ Govern behaviour and decisions	☐ Openness/honesty
☐ Integral to being human	☐ Community health – individuals, society, culture	☐ Personal motivating force
☐ Quality of life	☐ Ideals	☐ Primary reference points
☐ Right to be heard	☐ Morals	☐ Ethics
☐ Social values	☐ Principles	☐ Virtues
☐ Self respect	☐ Standards	☐ Sharing
☐ Valuing neighbours	☐ Conscience	☐ Touchstones/bases
☐ Guiding you	☐ Fluid/changeable	☐ Willing to sacrifice for
☐ Core beliefs		☐ Self-interested tenets
		☐ Areas of negotiation in relationships

Table 3.1 Some of the wide variety of words that "mean values to me"

The variety of values

The first thing you will notice when you compare your list with those of others is the sheer variety of meanings that different people associate with the word "values". The lists in Table 3.1 are the words from three training workshops in values-based practice for people all of whom had backgrounds in health care. As you would expect, there are some shared responses; we come to the importance of shared values later in this chapter. But what stands out is the huge variety of ways in which people, even people from similar backgrounds, respond to that simple question about what values mean to them.

Having read Chapter 2, you will not be surprised to find ethical values included. The word "ethics" itself is there, together with other ethics-related words such as "principles", "virtues" and "standards". You may well have included words along these lines in your own three words. But ethical values such as these reflect general norms that apply to everyone, whereas the lists also include a number of responses that are *highly personal and individual* – "your perspective on the world", "what you believe in", "personal motivating force".

Again, we think of ethical values as relatively unchanging but, for some people, values are "fluid and changeable". Many values are positive – for example, "justice", "self-respect", "self-esteem", "integrity", "sharing" – but there are also negative values, some of which (such as "self-interested tenets") are, by most people's standards, *un*-ethical.

> **Reflection point:** *Having opened up our ideas about values, can you think of any other kinds of values that come into health care? Try this for yourself before reading on.*

There are many varieties of values of which you may have thought: the Finnish philosopher G.H. Von Wright, in his book *The Varieties of Goodness* (1963), written during his time as Professor of Philosophy in Cambridge, catalogued several hundred!

First, there are other important ethical values. You may well have thought of "best interests" and "autonomy", for example, as discussed in Chapter 2. But, among values important in health care, we should also include "preferences", "needs and wishes", and prudential values such as "care", "wisdom" and "foolishness". Positive values – "strengths", "resilience" and "resources" – tend to be neglected in health care, overshadowed as they can be by the negatives of "distress", "difficulties" and "disease", with which we are so often dealing. But strengths, as we will see in Chapter 9, are especially important in mental health as a key to recovery.

Another somewhat neglected but potentially important area of health care values is aesthetics. You might think of aesthetic values (such as beauty and ugliness) in connection only with areas of health care such as dermatology and cosmetic surgery. But, in mental health, there is a long history of user/survivor work around the use of art in (self-) recovery (see, for example, Spandler et al., 2007; Shingler, 2008). Aesthetics, including environment and design, has also been known to have a positive effect in mental health care settings (Daykin et. al., 2008); recent developments have shown the potential therapeutic role of aesthetics in areas of mental health ranging from addiction (Musalek, 2010) to dementia care (Hughes and Beatty, 2013).

A first feature of values important in health care is, thus, their sheer variety. The focus on ethical values in health care is understandable, with almost daily scandals about poor standards of practice. Ethical values, therefore, really *are* important. But so, too, is a wide variety of other values, individual and cultural, positive and negative, and including personal needs and preferences, prudential and aesthetic values, and numerous others. This is why, as we will see, we need a whole tool kit for working with values.

Foreground and background values

> **Reflection point:** *Take another look at the lists in Table 3.1. Most of the words will be different from the words you came up with. But are there any words on the lists with which you actively disagree? Is there anything on the lists to which you reacted with "But that's nothing to do with values!"*

Most people's response to this second take on the three words exercise is to say: "Well, yes, on reflection, although I didn't come up with such-and-such a word myself, I agree it's something to do with values". In other words, although initially we all identify three different three words, we find on reflection that we usually agree with everyone else's suggestions.

This second-take agreement is important in various ways for understanding how values come into health care. First, it shows very clearly the extent to which our values are, to a greater or lesser extent, *in the background rather than the foreground of our thinking*. Our first three words were at the forefront of our minds – this is why we wrote them down. But what we now see is that these three words were just the tip of a whole iceberg of meaning that was there all the time in the background. Kim Woodbridge-Dodd, who was the lead author for the first training manual in values-based practice (Woodbridge and Fulford, 2004) described values in this respect as being like the air we breathe – they are there all the time and essential but, by and large, not something of which we are fully aware.

Again, we will be coming to the clinical importance of this later. For now, though, the point is that it adds a further dimension of difficulty to the challenge of working with values in practice. Much discussion of ethical issues focusses on dilemmas where the values in question are all, more or less, very much in the foreground. This, in itself, can be challenging, as we saw from the examples in Chapter 2. In this chapter, we have now added to these ethical challenges the challenge of the variety of other values as we just outlined. But the further challenge of working with values in practice is that the relevant values may be in the background rather than the foreground and, hence, may not be taken into account at all. We will see later in this chapter that moving the values of users/survivors from the background to the foreground of clinical decision making is a key step towards person-centred care.

Shared values: Complex and conflicting

A second and equally important point arising from the second-take agreement on our "three word" exercise is that, for all their variety, many values are widely shared. "Quality of life", for example, appears only on List 1. But most (all?) of us would, on reflection, sign up to this as a shared value. Most of us, that is to say, would agree that quality of life is important. Other widely shared values in health care include those noted in Chapter 2: "autonomy" and "best interests".

It is no coincidence that these shared values are among the ethical values discussed in Chapter 2. Quality of life is what utilitarianism (based on pleasure) and Aristotelianism (based on flourishing) have in common. "Autonomy" and "best interests" (beneficence), similarly, were two of the four principles identified by Beauchamp and Childress: the other two principles, you will recall, were the further widely shared values of "non-maleficence" (first, do no harm) and "justice". It is *because* they are widely shared values that these are all contenders for the basis of ethical theories. For ethical theories, as we saw in Chapter 2, are about "how to live well". It is for similar reasons that these and other shared values figure prominently in professional codes of practice: they provide a shared basis for decisions about "how to practice well". We will see in Chapter 4 that shared values also have an important place in values-based decision making. For all these reasons, then, shared values are important in the values tool kit of health care.

Reflection point: *If we have these shared values, why is ethical decision making so difficult?*

At one level, it seems obvious that, if we can just agree on a shared set of values, everything else will fall into place. This, as we have just seen, is the idea behind the ethical theories discussed in Chapter 2. But the reason that ethical decision making remains so difficult is that the shared values on which our ethical theories are based are both *individually complex* and *jointly conflicting.*

We will be looking at the complex and conflicting nature of shared values in more detail in the second part of this chapter, when we come to how values play out in practice. But as features of shared values, they are evident already in our "three words" exercise. Thus, "quality of life" may, indeed, be a shared value. However, what exactly *counts as* a good quality of life will vary widely from one individual to the next or, indeed, from one situation to the next for the same individual (at different stages in their life, for instance). An important example of this is provided by people with serious disabilities. A natural expectation might be that people with disabilities experience a poor quality of life. This, indeed, is assumed by the widely adopted measure of health care utility: the QALY (more on QALYs later in this chapter). But the *actual* experience of people with disabilities may be of a very good quality of life, even to the point that disabilities (such as deafness) may actually be preferred (Tucker, 1998). Understanding the individual uniqueness of quality of life is key to recovery practice in mental health (see Chapter 10).

It is in this specific sense, then, that shared values are individually complex: they *mean different things to different people and in different contexts*; thus, they have to be carefully interpreted from case to case, rather than applied in an unthinking manner. This is important in values-based practice, as we will see in Chapter 4. But shared values, however interpreted in a given context, come with the further challenge that they *tend to be in conflict one with another*. This is why, as we saw in Chapter 2, utilitarians and Aristotelians remain at loggerheads over whether pleasure or flourishing is the "top" value. And the conflicting nature of shared values is evident, too, at a more practical level in health care. "Community health", for example, is another shared value that appears in Table 3.1, this time in List 2. But "community health" may be in conflict with "quality of life" (List 1) in contexts in which personal and community values diverge.

A recent example of this divergence was a high-profile dispute over measles vaccination. This took the form of a stand-off between, on the one hand, individual parents refusing to have their children vaccinated for measles because they wanted to protect them from potential side effects, and, on the other hand, the wider community interest in universal vaccination as the basis of the "herd immunity" required to prevent the spread of the disease (Hutchinson and Read, 2014). In terms of the four principles, then, this stand-off represented a conflict between individual parent's values of non-maleficence (first, do no harm) and the wider community's value of beneficence (the best interests of the group as a whole).

Such conflicts between values are not exceptions; rather, they are the norm. You have only to reflect for a moment on your own values to recognise the extent to which we spend our whole lives balancing the tensions between different needs, preferences, wishes, and so on within ourselves (between our short- and longer-term interests, for example) and between ourselves and other people. Values-based practice, as we will see, faces the complex and conflicting nature of values head-on.

Values and clinical decision making

Reflection point: *What do you think unites all the variety of values? In what sense are all these very different things, foreground and background, shared, complex and conflicting, "values"? Again, try thinking about this for a few minutes before reading on. If you are working with others, see what ideas you come up with as a group.*

In one way, we all know what "values" means. We all *use* the word "values" most of the time without apparent difficulty. When you originally read the title of this book, we doubt if you asked yourself "Whatever is this book about?" And yet, as we saw with our "three words" exercise (pp. 24–5), what "values" means is considerably more complicated than we generally recognise. Indeed, the point of this exercise is to defuse a perhaps natural reaction to taking values seriously in health care – which is to say "It's obvious, isn't it? We don't need to spend time on this!"

Well, we hope you have got past "It's obvious". But we also need to navigate an equal and opposite reaction, that "It's all just *too* complicated. So there's no point spending time on this!" That it *is* complicated is why we need a tool kit of methods for working with values. And, as with tools for any other trade, it takes time and practice to use them appropriately and to good effect. This is why, in this book, we have included so many exercises and case examples. For now, though, a first step towards managing the complexity of values is to see that what all the variety of values has in common is that *they guide decision making*.

The role of values in decision making is signalled in the lists in Table 3.1: "personal motivating force" and "guide you" both make this explicit. And ethics is all about "the right thing" to do: recall from Chapter 2 how we turn to ethics "because we want answers and guidance on how to act". And, if you think about the other value words discussed in this chapter so far, they all come back, in one way or another, to influencing what we do. Even aesthetic values "draw" or "repel", and they may have a broader role in establishing the "mind set" of decision making: a *cared for* (aesthetically pleasing) environment is a *caring* environment.

Of course, evidence and experience are also important influences on decision making in health care. In Chapter 4, we will look at how these three – values, experience and evidence – come together in decision making. But, for now, values can be thought of as *anything positively or negatively weighted that, alongside experience and evidence, guides our decisions and actions.*

Part II – Values in health care

In this second part of the chapter, we will be exploring how values come into health care decision making through the story of a young woman called Sally Coombs. Sally's story is based on experience but Sally herself, and the other people involved, are all fictitious.

A journey of understanding

The focus here is on a brief episode in Sally's story in which she is admitted as an emergency to her local acute care ward. We will be returning to Sally's story later in this chapter, Chapter 4 and, again, in Chapter 9 (on values-based assessment). By the end of the book, you will thus understand much more of Sally's story than is given in the first brief episode described here. But please take each stage of her story as it comes, rather than reading ahead. The different stages of Sally's story are intended to take you through a "journey of understanding" about the values in play, not only in Sally's story, but also in corresponding situations in your own practice. So, it is important to follow the journey step-by-step, taking in the learning points as you go, rather than jumping to the end.

Box 3.1 An extract from Sally Coombs' story

Sally Coombs was a young art student who was brought to the Acute Care Ward of her local psychiatric hospital on a "Section 136" by two police constables. They had been called by the staff of a Mental Health Day Centre that Sally had been attending. The story was that Sally had walked out of the Day Centre after "going berserk" in the OT (occupational therapy) room during an art session. She had not hurt anyone but she had slashed her art work and broken up easels and other equipment and then just stormed out. The Day Centre staff and her parents (they had called them to check that she had not gone home) had been understandably worried about her wandering the streets on her own and called the police for help.

Sally had calmed down by the time the two police constables found her but she was withdrawn and appeared not to know where she was. She refused to talk with them but made it clear she would not go back to the Day Centre. After calling the Day Centre staff, they decided that they should take Sally to the nearest acute care ward on a "136". This is a short-term section of the UK's Mental Health Act that allows someone to be taken to a place of safety for assessment. The Day Centre staff called the ward who agreed to take Sally on this basis.

Source: Fulford et al. (2012)

Exercise 3.2

Sally Coombs' story

Read through the extract from Sally's story as given in Box 3.1. As you read, please think how the points about values set out in the first part of the Chapter apply here in the context of Sally's story. Think, in particular, about values in the background as well as those in the foreground.

Note: As with our first exercise, do not simply do this in your head. Write down your own answers before reading on. One way to do this is to go through the story with a high-lighter, marking key points about values as they occur to you.

Also, think about Sally's story as being real, rather than as a theoretical exercise. If you have worked in an acute care ward and/or have personal experience of a similar situation, you will have ample background from which to draw. If not, draw on your own knowledge and experience to fill out Sally's story, and to imagine what it would really have felt like to be there and involved in person. This is not always easy. But, if you do this and our other exercises in this way as though the situations and characters were real, you will be actively developing your skills for working with values in practice.

Values in the clinical encounter

Clearly, values of many kinds are in play in this story. In the foreground are two shared values, safety and health. In one sense, the whole story is about safety. It starts with Sally "going berserk" (as the Day Centre staff put it). It is concerns about safety that lead the staff to call Sally's parents and to ask for help from the police. It is a concern about safety, too, that lead the police constables to take Sally to a "place of safety", using Section 136 of the Mental Health Act (risk to self or others is a key criterion for the use of the Mental Health Act; see Chapter 7). And it was concerns for Sally's safety (it seems reasonable to assume) that motivated the Acute Care Ward's agreement to accept Sally.

Equally pervasive in this story, though, are concerns about Sally's health. We are not told in Box 3.1 why Sally was attending the Day Centre. But it was a *Mental Health* Day Centre; and she "stormed out" of an Occupational Therapy art group. The police constables similarly were concerned more for Sally's health than any immediate risk to others: recall that she had calmed down but "*was withdrawn and appeared not to know where she was*". They had enough experience of seeing people in confusional states to realise that, whatever else might be going on, Sally needed medical attention urgently to exclude, for example, a diabetic episode.

As values in the foreground, safety and health are thus both important here. But so, too, are other less obvious values that, to some extent, are hidden in the background. Among background values you may have thought of so far in Sally's story are issues of confidentiality: the Day Centre staff called Sally's parents (she lived at home) because of what they perceived as an acute threat to her safety: but what should her parents be told now? Other background values include resource issues: staff time is always under pressure; there may be local or national targets to meet; and, as often as not, there is a shortage of "beds". So, managerial and policy values are in play. What about virtues? Listening, for example, an important virtue in the ethics of care noted in Chapter 2, could be vital to how Sally perceives and responds to the ward staff at this critical juncture. Also important in this respect are first impressions of the ward, whether it is welcoming and cared for: so, aesthetics come into play. These and other "background values", are often critical to how we provide care.

> **Reflection point:** *But whose values are still hidden in the background to Sally's story as presented thus far?*

The key person whose values are missing from the story as presented thus far is Sally herself. We called her story "Sally's story". But, thus far, *we know nothing about Sally's actual values, about what actually mattered to her.* The story as presented assumes that she is concerned, as are others, about her health and, indeed, her safety. But we have no actual evidence of this. We have been told that Sally "had slashed her art work and broken up easels and other equipment and then just stormed out", and that she had subsequently refused to return to the Day Centre. Both are highly significant in Sally's story. But we have been told nothing at all about *why* she behaved as she did. Her values remain in the story as presented not only in the background, but also as invisible.

If you thought to ask about Sally's values – about why she "went berserk" and why she refused to go back – you are already well on the way to becoming a values-based practitioner. But, all too often, most of us (as health care professionals) fail actually to find out what matters to those with whom we are working. We just *assume* that we know. The result is that, while we may aspire to person-centred practice, the care we actually provide reflects our own values, rather than the values of those for whom we care.

This is why Sally's story is presented in the way that it is, as a "clinical case history". We return to the narrative in Chapter 6, which describes how the very language of our practice reinforces the dominance of the worker's perspective in the way that it frames and positions people.

This framing and positioning is evident in Sally's story as presented in Box 3.1. The "case report" language frames her story from the perspective of the professionals concerned to the point that we are not even aware that Sally's own values are nowhere to be found. We assume we know what matters but what *actually* matters is left implicit in the background. In Sally's story, as presented here, most workers assume she has had some kind of psychotic episode that (excluding organic causes such as hypoglycaemia) is, at best, "irrational" and, at worst, essentially meaningless. The chances of such assumptions being made would have been further increased had Sally's received diagnosis been included (during a previous in-patient stay, she had been given a diagnosis of schizophrenia). Again, we return to some of the misuses of diagnostic labelling in Chapter 8.

Person-values-centred practice

Kim Woodbridge-Dodd, in the early days of the development of training materials for values-based practice, describes a telling example of how user/survivor values can get lost in the background of clinical decision making (Fulford and Woodbridge, 2008). Kim had been asked by a local Assertive Outreach Team to provide them with training in values-based practice specifically to support their work as person-centred practitioners. As a first exercise, Kim recorded (with their agreement) the perspectives from which comments were made in one of their routine case review meetings. The result was a big wake-up call. As Figure 3.1 shows, the comments overwhelmingly reflected the workers' perspective and not that of the clients'. Not shown here, but equally important for recovery, the comments in the case review were largely concerned with team members' priorities of diagnosis and medication, rather than with their clients' priorities of housing, friends and employment.

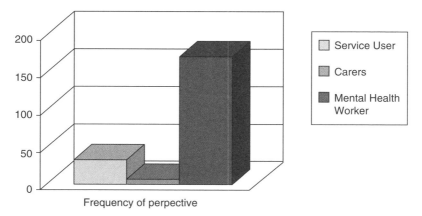

Figure 3.1 Perspectives from which comments made in a case review meeting

Source: Fulford and Woodbridge (2008)

This repeated tendency for user/survivor values to remain hidden in the background is why, as will see in Chapter 4, a key element in values-based practice is what is called "person-*values*-centred care", that is, care that is genuinely person-centred in being based on an understanding of what *really* matters to the client or patient concerned, rather than our *assumptions* about what matters. Bringing the individual client's or patient's values fully to the foreground is important in all areas of health care. But, in mental health, this is vital to recovery. Sally Coombs' recovery journey, as we will see later in Chapter 9), started with a background value that was so well hidden everyone (or almost everyone) missed it.

Your values matter, too

> **Reflection point:** *Why do you think that as workers, all too often, we fail to make good on our aspirations to person-centred care?*

Clearly, there are many negative ways to answer this question: lack of training, laziness and so forth. A positive answer is that it reflects *our own values* as workers. After all, we opt to go into "caring" professions. And we spend many years training in the knowledge and skills to deliver, within one specialist discipline or another, "good care". So, it is natural that we should have a distinctive perspective on what "good care" in a given context means; and, in many situations, this is vital. If someone has a "heart attack" while in our care, it is vital that we are able to act decisively. Acting decisively in this kind of context means drawing instinctively on our knowledge and experience guided by our professional (as well as personal) values. Overly-reflective practice in this kind of context can literally be fatal.

Even in acute situations, it is important to add, there may be advance directives, joint crisis plans or other considerations that should contribute to the values guiding decision making (Flood et al., 2006). Failure to attend to such considerations is commonly a factor where things go wrong from the service user/survivor's point of view in mental health crisis management (Mind, 2011). But the wider problem is that, as workers, we simply *fail to realise the extent to which our decisions reflect our own values, rather than those of our clients and patients.* This was the case with Kim Woodbridge-Dodd's team (p. 32): they believed they were being client-centred but the reality was they were being worker-centred.

This is why values-based practice emphasises that "your values matter too". Finding out what really matters to a particular individual is not always easy. It was not easy at this early acute stage in Sally Coombs' story. But an essential first step is to recognise the extent to which our own values may stop us from even realising the need to find out. This is what Kim Woodbridge-Dodd's team discovered for themselves from her initial case review exercise with them. What they realised was that, as workers, they had framed and positioned their case review within their own professional understanding of what was important, their own professional values. We will see in Chapter 9, in which we discuss values-based assessment, that Sally's values – the things that really mattered to her – were, in fact, very different from those assumed by the team and, indeed, everyone else. And, as already noted, finding out what really mattered to Sally was the turning point in her story towards recovery.

Ethics and clinical decision making

But, for now, this was all still some way off in the future. The immediate priority for the Acute Care Ward team was to decide what to do next. Here, as the further episode from Sally's story given in Box 3.2 describes, opinions were divided.

Box 3.2 – A further extract from Sally Coombs' story

Faced with an uncommunicative Sally Coombs, the team were split about what to do next. Dr Brown was concerned that the police constables thought Sally had been disoriented (she "appeared not to know where she was") and she wanted to exclude possible undiagnosed medical conditions as soon as possible. Nurse Matthews, however, took the view that Sally should be allowed to settle in with as little interference as possible. She was concerned that putting her through a physical examination and tests at this stage might prejudice the chance of establishing a trusting therapeutic relationship as the basis of longer-term support towards recovery.

Source: Fulford et al. (2012)

Exercise 3.3

What to do next

As you read through the further extract from Sally's story given in Box 3.2, think about the ethical issues raised by the difference of opinion between Nurse Matthews and Dr Brown about what to do next. You may find it helpful here to look back at the ethical theories covered in Chapter 2, asking how far, or in what ways, they contribute to clinical care in this particular situation.

When you first read through this further episode from Sally Coombs' story, you may well have found yourself asking whether the situation described is really a matter for ethics at all. The decision required is, after all, a *clinical* decision, rather than an ethical dilemma of the kind generally described in ethics textbooks. This is important. The focus in much ethics teaching and discussion on dilemmas has meant that the pervasiveness of values in clinical decision making has tended to be overlooked – an important example of values being pushed into the background.

However, further reflection in this instance shows that the difference of opinion between Nurse Matthews and Dr Brown is about what is the *right* thing to do. In the language of Chapter 2, therefore, this is a matter of ethical (individual) rather than moral (collective) norms. As a clinical decision, it is a matter to which (as noted earlier in this chapter) evidence and experience will both be relevant. But, in this instance at least, it is not the evidence and experience that is at issue. Nurse Matthews and Dr Brown have the same evidence on which to base their decision and both are equally experienced. The difference is, rather, in their *values* – their different perceptions of what is most important: to exclude undiagnosed medical conditions (Dr Brown), or to secure a therapeutic relationship (Nurse Matthews).

Each of the ethical theories described in Chapter 2 has important things to say about this. Deontology (rights-based ethics) emphasises the importance of respecting Sally Coombs' autonomy: this is reflected in relevant legislation such as the Mental Capacity Act and the Mental Health Act. Consequentialist ethics offers a balancing focus on outcomes. Virtues are important, too, in reminding us that it is not simply what you do that is important but also how you do it. Recall from Chapter 2 the relevance of virtue ethics in such practically relevant publications as the *6 Cs of Compassionate Care* and the *Capable Practitioner Framework*. The importance of "how as well as what" is further reinforced by the emphasis in the ethics of care on affective as well as cognitive aspects of decision making: we will see in Chapter 9 that the work of Carol Gilligan and others on "attentiveness" and "being with" (described in Chapter 2) was directly relevant to the eventually positive outcome of Sally Coombs' story.

Yet, while each of these theories illuminates the situation presented by Sally Coombs, none actually resolves the question of what to do.

> **Reflection point:** *Think about that last claim for a moment. Is it true? If you were Nurse Matthews or Dr Brown would any of the above theories have resolved the difference of opinion between you? If not, why not? In answering this question, look back to what we said in Part 1 of this chapter about the complex and conflicting nature of shared values.*

The key point here is that the ethical theories described in general terms in Chapter 2 rely on shared values: autonomy, good outcomes, capable practice, care and so forth. This is why they help to illuminate the particular situation faced by Nurse Matthews and Dr Brown. For Nurse Matthews and Dr Brown, as most other practitioners, share these same values. But shared values, as we saw in the first part of this chapter, are by their nature complex and conflicting. This, as we described, means that they have to be interpreted and balanced, one against another, in the particular circumstances presented by a given situation. And it is interpreting and balancing the values shared by Nurse Matthews and Dr Brown that is at the heart of the difference between them about what to do.

One way to see this is in terms of the four principles of Tom Beauchamp and James Childress, introduced at the end of Chapter 2 (Beauchamp and Childress, 1994 [1989]). As we indicated, the four principles – autonomy, beneficence, non-maleficence and justice – bring together elements of both deontology and consequentialism. As such, they reflect values that are widely shared within health care and in terms of which ethical difficulties (as in the present case) can be characterised. Ethical problems according to this approach break down into problems of interpreting and balancing the four principles one against another in the particular circumstances presented a given situation.

In terms of the four principles, then, we can see that, while Nurse Matthews was emphasising autonomy (as the basis of securing a trusting therapeutic relationship), Dr Brown was focussed on non-maleficence (avoiding the harm of a missed medical diagnosis). So far, then, we might say, so illuminated. But here, as Beauchamp and Childress themselves emphasise, when it comes to interpreting and balancing the principles in the context of a specific situation, the principles, as such, can take us no further. The principles themselves cannot tell us *how* they should be interpreted and balanced in a given case. We might turn for support to other ethical theories. But, as we saw in Chapter 2, it is at this point that virtue ethics, and even ethics of care, fail us for lack of content. For, in this instance, the difficulty is not whether Nurse Matthews or Dr Brown is either virtuous or caring. Both are virtuous (in the sense of the 6 Cs and the Capable Practitioner); and both are caring. But virtues and care are complex values meaning (as we saw earlier) different things to different people in different contexts. This is precisely why there is a problem about "what to do": Nurse Matthews and Dr Brown, in this instance, are both virtuous carers; the problem is precisely that they care virtuously about different things.

Something else, then, is needed to help us interpret and balance the complex and conflicting shared values of traditional ethical theory in the particular circumstances presented by individual clinical decisions. It is here that we turn to other tools in the values tool kit.

Introducing the values tool kit

As already noted, besides ethics, a whole tool kit of ways of working with values has appeared in recent years. We will not have space here to look at all of these in detail but it is important to be aware of them and of their usefulness for decisions of different kinds in health care. In this section, we will describe some of the main "tools" and the extent to which they might support Nurse Matthews and Dr Brown in deciding what to do.

> **Reflection point:** *As you read about the following ways of working with values in health care think about whether, and to what extent, each of them might help Nurse Matthews and Dr Brown decide what to do.*
>
> *We will be commenting on this as we go along but think about it for yourself and see whether you agree with us or not.*

Ethics and codes of practice

The most high-profile of the new tools is modern bioethics (as discussed in Chapter 2). Ethics, as such, is not new in health care – the Hippocratic code goes back over two thousand years. But a number of specific ethical tools have been introduced in recent decades in response to the particular challenges of modern health care. We looked at some of these in Chapter 2 and have seen in this chapter how they help to illuminate ethical problems but do not, as such, actually resolve them in individual cases.

One area that we have not examined in detail is professional codes of practice. As with ethical theories, though, turning to their respective codes of practice would not have helped to resolve the difference between Nurse Matthews and Dr Brown. For, as "virtuous carers" they were *both* acting entirely consistently with their respective professional standards. (For a more detailed worked example of the strengths and limitations of professional codes of practice in clinical decision making, see Fulford et al., 2012, ch. 2.)

Law

Law, too, is important in guiding health care decision making. As practitioners, we need to be aware of relevant legislation, both general and specific. In the present case, of general relevance are various anti-discriminatory policies and statutes, including the Human Rights Act and the UN Convention on the Rights of Persons with Disabilities (UNCRPD) which the UK has ratified; of specific relevance are the Mental Capacity Act and the Mental Health Act, already noted.

As with ethics, the law expresses widely shared values, in some cases explicitly so. The Mental Capacity Act, for example, requires workers to act in the "best interests" of the person concerned (Department for Constitutional Affairs, 2006); and the Mental Health Act incorporates a number of widely shared values such as the principle of employing the least restrictive option (Department of Health, 2008). Law, though – again, as with ethics and codes of practice – has to be interpreted in specific contexts and thus runs into the same problem: that the shared values it expresses are complex and conflicting. The Mental Capacity Act, for instance, (had Sally Coombs been assessed as lacking capacity) would not have helped Nurse Matthews and Dr Brown since what they disagreed about was what was in Sally Coombs' best interests.

Health economics: The QALY

Health economics has grown up around the problems of how to allocate scarce resources simultaneously in the most cost-effective and equitable ways. These are deeply value-laden problems raising similar difficulties of interpretation and balancing as those found in ethics and law, albeit in relation to different values. Efficiency and equity, for example, are both important values in health care economics that often conflict one with the other. Similarly, "costs" and "benefits" are both complex values, in the sense that what counts as a "cost" or a "benefit" will vary from person to person and situation to situation.

There is a whole research industry dedicated to working out the best way to resolve problems between economic values of these kinds. One widely used approach is the Quality Adjusted Life Year (QALY). As its name implies, the QALY is a measure of how many additional years of a given quality of life a health intervention will deliver. This is how the National Institute for Health and Care Excellence (NICE), for example, compares the potential benefits of competing treatments: NICE's review committees gather evidence of the effectiveness of different treatments in terms of QALYs and, on this basis, recommends which treatments will give the best value for money for patients in the NHS.

The many ethical problems raised by QALYs have been well-recognised from the start (Harris, 1991) – QALYs disadvantage minority interests, for example (Crisp, 1994). But faced with the impossibility of funding every possible treatment, the QALY is one way of guiding us how to spend what resources we have to best overall advantage. Other similar approaches have been suggested, such as the Disability Adjusted Life Year (DALY), although these, too, remain much disputed (Anand and Hanson, 1998); and there are moves towards more values-based methods encompassing a wider range of values (see "value-based pricing" in the Further Reading section). But, vital as all of these "tools" are with decisions of other kinds, they are clearly of little relevance to the decision facing Nurse Matthews and Dr Brown.

Decision aids

Where health economics is concerned with population-scale decisions, decision aids focus at the level of individual clinical decisions. A particular strength of such approaches is that they bring the values of the individual very firmly into focus. Developed in the form of web-based and other user-friendly resources, decision aids allow a worker and patient working together to feed in the relevant evidence together with the patient's values and to see how this affects their choices.

Although no substitute for careful discussion of options, decision aids can be very helpful with complex choices (Dowie, 2004). With Nurse Matthews and Dr Brown, however, the decision to be made is not between worker and patient but, rather, between two workers with different views about what to do.

The bottom line

The bottom line, then, is that none of the above "tools", although useful in other ways and for decisions of other kinds, can help Nurse Matthews and Dr Brown with their decision about what to do next. The problem in each case is similar to the problem we ran into earlier with ethics. These different tools all depend on shared values that, being complex and conflicting in nature, have to be interpreted and balanced when applied in individual cases. This, as we will see in Chapter 4, is where values-based practice comes into play.

Not quite the bottom line

Reflection point: *But whose values have once again dropped into the background in this discussion of the values tool kit?*

The missing values here are, once again, those of Sally Coombs herself. The discussion throughout this section has focussed, very much as such discussions traditionally focus, on the perspectives of the workers concerned. The whole set up was defined in terms of the different priorities of Nurse Matthews (autonomy) and Dr Brown (non-maleficence). Both were concerned *for* Sally Coombs. But their concerns were guided by their own values, their own ideas about what was important, rather than by those of Sally Coombs herself.

Establishing what matters to Sally will not be easy. And, if what we have said in this chapter about the need for values to be interpreted and balanced is right, establishing what matters to Sally will be only a first step towards resolving the complex and conflicting issues involved in working effectively with her in a way that genuinely reflects her values. But it is a first step that is all too often forgotten. And it is the essential first step towards values-based decision making.

CONCLUSION

In this chapter, we have looked at some of the features of values important in health care and explored how these play out in the clinical encounter. Values in health care are:

- *wider than ethics*: they include wishes, needs and preferences, they may be both positive and negative, and they extend across a number of areas including aesthetics;
- they are also present in both the *foreground and the background* of our thinking;
- they are often *shared* but, as such, are *always complex* (meaning different things to different people and in different contexts) and *often conflicting* one with another.

Taken together values can be thought of as *anything positively or negatively weighted as a guide to decision and action.*

We explored this action-guiding feature of values in the second part of the chapter through an episode in the story of Sally Coombs, a young woman admitted to an acute care ward. The key message from Sally's story was that *her values were all too readily lost in the background.* This, we suggested, corresponds with clinical experience and reflects the extent to which our own values as workers, although often unacknowledged, are important in framing and positioning how we view the world. For genuinely person-*values*-centred care, therefore, the message was that *your values matter too.*

As to how this can be achieved in practice, we found that ethics and a number of other "tools" in the values tool kit (codes of practice, law, health economics and decision aids) were all helpful, up to a point, in illuminating the complex and conflicting values issues arising in clinical decision making. But, when it came down to a particular decision to be made in a particular set of circumstances between particular individuals, none of these tools actually resolved the issues in question. It was at this point, as we indicated, that values-based practice comes into play.

GLOSSARY OF KEY TERMS

Values – anything positively or negatively weighted as a guide to decision and action

Foreground and background values – values respectively in the foreground and background of our minds

Shared values – values that are widely shared within a given group

Complex values – values that mean different things to different people and/or the same person in different contexts (shared values such as 'best interests' are often complex in this sense)

Conflicting values – values the demands of which tend to be in tension one with another (shared values are often conflicting in this sense – eg 'best interests' is often in tension with 'autonomy')

The values tool kit – the range of resources available to meet the challenge of working with values in healthcare; the tool kit includes ethics but also codes of practice, law, health economics, decision aids and values-based practice (see next chapter)

Person-values-centred-practice – clinical practice that is guided primarily by the actual rather than assumed values of the person in question

FURTHER READING

For a detailed account of the philosophy of values in health care, see Fulford (1989) *Moral Theory and Medical Practice.*

A recent review and overview is given in Fulford and van Staden (2013), with a critical commentary by Crisp (2013).

A more detailed description of the various tools in the values tool kit and how they play out in clinical decision making is given in the first two chapters of Fulford et al. (2012) *Essential Values-based Practice: Linking Science with People.*

Chapter 4 of that book, "Recovery in schizophrenia: A values wake-up call" gives a fuller version of Sally Coombs' story as seen not only through her eyes, but also those of her parents and of a wide range of others concerned with her at different times.

For further details of value-based pricing please see www.valuesbasedpractice.org and follow the links to VBP.

REFERENCES

Anand, S. and Hanson, K. (1998) "DALYs: Efficiency versus equity", *World Development*, 26: 30710.

Beauchamp, T.L. and Childress, J.F. (1994 [1989]) *Principles of Biomedical Ethics* (4th edn). Oxford: Oxford University Press.

Crisp, R. (1994) "Quality of life and health care" in Fulford, K.W.M., Gillett, G. and Soskice, J. (eds) *Medicine and Moral Reasoning.* Cambridge: Cambridge University Press.

Crisp, R. (2013) "Commentary: Values-based practice by a different route", in Fulford, K.W.M. and van Staden, W. (2013) "Values-based practice: Topsy-turvy take home messages from ordinary language philosophy (and a few next steps)" in Fulford, K.W.M., Davies, M., Gipps, R., Graham, G., Sadler, J., Stanghellini, G. and Thornton, T. (eds) *The Oxford Handbook of Philosophy and Psychiatry.* Oxford: Oxford University Press.

Daykin, N., Orme, J., Evans, D., Salmon, D., McEachran, M. and Brain, S. (2008) "The impact of participation in performing arts on adolescent health and behaviour: A systematic review of the literature", *Journal of Health Psychology,* 13(2): 251–64.

Department for Constitutional Affairs (2006) *Mental Capacity Act Code of Practice.* Code Number CP 05/06. London: TSO.

Department of Health (2008) *Mental Health Act 1983 Code of Practice – 2008 Revision.* London: TSO.

Dowie, J. (2004) "Research implications of science-informed, value-based decision making", *International Journal of Occupational Medicine and Environmental Health,* 17(1): 83–90.

Flood, C., Byford, S., Henderson, C., Leese, M., Thornicroft, G., Sutherby, K. and Szmukler, G. (2006) "Joint crisis plans for people with psychosis: Economic evaluation of a randomised controlled trial", *BMJ,* doi:10.1136/bmj.38929.653704.55 (16 August 2006).

Fulford, K.W.M. (1999 [1989, 1995]) *Moral Theory and Medical Practice.* Cambridge: Cambridge University Press.

Fulford, K.W.M. and Woodbridge, K. (2008) "Practising ethically: Values-based practice and ethics – Working together to support person-centred and multidisciplinary mental health care" in Stickley, T. and Basset, T. (eds) *Learning About Mental Health Practice.* Chichester: Wiley.

Fulford, K.W.M. and van Staden, W. (2013) "Values-based practice: Topsy-turvy take home messages from ordinary language philosophy (and a few next steps)" in Fulford, K.W.M., Davies, M., Gipps, R., Graham, G., Sadler, J., Stanghellini, G., and Thornton, T. (eds), *The Oxford Handbook of Philosophy and Psychiatry.* Oxford: Oxford University Press.

Fulford, K.W.M., Peile, E. and Carroll, H. (2012) "'Recovery in schizophrenia: A values wake-up call' values-based practice element 1: Awareness of values" in Fulford, K.W.M., Peile, E. and Carroll, H. *Essential Values-based Practice: Clinical Stories Linking Science with People.* Cambridge: Cambridge University Press.

Fulford, K.W.M., Peile, E. and Carroll, H. (2012) *Essential Values-based Practice: Clinical Stories Linking Science with People.* Cambridge: Cambridge University Press.

Harris J. (1991) "Unprincipled QALYs: A response to Cubbon", *Journal of Medical Ethics,* 17: 185–8.

Hughes, J.C. and Beatty, A. (2013) "Understanding the person with dementia: A clinicophilosophical case discussion", *Advances in Psychiatric Treatment* 19: 337–43 doi: 10.1192/apt.bp.112.011098

Hutchinson, P. and Read, R. (2014) "Reframing health care: Philosophy for medicine and human flourishing" in Loughlin, M. (ed.) *Debates in Values-based Practice.* Cambridge: Cambridge University Press.

Mind (2011) *Listening to Experience: An Independent Inquiry into Acute and Crisis Mental Health Care.* London: Mind.

Musalek, M. (2010) "Social aesthetics and the management of addiction", *Current Opinion in Psychiatry*, 23: 530–5.

Shingler, A. (2008) *One in a Hundred*. Derbyshire: Thorntree Press.

Spandler, H., Secker, J., Kent, L., Hacking, S. and Shenton, J. (2007) "Catching life: The contribution of arts initiatives to recovery approaches in mental health", *Journal of Psychiatric and Mental Health Nursing*, 14(8): 791–9.

Tucker, B.P. (1998) "Deaf culture, cochlear implants, and elective disability", *Hastings Center Report*, 28(4): 6–14.

Von Wright, G.H. (1963) *The Varieties of Goodness*. London: Routledge & Kegan Paul.

Woodbridge, K. and Fulford, K.W.M. (2004) *"Whose Values?" A Workbook for Values-based Practice in Mental Health Care*. London: Sainsbury Centre for Mental Health.

4 | Values-based practice

Chapter Summary

This chapter will:

- Present an overview of values-based practice.
- Discuss the clinical skills for values-based practice.
- Consider professional relationships in values-based practice:
  - Person-*values*-centred care
  - The *extended* multidisciplinary team.
- Discuss values and evidence in values-based practice.
- Consider partnership in values-based practice.
- Demonstrate how to pull it all together: making balanced decisions in individual situations.

Values-based practice is a new skills-based approach to balanced decision making where complex and conflicting values are involved. Within the values tool kit, values-based practice focusses on individuals. This is why it is important especially for person-centred care.

We start the chapter with an overview of values-based practice and then look at each of its elements in more detail. We will be exploring these elements not in a theoretical way but, rather, through a series of brief reflective exercises focussed around the story of Sally Coombs (see Chapter 3).

Overview of values-based practice

Values-based practice builds directly on the features of values introduced in Chapter 3. As Figure 4.1 shows, with its starting point in mutual respect, values-based practice is rooted firmly in the *variety of values*. It then employs key clinical skills (these include awareness, reasoning, knowledge and communication) to bring the values relevant to a given situation from the *background to the foreground* of our thinking. But, as we saw, values are often *complex and conflicting*. So, these clinical skills – together with a number of further elements (professional relationships, close links between values and evidence, and partnership within frameworks of *shared values*) – are needed to support balanced *clinical decision making* in individual situations.

Features of values (from Chapter 3)	Values-based practice
The variety of values	Starting point is… Mutual respect for differences of values ⬇
Foreground and background Complex and conflicting Shared values	Process involves… • Clinical skills • Professional relationships • Links between values and evidence • Partnership ⬇
Guide clinical decision making	Outputs are… Balanced decisions in individual situations

Figure 4.1 From values to values-based practice

The elements of values-based practice, as we will see, work closely together in practice. In this respect, values-based practice is like any other skills-based activity. Playing tennis, for example, involves learning a number of different shots (serve, forehand, and so on). We learn these shots separately and proficiency in each is useful in its own right; however, to play tennis really well we have to practice to the point that we can use all the different shots seamlessly and in a well-connected way.

We will be learning about the different elements of the process of values-based practice (its different "tennis shots" as it were) as we work through the chapter. In brief, they are

- *Four key clinical skills*: awareness of values and of the variety of values; reasoning about values; knowledge of values and how to get it; and two aspects of communication skills (eliciting values and conflict resolution);
- *Two aspects of professional relationships*: person-values-centred care (introduced in Chapter 3) and an extended understanding of the role of the multi-disciplinary team;
- *Three principles linking values and evidence*: the two feet]principle; the squeaky whee principle; and the science-driven principle;
- *Partnership in decision making* based on what in values-based practice is called "dissensus" within frameworks of shared values.

Exercise 4.1

Starting your own table of values-based practice

Draw up a table of the elements of values-based practice on the lines of the one shown in Table 4.1. As you will see, this covers the same elements of values-based practice as Figure 4.1 but now set out in the form of a list with spaces for you to add your own comments. So, try adding a brief comment against each element with your preliminary ideas about their relevance in principle in Sally Coombs' story.

Clearly, at this stage you have only just begun to read about values-based practice. But, as you will see in this chapter, values-based practice is very much about building on best practice. Draw on your own ideas about best practice, including some of the points we introduced in the last chapter. We will be coming back to this table and adding additional comments as we work through the chapter. You will thus be able to see how and in what ways values-based practice builds further on your preliminary ideas as set out here.

In Chapter 3, we touched in one way or another on each of the main areas of values-based practice but two that stand out here are awareness of values (Element 1) and person-values-centred care (Element 5). Awareness (or *lack* of awareness) of Sally Coombs' value was the key point about how, as professionals, we position and frame stories such as Sally' in terms of our own values, rather than those of the person concerned. Sally's values were so far in the background as to become, as we put it, 'invisible'. Recognising this was the first step towards the person-values-centred care of values-based practice. We drew on Kim Woodbridge-Dodd's study with the team who believed they were working in a person centred way but whose clinical case review meeting was framed almost entirely within their own professional values, rather than those of the users/survivors with whom they were

Elements of values-based practice	Relevance to Sally Coombs' story (for you to complete)
Premise of mutual respect	
Skills areas	
1. Awareness	
2. Reasoning	
3. Knowledge	
4. Communication	
Professional relationships	
5. Person-values-centred care	
6. Extended MDT	
Values and evidence	
7. Two feet principle	
8. Squeaky wheel principle	
9. Science-driven principle	
Partnership	
10. Dissensus within frameworks of shared values	
Balanced decisions in individual situations	

Table 4.1 The elements of values-based practice

working. This is vital since, as we will find in Chapters 9 and 10, person-values-centred care is the key-of-keys to recovery.

Practice for practice

In the rest of this chapter, we will be looking in more detail at these and other main elements of values-based practice. The table of elements as a whole may look rather daunting but, as with other skills-based areas, it all falls into place with practice (think tennis again). This is why, as we emphasised in Chapter 3, it is important to do the exercises for yourself, rather than just skipping ahead to what we say about them.

Clinical skills for values-based practice

With Sally Coombs in mind, we will start with the bedrock of values-based practice, its four key areas of clinical skill: awareness, reasoning, knowledge and communication.

Awareness of values: this includes raised awareness of values and of the variety of values   Training in values-based practice starts with raising awareness of values through one or more practical exercises. These can take various forms. One commonly used exercise is the "three words" exercise at the start of Chapter 3. Others are given in a training manual for values-based practice

(*Whose Values?*, Woodbridge and Fulford, 2004) that is available as a full text down-load from the VBP Website (see the Further Reading section at the end of this chapter).

Awareness of the variety of values includes awareness of the often surprising extent to which other people's values are different than we expect them to be. The beginning of wisdom in values-based practice is to recognise that we all make assumptions about each other's values and that, much of the time, these assumptions are wrong. We will see later that Sally Coombs' values, what was important to her, was very different from everyone's assumptions. This is why keeping the service user's values firmly at the forefront of our thinking is so important. It is also why raised awareness of our own values is vital: as you will recall from Chapter 3, it is our own values as professionals that tend to eclipse those of the service users/survivors with whom we are working.

Reasoning about values: using a range of methods including, in particular, principles reasoning and case-based reasoning (or casuistry)   You will hear people say that values are not something about which you can reason. Well, they are wrong. As we saw in Chapters 2 and 3 there are many methods available for reasoning about values. In fact, you can use any of the methods used for ethical reasoning (as covered in Chapter 2) to reason about values of other kinds. What is distinctive about values reasoning in values-based practice is that it is used not to find answers as such but, rather, to help expand our understanding of the values in play in a given situation.

> **Reflection point:** *Think back to Chapter 3. Did we use values reasoning at any point in thinking about Sally Coombs?*

We used principles reasoning in thinking about Sally Coombs. You will recall that Beauchamp and Childress' four principles helped us to understand the difference of view between Nurse Matthews and Dr Brown as a difference between autonomy (Nurse Matthews) and non-malef-icence (Dr Brown). This approach is sometimes described as "top down" reasoning because it applies high-level principles to individual cases. Case-based reasoning (sometimes called "casu-istry") is complementary, in that it is bottom-up reasoning, starting as its name suggests from actual cases using case-based reasoning. Case-based reasoning explores our values by asking how our thinking would change if this or that detail of the case in question were different. In Sally Coombs case, for example, case-based reasoning would ask questions such as "If Sally had a history of attempted suicide, what difference would that make to what we should do?"

Of the many methods for reasoning about ethics and values described earlier, principles reasoning and case-based reasoning are often the most helpful in a clinical context. Again, neither in themselves can resolve issues, as such. But particularly, used together, they may help to illuminate the values in play. This is important, especially with values (such of those of Sally Coombs, in this case) that are at risk of being lost in the background.

Knowledge of values: including both how to get it and its limitations   As with any other subject, there is a great deal you can learn about values from research. It is worth repeating the point noted in Chapter 3: that, besides research, personal and clinical experience are important sources of information when it comes to decision making. We will see later in this chapter that evidence-based medicine, properly understood, also makes this clear. That said, it is important to be aware that there is a wide range of research methods available for working with values. These include empirical social science methods – such as ethnography and anthropology, as well as philosophical methods – such as phenomenology (important, particularly, in mental health) and hermeneutics.

> **Reflection point:** *What are the possible limitations of research knowledge of values in Sally Coombs' story?*

The key thing to remember with research knowledge of values is that it should never be used to trump or replace the actual values of the individual concerned in a given situation. Everyone is unique. Everyone has their own unique "values fingerprint". So, research may help us by suggesting the values *likely to be in play* in a given type of situation. But you should never jump from the general to the particular. This is well-recognised in cultural studies, for example. The danger of learning about other cultures is that we risk generalising from the group to the individual. Just because someone is, say, a Moslem, we should not assume that they only eat Halal meat.

Sally Coombs' story offers a clear illustration of not only the strengths, but also limitations of research knowledge of values. You will recall that she was described as going along "willingly" with the police constables who found her (Box 3.1). Well, she may have been willing. But it is equally possible that she may have gone along because she was afraid of what would happen if she resisted. We would only know if Sally had an opportunity to tell us her version of events. It is important to be aware of this possibility in working with people in Sally's situation (those admitted under "Section 136") when deciding what to do next.

But again, we should not just *assume* this to be the case. In fact, as we will see later, it was *not* the case for Sally. Far from being afraid, she had good reasons for going along willingly. Understanding these reasons was to prove important later on in helping her turn the corner towards recovery. But Sally's reasons reflected values that were unique to her at that time and arising from her particular personal situation.

So, knowledge, including research knowledge, can be helpful in suggesting what values are likely to be in play in this or that type of situation. But you always have to find out for a given individual in a particular situation exactly what values actually *are* in play.

Communication skills: especially for eliciting values and of conflict resolution   Communication skills in general are important in values-based practice as in any other aspect of health care. Indeed, "values-based practice", as Fulford et al. emphasised (2012, ch. 7), is nothing without communication skills. But the relationship is two-way. Communication skills are important to values-based practice: two skills in particular are essential – skills for eliciting values and skills of conflict resolution. But values-based practice is also important to communication skills. This is because, in health care, what is important is not just skills, but also what we do with them. Communication skills may otherwise be used as readily to misinform as to inform.

Values-based practice thus helps to give content to communication skills. An important example of this in relation to recovery practice is the emphasis in values-based practice (noted in Chapter 3) on looking for positives as well as negatives. In communication skills training, you may have come across the acronym ICE: it reminds us to explore Ideas, Concerns and

Expectations. Values-based practice makes ICE into ICEStAR (Fulford et al., 2012, ch. 7). It reminds us to explore not only ICE, but also the positives of Strengths, Aspirations and Resources.

> **Reflection point:** *What strengths can you identify in Sally Coombs' story? How might the StAR in ICEStAR contribute to her recovery?*

Focussing on strengths as well as problems transforms how we perceive someone. Sally is described, as is consistent with most clinical case histories, in mainly negative terms as presenting a "problem". But, even here, reading between the lines we begin to see real strengths: despite her distress and lack of immediate support, she took a strong line with the police constables on what she was or was not prepared to do. In the original of the story, we find that, among other strengths and resources, she was an excellent artist who had a wide circle of friends and a supportive family.

In the event, as we will see, these were all mixed blessings. But the real key to her recovery was the A in ICEStAR: her personal aspirations. Again, we will come back in Chapter 9 to what these aspirations were. But the point for now is that personal aspirations, although widely neglected in how an episode of mental distress is understood, are often the key to recovery.

Exercise 4.2

Clinical skills for values–based practice and Sally Coombs' story

Now try filling in the first part of your table of values-based practice. We have already seen that awareness of values was important in Sally's story. But try adding what was important also from the other skills areas of reasoning, knowledge and communication. Then compare your summary with ours, as given in Table 4.2.

The message is now clear. Each of the skills areas may contribute separately and together in Sally Coombs' story. Skills though as noted earlier (under communication skills) are important not in themselves but, rather, for what we do with them. So, rather than considering these various skills further in isolation, we will now look at how they played out in the way Sally Coombs' emergency admission was actually handled by the ward staff. This brings us to the second main group of elements of values-based practice: professional relationships.

Professional relationships in values-based practice

In Chapter 3, we introduced the first of the two aspects of professional relationships important in values-based practice, person-values-centred care. In this section, we take a further look at what person-values-centred care means in practice and then show how this is supported by the second aspect: the extended multidisciplinary team.

Person-values-centred care: putting the values of the individual service user at the centre of clinical decision making   "Person-centred care" is something of a buzz word in contemporary health care and, as with other buzz words, it carries different meanings in different contexts. The closely related idea of "personalised medicine", for example, is widely used in physical medicine to mean targeting drug treatment according to an individual's particular genetic profile (Fulford et al., 2012, ch. 8). In mental health, the concept of person-centred

Elements of values-based practice	Relevance to Sally Coombs' story
Premise of mutual respect	
Skills areas	
1. Awareness	Awareness of Sally Coombs' values is important – including awareness that we do not yet know what they are!
2. Reasoning	Principles reasoning proved helpful in Chapter 3 in understanding the difference of view between Nurse Matthews and Dr Brown about what to do next. (Casuistry might have been used to extend this.)
3. Knowledge	There is relevant knowledge of the values likely to be in play in crisis situations, particularly from service user/survivor research – but Sally is a unique individual and we must not assume that these actually are *her* values.
4. Communication	Communication skills generally are important especially: (1) for eliciting values (notably Sally's values) and,(2) of conflict resolution (as between Nurse Matthews and Dr Brown). We should look in particular for positive (StAR) values with Sally's aspirations likely to be important to her recovery.
Professional relationships	
5. Person-values-centred care	
6. Extended MDT	
Values and evidence	
7. Two feet principle	
8. Squeaky wheel principle	
9. Science-driven principle	
Partnership	
10. Dissensus within frameworks of shared values	
Balanced decisions in individual situations	

Table 4.2 The clinical skills for values-based practice and Sally Coombs' story

care has been hard-fought over as a highly significant issue from the perspective of service users/survivors: key insights have come into this debate from discussions within social models of disability and work undertaken by the user-led organisation Shaping Our Lives in collaboration with others (see, for example, Glynn and Beresford, 2008; Croft et. al., 2011). The primary shift that the person-centred approach makes is putting the person who is in need of support, rather than the concerns of the service itself, at the centre of decision making, work planning and delivery.

In values-based practice, as we saw in Chapter 3, person-centred care means putting the individual service user's values at the heart of clinical decision making. This is why it is called "person-*values*-centred care". But, here, we need to be careful. For important as the values of the individual service user certainly are, and all too often neglected as they certainly may be, they are not the only values involved in clinical decision making. This was clear from Sally Coombs' story in Chapter 3. Besides her values (still undefined, by the way) there were many other values in play: of staff, of family and others immediately concerned; and deeper in the background there were all the economic and social values that go into shaping service provision. These values, moreover, (as do values in general) often have competing claims. The confidentiality, for example, that Sally Coombs had the right to expect was in tension with her family carers' needs for reassurance and support.

One response to such conflicts is to make the service user's values paramount – trumping all others in whatever circumstances. Values-based practice, by contrast, with its aim of balanced decision making, puts the service users' values at the heart of clinical decision making but recognises the need to balance these against other relevant values according to the particular circumstances presented by a given situation.

Person-values-centred care in the NIMHE Values Framework

This approach was adopted in a framework for values-based decision making developed by a group of service users and service providers to support the work of a policy-delivery body set up under the first New Labour government in the UK in the late 1990s, the National Institute for Mental Health England (NIMHE). Although NIMHE no longer exists, it had a strong commitment to service user-led service development and its values framework remains resonant for contemporary mental health services as the basis of recovery practice (see Box 4.1).

BOX 4.1 The NIMHE values framework

The work of the National Institute for Mental Health in England (NIMHE) on values in mental health care is guided by three principles of values-based practice:

1. **Recognition** – NIMHE recognises the role of values alongside evidence in all areas of mental health policy and practice.
2. **Raising awareness** – NIMHE is committed to raising awareness of the values involved in different contexts, the role(s) they play and their impact on practice in mental health.
3. **Respect** – NIMHE respects diversity of values and will support ways of working with such diversity that makes the principle of service-user centrality a unifying focus for practice. This means that the values of each individual service user/client and their communities must be the starting point and key determinant for all actions by professionals.

Respect for diversity of values encompasses a number of specific policies and principles concerned with equality of citizenship. In particular, it is anti-discriminatory because

discrimination in all its forms is intolerant of diversity. Thus, respect for diversity of values has the consequence that it is unacceptable (and unlawful, in some instances) to discriminate on grounds such as gender, sexual orientation, class, age, abilities, religion, race, culture or language.
Respect for diversity within mental health is also:

- *User-centred* – it puts respect for the values of individual users at the centre of policy and practice.
- *Recovery oriented* – it recognises that building on the personal strengths and resiliencies of individual users, and on their cultural and racial characteristics, there are many diverse routes to recovery.
- *Multidisciplinary* – it requires that respect be reciprocal, at a personal level (between service users, their family members, friends, communities and providers), between different provider disciplines (such as nursing, psychology, psychiatry, medicine, social work), and between different organisations (including health, social care, local authority housing, voluntary organisations, community groups, faith communities and other social support services).
- *Dynamic* – it is open and responsive to change.
- *Reflective* – it combines self-monitoring and self-management with positive self-regard.
- *Balanced* – it emphasises positive as well as negative values.
- *Relational* – it puts positive working relationships supported by good communication skills at the heart of practice.

NIMHE will encourage educational and research initiatives aimed at developing the capabilities (the awareness, attitudes, knowledge and skills) needed to deliver mental health services that will give effect to the principles of values-based practice.

he key drafting comes at the heart of the framework in the definition of the starting point or values-based practice: respect – the third of the three "Rs" at the start of the framework). n this context, "respect" means that NIMHE will support "ways of working with diversity (of values) that makes the principle of service-user centrality a unifying focus for practice. This means that the values of each individual service user/client and their communities must be he starting point and key determinant for all actions by professionals"

This wording is important for values-based practice in a number of respects. First, it was produced by Simon Allard, a member of the group with several years' experience as a service user. As such, it is all the more persuasive in making clear that a range of values is in play and have to be taken into account in clinical decision making: the values of the individual service user are the "starting point" – but not, this implies, the *only* point; and they are the key determinant" – but not, therefore, the *sole* determinant of actions by professionals. At he same time, though, the drafting makes unequivocal the centrality of the values of the individual service user.

This is reflected, too, in other parts of the values framework: it is explicit, in particular, n the first of the bulleted points in the second half of the framework. But, as Element 1 of values-based practice ("awareness of values") reminds us, the essential first step toward making the service user's values central is the active discovery (not simply the assumption) of what the values of the person concerned actually are. This is where the second key aspect of professional relationships in values-based practice – the "extended" multidisciplinary team – comes into play.

The extended multidisciplinary team: the importance of multidisciplinary teamwork in values-based practice is extended from providing a range of different knowledge and skills to include also a range of different values.

> **Reflection point:** *Before reading on think about multidisciplinary teamwork for a moment. If person-values-centred care means putting the individual service user's values at the centre of decision making, why should team values be so significant? In particular, what role or roles might team values have in supporting person-values-centred care?*

In values-based practice, as we have said, the importance of multidisciplinary teamwork is extended from providing a range of different knowledge and skills that also includes a range of different value perspectives. This is the sense in which the multidisciplinary team of values-based practice is an "extended" multidisciplinary team. It is extended from knowledge and skills to values.

The stand-off between Nurse Matthews and Dr Brown illustrates one aspect of the importance of this. As we described in Chapter 3, this was a stand-off of values. Nurse Matthews and Dr Brown started from the same evidence base, and were equally skilled and experienced. But their respective professional values led them to prioritise different aspects of Sally Coombs' situation: Nurse Matthews, concerned for the longer-term therapeutic relationship as the basis of recovery (see Chapter 10), prioritised autonomy; Dr Brown, concerned for missed medical diagnoses, prioritised non-maleficence. Neither was right or wrong. Both had a point. Unacknowledged, such differences of values can be a source of disagreement and failed communication (Colombo et al., 2003). But, if differences of values are acknowledged, they can provide a *balance of perspectives within which a shared decision becomes possible.* This, as we will see later, is what happened in Sally's case.

One aspect, then, of the importance of different values as well as different knowledge and skills in the extended multidisciplinary team is that they contribute to balanced decision making. Fulford et al. (2012, ch. 9) give a worked example from child protection of the clinical significance of this. In Sally's story, though, the key issue is not about the difference in values between Nurse Matthews and Dr Brown. The key issue is, rather, that neither is basing their ideas about what to do on Sally's values. Neither, then, is thinking in the person-values-centred way of values-based practice required by the NIMHE framework. Nurse Matthews and Dr Brown (as for us so far in this book) have no idea what Sally's values actually are.

We have already looked at a number of elements of values-based practice that might contribute to finding out what Sally Coombs' values really are – the skills of awareness and communication, for example. But it is here, too, that a second aspect of the importance of different values in the extended multidisciplinary team comes into play. We owe this second aspect to an innovative study carried out by the social scientist, Anthony Colombo (2003).

The Colombo Models Project

We do not have space here to describe Colombo's work in detail (see Further Reading). His key finding, for present purposes, was that the differences in value perspectives of team members corresponded with *closely similar differences of values between service users*. This was significant for values-based practice because we are all better at identifying values similar to our own. So, what Colombo's finding showed was that differences in team values were *a resource for understanding the values of individual service users*.

It was this finding that led directly to the recognition of the importance of the *extended multidisciplinary team* as a key resource for person-*values*-centred care. Colombo's methodology, as well as his findings, played an important role in the early development of training materials for values-based practice (see Fulford and Woodbridge, 2004, s. 5; also available through the VBP website, see Further Reading).

Exercise 4.3

Professional relationships in values-based practice and Sally Coombs' story

At this point, please go back to your table of values-based practice and add in the relevance of professional relationships. You may well have included already person-values-centred care. But see what you can add about the extended multidisciplinary team. We give our own additions in Table 4.3.

Values and evidence in values-based practice

We have noted at several points in this chapter the close relationship between values-based practice and evidence-based practice. This sometimes comes as a surprise. Evidence-based practice is often presented as a value-free basis for clinical decision making. It aims to provide best evidence for clinical decision making. That is, after all, what science is all about. But what exactly is "evidence-based practice"? And how does it link up with values in clinical decision making? In this section, we will be thinking about these two questions before coming back to the three principles linking values with evidence in values-based practice.

Evidence, experience and values

We begin with a brief reflection point.

> **Reflection point:** *What is evidence-based practice? Reflect for a moment on what you understand by evidence-based practice before reading on.*

Most people think of evidence-based practice much as we described it just now, as being about "best research evidence". It *is* about best research evidence. But the point of this section is to drive home the message that, properly understood, evidence-based practice is not *just* about best research evidence. Or, at any rate, it was not originally intended to be *just* about best research evidence. David Sackett, one of the early leaders of evidence-based practice, made this clear on the very first page of his foundational book, *Evidence-Based Medicine: How to Practice and Teach EBM*. He defined evidence-based medicine there *as bringing together best research evidence with experience and with values* (Sackett et al., 2000: 1).

Elements of values-based practice	Relevance to Sally Coombs' story
Premise of mutual respect	
Skills areas	
1. Awareness	Awareness of Sally Coombs' values is important – including awareness that we do not yet know what they are!
2. Reasoning	Principles reasoning proved helpful in Chapter 3 in understanding the difference of view between Nurse Matthews and Dr Brown about what to do next. (Casuistry might have been used to extend this.)
3. Knowledge	There is relevant knowledge of the values likely to be in play in crisis situations, particularly from service user/survivor research – but Sally is a unique individual and we must not assume that these actually are *her* values.
4. Communication	Communication skills generally are important especially: (1) for eliciting values (notably Sally's values) and, (2) of conflict resolution (as between Nurse Matthews and Dr Brown). We should look in particular for positive (StAR) values with Sally's aspirations likely to be important to her recovery.
Professional relationships	
5. Person-values-centred care	Sally's (still to be defined) values should be the starting point and key determinant of what Nurse Matthews and Dr Brown decide to do
6. Extended MDT	The different value perspectives of team members are a resource: (1) for balanced decision making about what to do, and (2) for coming to understand what Sally's values actually are
Values and evidence	
7. Two feet principle	
8. Squeaky wheel principle	
9. Science-driven principle	
Partnership	
10. Dissensus within frameworks of shared values	
Balanced decisions in individual situations	

Table 4.3 Professional relationships in values-based practice and Sally Coombs' story

Sackett's definition of evidence-based medicine thus adds to best research evidence the importance of both experience and values. Yet, this is widely neglected among today's advocates of evidence-based practice. We have moved from Sackett's rich three-way model to a one-way-only model in which research-based evidence alone is recognised. We return to values and experience later in the chapter. But even the evidence in evidence-based practice has become increasingly limited. Worse still, the kind of research that is acceptable has become narrowed – first, to quantitative research and, then, to specific paradigms such as RCTs (randomised controlled trials). This thinned-down version of evidence-based medicine might be summed up as "What can't be measured doesn't count; and what can't be counted won't be measured!"

To be clear, there is nothing wrong with RCTs. RCTs are essential for certain kinds of research question crucial to health care decision making. The problem is the *limitation* of the evidence-base of decision making to evidence of just this one particular kind. We need, as it were, other research horses for other research courses. There are other quantitative research paradigms with much to offer health care; there are many qualitative paradigms; there are philosophical paradigms, too – analytic philosophy, for example, was a partner discipline in Colombo's study (p. 53; see Fulford and Colombo, 2004). There are important issues, too – not simply about *how* research is done, but also *by whom* it is done. In mental health, there is a growing resource of service user/survivor research (Wallcraft et al., 2009).

To all these research-based sources of knowledge, furthermore, Sackett reminds us, should be added the further resources of *experience*-based knowledge. In his original definition, Sackett specifies clinical experience. But again, in mental health (and increasingly in other areas of health care), we are adding to the expertise-by-training, represented by clinical experience, a whole new resource of expertise-by-experience from service users/survivors. (For a collection of narratives of service user/survivor perspectives, see Basset and Stickley, 2010).

As resources for health care, these different components of the evidence-base of decision making are complementary. Sackett, again, makes this clear from the perspective of evidence-based practice. "When these three elements (evidence, experience and values) are integrated", he continues (Sackett et al., 2000: 1), "clinicians and patients form a diagnostic and therapeutic alliance which optimises clinical outcomes and quality of life."

Three principles linking values and evidence

The importance of experienced-based knowledge in values-based practice is an area of ongoing active development (see Further Reading), but the complementarity between values and evidence in values-based practice is explicitly spelled out in its three principles, directly linking values with evidence.

Reflection point: *As you read about the following three principles of values-based practice, think back to Sally Coombs' story. Ask yourself whether – and, if so, in what way – each of these might be helpful clinically.*

The "two feet" principle: all decisions stand on the two feet of values as well as evidence   This principle reflects the point made in Chapter 3 about values "weighting" evidence and, thus, guiding decisions. It is an important point to emphasise clinically because, in the pressures of everyday practice, is easy to lose sight of the values guiding decision making where there is a strong evidence base. Evidence in such situations tends to eclipse values. The "two feet" principle reminds us to keep a careful eye on the values in play, especially where there is a strong evidence base for the decision in question.

The "squeaky wheel" principle: we notice values when they are complex and/or conflicting and hence cause trouble   This principle trades on the idea that we notice things when they cause trouble and draw themselves to our attention – "It is the squeaky wheel that gets the grease", as the saying goes. What this means in values-based practice is that (as with wheels) values are noticed when they cause trouble and thus force themselves on our attention. This happens – for example, clinically – where there is an ethical dilemma about what to do. But the danger is that, in such situations, the values in question tend to eclipse the relevant evidence. So, the message of the "squeaky wheel" principle is to keep a careful eye on the evidence base of decision making, especially where there are strong values issues in play.

The "two feet" and "squeaky wheel" principles thus balance each other. The "two feet" principle tells us not to lose sight of the values when focussing on the evidence. The "squeaky wheel" principle takes this observation in the other direction: it tells us not to lose sight of the evidence when focussing on the values. The third principle brings evidence and values fully together.

The "science-driven" principle: advances in science and technology drive the need equally for values-based as for evidence-based practice   This principle addresses head-on the supposed opposition between values-based and evidence-based approaches. One aspect of this opposition is the idea that as health care becomes more scientific, it will become less value-laden. The science-driven principle says, to the contrary, that more science will mean *more values* not fewer. The reason for this is to do with the way values link science with people. Science and technology as human activities are not value-free. But, even if they were, their effect in health care is to increase the choices available to us – and with choices go values.

There are many areas of health care where this values-raising effect of scientific and technological advances is all too evident. Consider assisted fertility, for example. Decision making in a "fertility clinic" is as much about values as it is about science (Fulford et al., 2012, ch. 12). This is not because infertility treatment has become somehow less scientific. It is because the remarkable advances we have seen in infertility treatment in recent decades have opened up a whole range of choices to which the values of those concerned are irreducibly linked.

Exercise 4.4

Values and evidence in values–based practice and Sally Coombs' story

In this exercise, we come back once again to our table of values-based practice with Sally Coombs in mind. Try adding a brief comment about the relevance (or otherwise) of the "two feet", "squeaky wheel" and "science-driven" principles in her story.

We give our own additions to Table 4.4. As this indicates, the key principle here is the "two feet" principle. This is because, at the stage in Sally's story described, the focus is on assessment: Dr Brown, you will recall, wanted to do an immediate "medical"; Nurse

Elements of values-based practice	Relevance to Sally Coombs' story
Premise of mutual respect	
Skills areas	
1. Awareness	Awareness of Sally Coombs' values is important – including awareness that we do not yet know what they are!
2. Reasoning	Principles reasoning proved helpful in Chapter 3 in understanding the difference of view between Nurse Matthews and Dr Brown about what to do next. (Casuistry might have been used to extend this.)
3. Knowledge	There is relevant knowledge of the values likely to be in play in crisis situations, particularly from service user/survivor research – but Sally is a unique individual and we must not assume that these actually are *her* values.
4. Communication	Communication skills generally are important especially: (1) for eliciting values (notably Sally's values) and, (2) of conflict resolution (as between Nurse Matthews and Dr Brown). We should look in particular for positive (StAR) values with Sally's aspirations likely to be important to her recovery.
Professional relationships	
5. Person-values-centred care	Sally's (still to be defined) values should be the starting point and key determinant of what Nurse Matthews and Dr Brown decide to do.
6. Extended MDT	The different value perspectives of team members are a resource: (1) for balanced decision making about what to do, and (2) for coming to understand what Sally's values actually are.
Values and evidence	
7. Two feet principle	In focussing, respectively, on the therapeutic relationship and missed medical conditions, Nurse Matthews and Dr Brown may well see the difference between them as one of evidence only, thus losing sight of the values in play.
8. Squeaky wheel principle	Not directly relevant here – but reminds us that, where values are more up-front in clinical decision making (as in ethical dilemmas), we should not to lose sight of the evidence in play.
9. Science-driven principle	Again, not directly relevant here but provides a reminder that values, as well as evidence, remain no less crucial in "high tech" decision making (as in fertility treatment).

Table 4.4 Values and evidence in values-based practice and Sally Coombs' story

Elements of values-based practice	Relevance to Sally Coombs' story
Partnership	
10. Dissensus within frameworks of shared values	
Balanced decisions in individual situations	

Table 4.4 (Continued)

Matthews thought this should be deferred in favour of allowing Sally to settle in and gain confidence in the team as the basis of future therapeutic work. And assessment is one of those areas where values are all too readily eclipsed by evidence. This is particularly so with medical assessment: "diagnosis" is widely thought of as an exclusively scientific process that is very much the preserve of doctors. And we have already seen that, at that this assessment stage in Sally's story, her values, although crucial, remained invisible in the background.

We will be looking at the issues this raises in detail in later chapters: at meaning in mental distress, in Chapter 8; at the resources of values-based assessment, in Chapter 9 – where Sally's values will finally come to light, though from an unlikely source; and at the importance of values in assessment to recovery, in Chapter 10.

Partnership in values-based practice

The need for partnership in health care decision making may seem obvious, with multidisciplinary team work now well-established as the basis of increasingly person-centred care. Partnership in practice, however, is all too often unequal. Service users/survivors in mental health, in one way or another, find themselves pushed into essentially passive roles. Within multidisciplinary teams, there is often one or another discipline that is dominant. And service users and providers alike find themselves subordinate to managers and policy makers. These facts of health care life raise issues of power to which we return in Chapter 5. Values-based practice, though, seeks an equality of partnership in decision making based on dissensus within frameworks of shared values.

'Dissensus' sounds rather technical. But, as we will see, it captures an important idea that is at the heart of how the various elements of values-based practice described in this chapter come together in balanced decision making. In this section, we give a brief introduction to dissensus and how it works within shared framework values. In the next and final section of the chapter, we will see how dissensus draws together the elements of values-based practice to support balanced decision making in practice.

Dissensus

One way to understand what "dissensus" means is by contrast with the more familiar idea of "consensus". Consensus means coming to an agreed view by deciding between different options. This is what happens in evidence-based medicine, in which we aim to "reach a consensus" between different views on what current research is telling us about this or that medical problem. A corresponding process in ethics is to make this or that value – autonomy, confidentiality, best interests, and so on – paramount; a top or overriding value that trumps all others. In values-based practice, by contrast, dissensus involves *different values remaining fully in play to be balanced sometimes one way and sometimes another according to the particular circumstances of a given situation.*

> **Reflection point:** *What role might dissensus as just described have in resolving the situation between Nurse Matthews and Dr Brown in Sally Coombs' story?*

Nurse Matthews and Dr Brown, you will recall, differed over what to do next in Sally Coombs' story because of a difference between them neither of evidence nor experience but, rather, of values. In terms of Beauchamp and Childress' four principles, Nurse Matthews' priority was autonomy (concerned in this instance with establishing a therapeutic relationship); Dr Brown's priority was non-maleficence (concerned in this instance with avoiding the harms arising from a missed medical condition such as diabetes).

One way of resolving such differences is to agree on an overriding value. In contemporary practice, autonomy is an example of a value that is often taken to be overriding in this sense. So, Nurse Matthews' autonomy would trump Dr Brown's non-maleficence. This is resolution by consensus. It depends on one value or set of values being discounted in favour of another.

The dissensus of values-based practice, by contrast, makes no claim to any such overriding value. It requires instead that the values in play be balanced according to the particular circumstances presented by the particular situation in question. As between Nurse Matthews and Dr Brown, then, this means a balance has to be drawn between their respective values. We will look in the next section at how this might be achieved. But the key point of dissensus is that, however the balance came out, in this instance their respective values *would remain fully in play*, to be balanced sometimes in the same way and sometimes in quite different ways according to the specific circumstances of the decision in question.

Shared framework values

To those inclined towards overriding values, this may seem like a recipe for "anything goes". Similar concerns might be raised by the starting point of values-based practice in mutual respect. There are, though, clear limits imposed by values-based practice. In the first place, the premise of mutual respect precludes racist and any other discriminatory values, since these by definition are not *mutually* respectful. This point was recognised and made explicit in the NIMHE values framework (see Box 4.1).

Equally important in values-based decision making are the shared values that, as we saw in Chapter 3, are a feature of any "values landscape". The shared values in question vary from situation to situation and it is part of the process of applying values-based practice to make explicit the shared values of those concerned. The development of the NIMHE values framework is a case in point: Fulford et al. (2012, ch. 14) give an example of a different approach adopted by a GP practice working with their local patients' forum.

> **Reflection point:** *What are the shared values between Nurse Matthews and Dr Brown in Sally Coombs' story? And in what sense do these provide a framework for balanced decision making? You may find it helpful here to think back to what we said in Chapters 2 and 3 about Beauchamp and Childress' four principles.*

With that final large hint, it is easy to see that the values shared between Nurse Matthews and Dr Brown were those defined by Beauchamp and Childress in their four principles. The point of these particular four principles, you will recall, was that they are widely shared within health care. They thus form a framework for decision making, in the sense that decision making involves balancing one against the other in a given case. So, no one principle (not even autonomy) is over-riding. There are no trumping values. They form, instead, a kind of values "round table" with no one at the head of the table. This leaves open, as Beauchamp and Childress make clear, the question of precisely how the balancing is to be carried out in a given case. It is here, as we said at the end of Chapter 3, that the elements of values-based practice come into play.

Exercise 4.5

Partnership in values–based practice and Sally Coombs' story

At this point, go back to your table of values-based practice and try adding dissensus and the framework values involved from the Reflection Points immediately above.

Our additions are given in Table 4.5. As we discussed in this section, the stand-off between Nurse Matthews and Dr Brown can be understood in terms of Beauchamp and Childress' four principles as a tension or conflict between autonomy and non-maleficence. The stand-off, though, is not that Nurse Matthews believes in autonomy while Dr Brown believes in non-maleficence. These are, instead, both values that *they share*. So, the stand-off is about the weights each of them gives to these two shared values in the particular situation presented by Sally Coombs at this time. Consensus in a situation such as this means agreeing which of them is right – Nurse Matthews with her value of autonomy, or Dr Brown with her value of non-maleficence. Dissensus, by contrast, means keeping both values in play but balanced one against the other in deciding what to do.

Pulling it all together: balanced decisions in individual situations

So, how does all this work out in practice?

Exercise 4.6

Balanced decisions in individual situations and Sally Coombs' story

In the final exercise in this chapter, look back to the comments you added earlier and think about which of the various elements of values-based practice might support balanced values-based decision making between Nurse Matthews and Dr Brown.

Finally, what do you think they decided to do?

Elements of values-based practice	Relevance to Sally Coombs' story
Premise of mutual respect	
Skills areas	
1. Awareness	Awareness of Sally Coombs' values is important – including awareness that we do not yet know what they are!
2. Reasoning	Principles reasoning proved helpful in Chapter 3 in understanding the difference of view between Nurse Matthews and Dr Brown about what to do next. (Casuistry might have been used to extend this.)
3. Knowledge	There is relevant knowledge of the values likely to be in play in crisis situations, particularly from service user/ survivor research – but Sally is a unique individual and we must not assume that these actually are *her* values.
4. Communication	Communication skills generally are important especially: (1) for eliciting values (notably Sally's values) and, (2) of conflict resolution (as between Nurse Matthews and Dr Brown). We should look in particular for positive (StAR) values with Sally's aspirations likely to be important to her recovery.
Professional relationships	
5. Person-values-centred care	Sally's (still to be defined) values should be the starting point and key determinant of what Nurse Matthews and Dr Brown decide to do.
6. Extended MDT	The different value perspectives of team members are a resource: (1) for balanced decision making about what to do, and (2) for coming to understand what Sally's values actually are.
Values and evidence	
7. Two feet principle	In focussing, respectively, on the therapeutic relationship and missed medical conditions, Nurse Matthews and Dr Brown may well see the difference between them as one of evidence only, thus losing sight of the values in play.
8. Squeaky wheel principle	Not directly relevant here – but reminds us that, where values are more up-front in clinical decision making (as in ethical dilemmas), we should not to lose sight of the evidence in play.
9. Science-driven principle	Again, not directly relevant here but provides a reminder that values as well as evidence remain no less crucial in "high tech" decision making (as in fertility treatment).

Table 4.5 Partnership in values-based practice and Sally Coombs' story

Elements of values–based practice	Relevance to Sally Coombs' story
Partnership	
10. Dissensus within frameworks of shared values	A decision has to be made between autonomy (Nurse Matthews) and non-maleficence (Dr Brown) but, as shared values, *both* remain in play – this is partnership in decision making based on dissensus within shared framework values (represented here by the four principles).
Balanced decisions in individual situations	

Table 4.5 (Continued)

Elements of values–based practice	Relevance to Sally Coombs' story
Premise of mutual respect	Underpins the whole process – partnership in decision making impossible without mutual respect
Skills areas	
1. Awareness	Awareness of Sally Coombs' values is important – including awareness that we do not yet know what they are!
2. Reasoning	Principles reasoning proved helpful in Chapter 3 in understanding the difference of view between Nurse Matthews and Dr Brown about what to do next. (Case-based reasoning might have been used to extend this.)
3. Knowledge	There is relevant knowledge of the values likely to be in play in crisis situations, particularly from service user/survivor research – but Sally is a unique individual and we must not assume that these actually are *her* values.
4. Communication	Communication skills generally are important especially: (1) for eliciting values (notably Sally's values) and, (2) of conflict resolution (as between Nurse Matthews and Dr Brown). We should look in particular for positive (StAR) values with Sally's aspirations likely to be important to her recovery.
Professional relationships	
5. Person-values-centred care	Sally's (still to be defined) values should be the starting point and key determinant of what Nurse Matthews and Dr Brown decide to do.

6. Extended MDT	The different value perspectives of team members are a resource: (1) for balanced decision making about what to do, and (2) for coming to understand what Sally's values actually are.
Values and evidence	
7. Two feet principle	In focussing, respectively, on the therapeutic relationship and missed medical conditions, Nurse Matthews and Dr Brown may well see the difference between them as one of evidence only, thus losing sight of the values in play
8. Squeaky wheel principle	Not directly relevant here – but reminds us that where values are more up front in clinical decision making (as in ethical dilemmas) we should not to lose sight of the evidence in play
9. Science-driven principle	Again not directly relevant here but provides a reminder that values as well as evidence remain no less crucial in "high tech" decision making (as in fertility treatment)
Partnership	
10. Dissensus within frameworks of shared values	A decision has to be made between autonomy (Nurse Matthews) and non-maleficence (Dr Brown) but as shared values *both* remain in play – this is partnership in decision making based on dissensus within shared framework values (represented here by the four principles)
Balanced decisions in individual situations	The "wait and watch" decision balanced both values appropriately in the particular circumstances presented by Sally Coombs at this time

Table 4.6 Balanced decisions in individual situations and Sally Coombs' story

The answer to the first part of this exercise is, of course, all the elements you have already added to the table – and more.

- The skills of values-based practice are crucial: raised awareness of values, but also the ability to reason about values (in this case, using, in particular, principles reasoning); we will see in Chapter 9 that communication skills (especially listening skills) were decisive at a later stage.
- The story thus far is not yet person-values-centred because Sally Coombs' values are as yet unknown. Again, multidisciplinary working will be important in this and it is in play already between Nurse Matthews and Dr Brown as the basis of a balanced decision about what to do next.
- As between values and evidence, it is the "two feet" principle, with its reminder to keep the relevant values firmly in sight in the context of this clinical decision, that is most relevant.

Switching back to the top of the table, though, we need now to add "mutual respect". This is the starting point for values-based practice in the sense that, without mutual respect, there would be no possibility of partnership between those involved in coming to the balanced values-based decisions that need to be made.

As to what they actually decided to do, your experience may suggest that either Nurse Brown or Dr Matthews simply "won the argument"! But, in the event, they agreed that, as Sally appeared to be settling down, they could afford to "wait and watch", rather than insisting on an immediate medical examination. A health care assistant, Jenny Khan, offered to sit with Sally. Jenny was, in fact, a support, time and recovery (STR) worker. STR workers are people with minimal professional training who work alongside others in mental health teams to support recovery. We will see, in Chapter 9, that, in her role as an STR worker, Jenny Khan was to play a crucial role in Sally Coombs' recovery.

For now, though, the "wait and watch" decision meant that the team could monitor Sally's mental state closely and thus respond promptly were there any deterioration. But, at the same time, it allowed this to be done in an unobtrusive and unthreatening way consistent with the need to establish a trusting relationship as the basis of future therapeutic work. This was not based on Nurse Matthews or Dr Brown giving up their respective nursing or medical perspectives on what was important, their respective values. Instead, their two perspectives remained in play but balanced one against the other. This dissensus was important because the right balance between them depended on the details of how Sally presented. Suppose, for example, that Sally had started to show new symptoms: the balance would then have shifted sharply to excluding an undiagnosed medical condition.

> **Reflection point:** *But whose values are still missing from the story to date and, correspondingly, from the decision made at this stage about what to do next?*

As noted, it is Sally's values that once again are still missing. In a sense, this is understandable, since the team have not yet had a chance to get to know her. This is often the case at an early and acute stage in a story such as that of Sally Coombs. Things go wrong though when, as professionals, we are simply blind to the fact that we do not know what really matters to the person concerned. This was very nearly what happened here, as we shall see in Chapter 9. Everyone simply assumed they knew what mattered to Sally Coombs. But they (like most of us, when we make the same assumption) were wrong.

CONCLUSION

This chapter has introduced the key elements of values-based practice – part of a tool kit of new ways of working with complex and conflicting values developed in health care in recent years. Among other tools in the tool kit, values-based practice offers a process to support balanced decision making in individual situations where complex and conflicting values are in play. In this respect, values-based practice is a partner to evidence-based practice. The processes involved are different. Notably, values-based practice depends critically on clinical skills. But both are decision support tools: values-based practice is a decision support tool for working with complex and confliction values; evidence-based practice is a decision support tool for working with complex and conflicting evidence.

Values-based practice is no sinecure. This is why as we have repeatedly emphasised that we need a whole tool kit of ways of working with values in health care. Values-based practice, in particular, as some of its critics have pointed out (Brecher, 2014), fails to address issues of power. Such issues are crucial at times of cutbacks in health and social care provision, as has been experienced in the UK and in many other parts of the world in recent years. Issues are crucial from top to bottom in values-based practice. The mutual respect from which values-based practice starts is meaningless in a power vacuum. Meaningless, too, is the dissensus on which the outputs of values-based practice depend: what chance is there for balanced decision making in a power vacuum? In the situation presented by Sally Coombs, it was her powerlessness relative to the professionals involved that allowed her values to remain, at this stage, invisible. It is to issues of power in mental health practice that we turn next.

GLOSSARY OF KEY TERMS

Values-based practice – provides a new skills-based approach to balanced decision making where complex and conflicting values are in play.

Awareness of values – this includes raised awareness of values and of the variety of values

Reasoning about values – using values reasoning to explore the variety of values in play in a given situation – methods useful clinically include principles reasoning and case-based reasoning (or casuistry).

Knowledge of values – research and experience-based knowledge of the values likely to be in play in a given situation – but such knowledge should never be assumed to apply to any particular individual (everyone has a unique 'values finger print')

Communication skills – important generally but especially skills for eliciting values and of conflict resolution

Person-values-centred care – putting the values of the individual service user/survivor at the centre of decision making

The extended multidisciplinary team – in values-based practice the importance of multi-disciplinary teamwork is extended from providing a range of different knowledge and skills to include also a range of different values

The "two feet" principle – all decisions stand on the two feet of values as well as evidence: so when a decision looks strongly evidence-based don't forget to look out also for the relevant values (in particular those of the service user/survivor concerned)

The "squeaky wheel" principle – we notice values particularly when they are complex and/or conflicting and hence cause trouble: so when a decision looks strongly values-based (as in an ethical dilemma) don't forget to look out also for the relevant evidence (in particular based on the knowledge and experience of the service user/survivor concerned)

The "science-driven" principle – advances in science and technology drive the need equally for values-based as for evidence-based practice: so in a high-tech situation it is particularly important to look out for both the values and the evidence involved

Partnership in values-based practice – based on dissensus within frameworks of shared values.

Dissensus – involves different values remaining fully in play to be balanced sometimes one way and sometimes another according to the particular circumstances of a given situation

Shared framework values – values shared between decision makers in a given situation thus providing a framework for balanced decision making: such values are usually complex and conflicting and thus have to be interpreted and balanced according to the situation in question

Balanced values-based decision making – decision making in an individual situation that uses the skills and other elements of values-based practice to interpret and balance the relevant shared framework values

FURTHER READING

Clinical stories illustrating the roles of the various elements of values-based practice across a range of health care scenarios are given in Fulford et al. (2012), *Essential Values-based Practice: Linking Science with People* (Cambridge University Press). This is the launch volume for a new book series on values-based practice. Other volumes in the series explore team work (Thistlethwaite, 2012) and commissioning (Heginbotham, 2012).

Chapters 2 and 6 of Fulford et al. (2012) explore the importance of experience-based knowledge, respectively, in individual judgement (see Peile's concept of "squaring down") and in the knowledge base of decision making. For a philosophical account connecting tacit knowledge and individual judgement, see Thornton (2006).

Work on values and models building on Colombo et al. (2003) (discussed in this chapter) is described in Fulford and van Staden (2013). The researcher and ex-service user Colin King has extended Colombo's approach to ethnic and spiritual aspects of models of mental distress in King et al. (2009). For other work on the theory underpinning values-based practice, see the Further Reading section to Chapter 3. The VBP website gives further information on all aspects of values-based practice. Also available on the website are downloadable versions of key resources such as the training manual for values-based practice in mental health care, *Whose Values?* (Woodbridge and Fulford, 2004). See http://www.go.warwick.ac.uk/values-basedpractice or simply search for "values-based practice".

REFERENCES

Allott, P. (2004) "What is mental health? Illness and recovery", in Ryan, T. and Pritchard, J. (eds) *Adult Mental Health*, Good Practice Series 10. London: Jessica Kingsley Publishers.

Basset, T. and Stickley, T. (eds) (2010) *Voices of Experience: Narratives of Mental Health Survivors*. Chichester: Wiley.

Brecher, B. (2014) "VBP: But which values? And whose?" in Loughlin, M. (ed.) *Debates in Values-Based Practice*. Cambridge: Cambridge University Press.

Colombo, A., Bendelow, G., Fulford, K.W.M. and Williams, S. (2003) "Evaluating the influence of implicit models of mental disorder on processes of shared decision making within community-based multi-disciplinary teams", *Social Science & Medicine*, 56: 1557–70.

Croft, S., Bewley, C., Beresford, P., Branfield, F., Fleming, J., Glynn, M. and Postle, K. (2011) *Person-centred Support: A Guide to Person-centred Working for Practitioners*. York: Shaping Our Lives and Joseph Rowntree Foundation.

Fulford, K.W.M. and Colombo, A. (2004) "Six models of mental disorder: A study combining linguistic-analytic and empirical methods", *Philosophy, Psychiatry, & Psychology*, 11(2): 129–44.

Fulford, K.W.M. and van Staden, W. (2013) "Values-based practice: Topsy-turvy take home messages from ordinary language philosophy (and a few next steps)" in Fulford, K.W.M., Davies, M., Gipps, R., Graham, G., Sadler, J., Stanghellini, G. and Thornton, T. (eds), *The Oxford Handbook of Philosophy and Psychiatry*. Oxford: Oxford University Press

Fulford, K.W.M., Peile, E. and Carroll, H. (2012) *Essential Values-based Practice: Clinical Stories Linking Science with People*. Cambridge: Cambridge University Press.

Glynn, M. and Beresford, P. with Bewley, C., Branfield, F., Jabeer Butt, Croft, S., Dattani Pitt, K., Fleming, J., Flynn, R., Patmore, C., Postle, K. and Turner, M. (2008) *Person-centred Support: What Service Users and Practitioners Say*. York: Joseph Rowntree Foundation.

Heginbotham, C. (2012) *Values-based Commissioning of Health and Social Care*. Cambridge: Cambridge University Press.

King, C., Bhui, K., Fulford, K.W.M., Vasiliou-Theodore, C. and Williamson, T. (2009) *Model Values? Race, Values and Models in Mental Health*. London: The Mental Health Foundation.

National Institute for Mental Health England (2004) "The National Framework of Values for Mental Health". Originally published on the NIMHE website at www.nimhe.org.uk/ValuesBasedPractise. Now available online at the Values-based Practice website (accessed 29 May 2015) or in Woodbridge, K. and Fulford, K.W.M. (2004) *"Whose Values?" A Workbook for Values-based Practice in Mental Health Care*. London: Sainsbury Centre for Mental Health.

Sackett, D.L., Straus, S.E., Scott Richardson, W., Rosenberg, W. and Haynes, R.B. (2000) *Evidence-Based Medicine: How to Practice and Teach EBM* (2nd edn). Edinburgh and London: Churchill Livingstone.

Thistlethwaite, J. (2012) *Values-based Interprofessional Collaborative Practice*. Cambridge: Cambridge University Press.

Thornton, T. (2006) "Tacit knowledge as the unifying factor in EBM and clinical judgement", *Philosophy, Ethics, and Humanities of Medicine*, 1:2doi:10.1186/1747-5341-1-2. Available at http://www.peh-med.com/content/1/1/2. BioMed Central Ltd (accessed 29 May 2015).

Wallcraft, J., Schrank, B. and Amering, M. (eds) (2009) *Handbook of Service User Involvement in Mental Health Research*. London: Wiley.

Woodbridge, K., and Fulford, K.W.M. (2004) *"Whose Values?. A Workbook for Values-based Practice in Mental Health Care*. London: Sainsbury Centre for Mental Health.

5 | The importance of power

Chapter Summary

This chapter will:

- Introduce the reader to definitions of power and the importance of considering issues of power when thinking about values and ethics in mental health care practice.

- Outline liberal theories of power and consider their application in mental health care, and consider critiques of psychiatry based around notions of liberal power and freedom.

- Outline Marxist theories of power, and consider the concept of ideological power in mental health practice.

- Outline Foucault's theories of power and consider critiques of power, based around Foucault's ideas and questions of the medicalisation of everyday life by psychiatry.

- Outline theories of power as empowerment and consider application to ideas of co-production when working in mental health practice.

Up to this point in the book, we have largely considered the issues of ethics and values as though they occur without a societal context. We have particularly not been addressing the question of differentials in power relationships within situations where conflicts over values arise. In this chapter, we consider the important question of power and how different ways of conceptualising power impact on our understanding of values and ethics in mental health practice.

What is power?

Power can be defined in simple terms as the ability of one individual to compel another to do something that they would otherwise not want to do (Lukes, 2004). Power is a social relation which situates two agents in a hierarchy of dominant and dominated (Scott, 2001), and can be exercised in a variety of ways ranging from the least violent to the most violent. In analysing power relations, we can move from notions of influence and authority towards more direct interpersonal relations of coercion and force (Lukes, 2004).

In this chapter, we will outline four broad themes in the analysis of power: liberal conceptions, Marxist accounts, a plural concept of power drawn from Foucault's work, and a concept of communicative power.

First, we consider liberal conceptions of power that start from the moral values of autonomy and liberty. Typical of such theories is the work of the nineteenth-century English philosopher J.S. Mill (Mill, 2006). They have been used to seek to justify restrictions on liberty based on notions of paternalism (Gert et al., 2006). These concepts of power justify political authority through the necessity for a societal contract to maintain good order and the equal liberty of citizens (Anderson, 2014). The underlying concept of power at play in liberal theories is one of a necessary but undesirable restriction of liberty.

Second, there are Marxist accounts of power that view power as a means of justifying particular societal inequalities and privileges. Derived from the work of the nineteenth-century political philosopher, Karl Marx (Marx, 1988), central to this analysis of power is the specific concept of ideology. Ideologies are ideas that permit the continuation of inequalities of power through the masking of those inequalities in supposedly neutral ideas that really serve the interests of a ruling group (Eagleton, 2007). The underlying analysis of power in Marxist theories is one of a societal domination of one class by another.

The third account of power is drawn from the work of a twentieth-century French philosopher and historian, Michel Foucault. Foucault focuses on power as both repressive and productive (Lupton, 1997). Power always exists in a relationship with concepts of truth and knowledge, and there is no fixed position beyond power that we can adopt to critique regimes of power (Foucault, 2002). In significant ways, we are who we are as human beings, because of power as both a productive and a repressive force.

The fourth and more recent understanding of power is what is called "communicative" power. This is distinctive, in that it attempts to separate a concept of power from a concept of force (Arendt, 1970). It is what Scott (2001: 6) has termed a "second stream of power research" that focuses on power as the abilities and capacities to carry out actions. This is the connotation of power as empowerment, as the ability to enact a full range of capacities as a political citizen.

Liberal theories of power

Liberal theories of power take as their starting point the importance of individual liberty and the right of individuals to make autonomous decisions (Mill, 2006). These rights can only be interfered with if there are overriding demands for specifically beneficial outcomes that will involve coercion. Coercion can be justified on paternalistic grounds but only if it meets strict criteria (Gert et al., 2006). We can override a person's autonomy and coerce them for their own benefit if they lack capacity to rationally decide their future or if their behaviour is criminal and thus threatens other individuals.

In *On Liberty*, Mill argues that the only grounds for interference with liberty are for public protection. We should not coerce other people through a belief that what they are doing is bad for them, but only if their actions threaten public safety in one form or another (Mill, 2006). We can reason with individuals about their behaviour, but as long as they are rational agents, then they are capable of making free choices about their lives.

Liberal political theorists have argued that, in forming societies, people may choose to give up elements of their autonomy in order to preserve a stable and safe political order. Hobbes famously argues that people freely choose to give up their autonomy to a sovereign ruler in order to provide a harmonious and safe environment for, without such a contract, a peaceful society is not possible (Hobbes, 2008). However, this is a freely chosen contract to institute a form of power and authority for public protection.

Liberal theories of power and critical psychiatry

Throughout the 1960s and the early 1970s, a range of critical voices were raised against the power of psychiatry to coerce, segregate and treat people against their will (Szasz,1972; Laing, 1990; Basaglia, 2004). Although retrospectively labelled "anti-psychiatry", these were a diverse group of people, many of whom were psychiatrists, arguing that psychiatry was illegitimately infringing the liberty of individuals diagnosed with mental illness through enforced sectioning and treatment. Bracken and Thomas (2005) have noted that, at the heart of this critique of power, was a liberal idea concerned with the suppressing of individual freedom and an understanding of power as the restriction of individual liberties.

The most consistent liberal and libertarian approach to a critique of psychiatry was taken by the American psychiatrist Thomas Szasz. Szasz (1976) argued that the diagnosis of mental illness had no valid basis in pathophysiology and therefore amounted to a value judgement. Throughout his life, Szasz (2010) argued that mental illnesses were life problems which people should be free to solve through seeking help from professionals if needed, but that they should not be coerced into treatment (Buchanan-Barker and Barker, 2009).

Szasz's consistent liberalism outlines the strengths and the failures of such an approach. Commentators have criticised his approach for its too simplistic equation of power with a restriction of liberty and his downplaying of the need for intervention in the name of care (Sedgwick, 1982). Treffert (1973) famously characterised this liberal approach to mental illness as enabling people to die with their "rights on". The argument was that liberalism was not much use if it amounted to an abandonment of care for those who needed it most. However, as we will see throughout this book, the liberal critique of psychiatric coercion remains an important and central theme to many recent debates on psychiatry (Bentall, 2009).

Exercise 5.1

- Write a list of the legal powers to coerce service users that exist within your particular professional group. You might want to consult the Mental Health Act 1983/2007 and the Mental Capacity Act, 2005.
- Write a list of the informal powers of influence and authority that exist within your particular professional group. Think about examples from practice where you have seen informal powers of influence used.
- Compare this list of powers with the list of values that you constructed earlier. Is it possible to reconcile your values with your powers to influence and coerce?

Marxist theories of power

While Szasz followed a consistent libertarian approach in his critique of psychiatric power, other critics of psychiatry were interested in a critique of the institutional power of psychiatry and the role it played in a wider capitalist society (Laing,1967; Basaglia, 2004). They drew on Marxist theories of power and ideology (Gramsci, 1999). Marxist theories of ideology define ideology as a set of ideas that represent specific interests, and consider that the ruling ideas within a society are ideas that represent the ruling class of society. Marx and Engels wrote that:

> "What else does the history of ideas prove, than that intellectual production changes its character in proportion as material production is changed? The ruling ideas of each age have ever been the ideas of its ruling class" (Marx and Engels, cited in Marx, 1988: 236).

Ideologies, according to Marxist theory, function in the following five ways:

- Ideologies mask reality; they outline a state of affairs, which is a way of hiding material realities. Marx's key example is the idea of free and equal commodity exchange that masks the exploitative reality of unequal labour relations. Capitalist markets are termed "free" when they are really exploitative and dominating.
- This masking of reality also functions as an "inversion" of the real state of affairs. Ideologies not only mask reality, but also turn the world on its head. For example, many writers have argued that the claim that psychiatry is developing progressively more evidence-based practice that offers better treatments is an ideological inversion of a reality where treatments on offer fail and mental illnesses proliferate (Bentall, 2009; Whitaker, 2010).
- Ideologies are socially necessary illusions; they enable the stability of society. Functionalist accounts of power would see this aspect of ideology in a positive light, so Parsons argues that such "illusions" are necessary for a stable order (Lukes, 1986). Marxists tend to view them as means of stabilising an unjust order (Horkheimer, 1973)
- Ideologies naturalise social processes. The Marxist theorist, Georg Lukács terms this process "reification" – the way that human and social processes that are the product of the struggles of history are treated as natural facts (Lukács, 1971). We often hear statements such as the "market will decide"; a statement that "reifies" the social processes

that constitute a market economy into a natural entity above, beyond and impervious to human action – the "market" comes to function as do natural weather fluctuations.

- Ideologies always have a "truth content" (Adorno, 1990). There is an aspect of an ideology that wants to move beyond exploitation and propose a better world. An example of this, for Marx, is religion. Marx believes that religion masks, distorts, serves the interests of the ruling class and naturalises states of affairs that are more properly treated as social. However, he also writes that religion is the "sigh of a soulless world"; within the religious hope for a better world lies a truth but only if that hope can be turned towards revolutionary purpose in this world rather than the next (Marx, 1988).

The ideology of mental "illness"

Critics of psychiatry, such as the democratic psychiatry movement in Italy and the increasing political texture of R.D. Laing's work in the UK, argued that the power of psychiatry is broadly ideological, and the ideology at play in psychiatry is around the nature and existence of mental illness (Crossley, 1998). Rather than arguing that the categorisation of mental illness is a "category mistake" (Szasz, 1972), they claim that constructing certain human behaviours as "mental illnesses" serves an ideological function through policing and defining social problems as "deviant behaviours" (Foucault, 1993).

The dominant thought and practice within psychiatry is one that sees "mental illness" as biomedical, as an illness like any other. Biomedical psychiatry assumes that mental illness should be treated primarily as diseases with a biological origin, that they should be subject to mainly medical treatments (Klerman, 1978).

Mental illnesses are ideologies, in the Marxist sense, for the following reasons:

- The statement that mental illnesses are biological in nature masks the social and material causes of distress in society (Parker et al., 1995).
- The belief in categories such as schizophrenia and bipolar disorder as natural constructs is an inversion of reality, as they are produced historically in a process of labelling and the refining of labels through diagnostic manuals. As the authors of the research agenda for the *Diagnostic and Statistical Manual of Mental Disorders* (5th edn) (DSM-5) wrote, there is not one biological marker of any of the DSM-defined syndromes that has been found (Kupfer et al., 2002). Schizophrenia and bipolar disorder are treated as identifiable disorders when they are social constructs.
- The ideology of mental illness enables a classification of groups of people who do not fit into the norm of society and their confinement in institutions. The idea of discrete classifiable mental illnesses enables a means way of treating and confining mental illness to continue, which serves wider interests of social control in society (Laing, 1967).
- Mental illnesses naturalise as facts entities that are social in production. Schizophrenia is a social and cultural concept, produced through an encounter in asylums between a medical classifying gaze and confined patients, but it is treated as an objective, naturally occurring entity.
- The truth content in the idea of mental illness is the need to respond to mental distress and suffering. Critical psychiatrists such as Laing and Basaglia wanted to take this impulse and move it in a more social direction; for example, the attempt to set up alternative means of care through deinstitutionalisation in Italy (Donnelly, 1992).

Critiques of the concept of ideology

Bracken and Thomas (2010) have criticised this form of critical psychiatry on a number of grounds. They argue that it stems from an era when institutions were predominant and there was a need for a critique of exclusion and confinement. However, the power of psychiatry is now far more dispersed than the focus on the asylum (Miller and Rose, 1986), and there is a need to develop tools of critique that are more adequate to a form of power that is more dispersed and less unitary.

Bracken and Thomas (2005) write of the way that the "anti-psychiatry" of the 1960s and 1970s was too focussed on an interrogation of individual madness and an understanding of power as repressing madness. Miller and Rose (1986) similarly argue for a shift in the understanding of the power of psychiatry away from notions of repression towards an understanding of a dispersed power that is contained in a range of health care disciplines, and that is both productive and repressive. Bracken and Thomas write about this in the following terms:

> "Instead of repression, psychiatric power is now operating to produce an enhanced notion of subjectivity, an expanded sense of selfhood, through the production of new discourses of the self" (Bracken and Thomas, 2005: 94).

This focus on psychiatric power as both productive and repressive is reliant on the complex analysis of power that is contained in the work of Michel Foucault.

Foucault on power

While Foucault's work on power is highly complex and it could be argued that he develops multiple strands in his analysis of power, his broad understanding of power is different from Marxism as he stresses that power is productive as well as repressive (Foucault, 2002. For Foucault, there is no space in society free from power and without power there are no possibilities for individuals to exist. We are products of power as individuals; we do not pre-exist and then become repressed by power.

The medicalisation of misery: An example

One of the ways of understanding what he means by this is to think about the dispute over medicalisation in society. Many authors have been worried recently that psychiatry is increasingly treating normal sadness and over-medicalising individuals (Davies, 2013; Frances, 2013).

A recent example of this dispute was in the controversy about depression and the bereavement exclusion in the new DSM-5 (APA, 2013). In the US revision of the manual that classifies disorder, there was a decision to remove the bereavement exclusion when diagnosing depression. Previously, psychiatrists were recommended to refrain from diagnosing severe depression for two months following bereavement (APA, 2013). It was felt that being depressed for two months after a loss was actually quite normal. However, in DSM-5, this exclusion has been removed, as it was argued that it is possible to distinguish between normal grieving and depression, and that neglecting to intervene early may mean poorer outcomes for people whose major depression may be triggered by the loss of a loved one (APA, 2013).

Liberal critics might be worried about this move because it is an unnecessary interference in normal and important processes of suffering in human life (Davies, 2013). Marxist critiques might see the process of pathologising bereavement as entwined with agendas from pharmaceutical companies to medicalise sadness and loss (Whitaker, 2010).

Critics who take a perspective informed by Foucault, such as the sociologist Nikolas Rose, are less likely immediately to criticise the removal of the bereavement exclusion. Rose (2007) has argued that who we are as subjects in the early twenty-first century is dependent on a historical process of medicalisation; advances in antibiotics, vaccines and preventive medicine have changed what it means to be human in ways we cannot imagine. There is no fixed meaning to humanity, and the power of medical science has importantly produced who we are as individuals and societies just as much as it has repressed us. There is no specific reason why we should not take anti-depressant drugs to alleviate our misery, and nothing inherently good about suffering (Rose, 2007).

Exercise 5.2

The journalist Robert Whitaker has written a book that poses a simple but startling dilemma for modern evidence-based psychiatry: if psychiatry is becoming more and more successful in treating mental illness, then why are more and more people becoming mentally ill? (Whitaker, 2010)

For the sake of this exercise, let us accept Whitaker's premise that there is an "epidemic" of mental illness, as he puts forward compelling statistics for growth in the numbers of people diagnosed and treated with depression and with bipolar disorder (Whitaker, 2010).

Write a list of reasons why this is a positive development and a list of reasons to state why this is a negative development. Reflect on this list to see where you stand on the debate on medicalisation.

Foucault's three forms of power

As we have seen, the first modification of traditional notions of power in Foucault's work is the stress on power as productive as well as repressive, and as a process that forms who we are as individuals, rather than repressing our inherent abilities and qualities.

The second focus of Foucault's analysis of power is concerned with the exercise of power and the manner in which power is not exercised in a unitary manner but, rather, dispersed throughout society. He argues for a diverse account focussing on three discrete but overlapping modes of power: sovereign power, governmental power and biopower.

Sovereign power is a dominating, repressive form of power; a power that lay in the right of the sovereign to "foster life or disallow it to the point of death" (Foucault, 1976: 138). This form of power is increasingly displaced in democratic states, although it never quite disappears, and may be reinstated even within democracies at moments of emergency or crisis. Democratic states may even create zones of exception to normal democratic rules where sovereign power holds sway, as when the US government introduced internment camps for terrorist suspects in Guantanamo Bay (Agamben, 2005).

Governmental power is diffused through a range of institutions within society that determine our education, health care, punishment in prisons and the way that we are formed as subjects in society. Foucault's focus here remains on repressive notions of power and how diffused institutions produce "docile" bodies and subjects through discipline (Foucault, 1991). Governmental power is a key dispersed form in which power operates in societies.

This question of governmental, disciplinary power is central to understanding the way that notions of mental illness intersect with other discriminatory judgements, particularly when applied to minority and oppressed groups within society. There is a long negative association with ideas of madness, irrationality and the feminine which has often resulted in the use of ideas of mental illness as a means of keeping women in a subordinate role in society (Showalter, 1987). We saw in the chapter on ethics how racist attitudes and values can impact upon minority ethnic groups, particularly in assessments of risk and dangerousness. Escobar (2012) has written of how psychiatric diagnosis, which we will see is an inherently value-laden activity, can unconsciously draw on inherent prejudices and stereotypes. For example, he writes that the over-diagnosis of schizophrenia amongst the African-American population in the USA may be influenced by cultural misapprehensions around notions of bizarre and strange behaviour (Escobar, 2012). We will return to the thorny question of the over-diagnosis of schizophrenia amongst minority ethnic populations in the UK in Chapter 8.

Finally, Foucault developed a concept of "biopower", which is a way in which power operates productively to produce forms of life. Power here takes as its object neither the right to kill (as in sovereign power), nor the right to discipline (as in governmental power) but, rather, the fostering of life and the production of life. Here, there is a focus on population health, on life expectancy, on the possibilities of increased fertility and potency (Foucault, 1986). Technologies and political power increasingly focus on aspects of life that were previously private and domestic (Rose, 2006). One need only to think of medical interventions such as Viagra, IVF and Prozac to think in different ways how medical technologies have started to invest our life processes and to increase and improve our desires, rather than discipline and model them (Rose and Abi-Rached, 2013).

In mental health care, we can see echoes of this focus on biopower in the emphasis on wellness, health and resilience (Layard, 2011). There is a growing focus on maintaining health and preventing mental distress through activities such as mindfulness. Mental health care and research is focussing progressively more on early detection, prevention and intervention in order to develop an individual's health and wellbeing. This is often being conceptualised in a biological way as a process of working on and through the brain (Cromby, 2011). The mental health disciplines are focussing on wellness as well as sickness and disease.

A "communicative" concept of power

The final concept of power that we will refer to, a "communicative" concept of power, has deep philosophical roots in Ancient Greek thought, but has been revived in modern philosophy by Hannah Arendt.

Arendt (1970) tries to distinguish conceptually between a concept of power and a concept of violence. Although she accepts that power can combine with force in specific situations; these are situations when power has failed or broken down. For Arendt, power is a word for a capacity to "act in concert" and represents a political and communal capacity for collective, democratic action (Arendt, 1986: 64). When force enters the arena, then we lose the collective power that is a possibility for political action. Arendt (1970) aims to outline a positive concept of democratic, political power that is separate from notions of domination and violence, although she accepts that the two concepts are often related. She writes that:

> "Power and violence are opposites; where the one rules absolutely the other is absent. ... violence can destroy power; it is utterly incapable of creating it (Arendt, 1986: 71).

This notion of power as a capacity that needs to be built communally is central to ideas of "co-production" in mental health services. The concept of co-production in mental health services has been defined in a recent document published by the New Economics Foundation (2013) as:

> "A relationship where professionals and citizens share power to plan and deliver support together, recognising that both partners have vital contributions to make in order to improve quality of life for people and communities (NEF, 2013: 6)."

The goal is to produce practice in mental health care which uses every participant's powers equally to produce truly democratic participatory decisions. This concept is complementary to the ideas of values-based practice that we saw outlined in Chapter 4 (Woodbridge and Fulford, 2004). The co-production report identifies a dynamic model of wellbeing that is concerned with the individual and the material conditions for living well (NEF, 2013: 15). However, there can still be questions that this notion of participatory power, while an important corrective to the idea of power and domination, ignores continuing inequalities and hierarchies within society (Habermas, 1986). There have been critiques of values-based practice for its too neutral notion of values and its downplaying of problems of power and hierarchy (Brecher, 2011).

❑ Case example 5.1

You are a professional from any discipline working closely alongside a service user who is sectioned under Section 3 of the Mental Health Act in an in-patient acute setting. Working with the service user, you have developed an outline of an argument for the person's medication to be reduced as she feels that it is being prescribed at too high a dosage, and it has previously been more beneficial at half the dose she is currently prescribed.

The service user wants to present this plan at a forthcoming ward round but is scared to do so, as she finds the atmosphere intimidating, with many people present she does not know. Also, she knows that the rest of the health care team do not want to reduce her medication. She asks you to present the plan for her. Here are a range of responses: which would you choose?

- Insist that she must present the plan herself, as she initiated it and has to take responsibility for it.
- Agree to take responsibility for her and present the plan.
- Argue that presenting this plan as her advocate compromises your position, so you will obtain the help of an Independent Mental Health Advocate to present the plan.
- Make a determined attempt to change the nature of the ward round meeting so that the service user feels comfortable to be present; insist that the service user has the first input, is not interrupted, and that only those who she wants to be present are present.

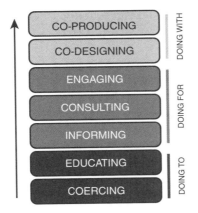

Figure 5.1 Identify where your responses fit in relation to this ladder of participation

Source: Slay and Stephens (2013)

CONCLUSION

This chapter has highlighted the importance of considering concepts of power when thinking about values and ethics in mental health practice. Four different strands of power have been identified from the philosophical tradition: liberal, Marxist, Foucault's ideas on power, and communicative concepts of power. This chapter has related these concepts to concrete examples in mental health practice: medicalisation, diagnosis and co-production in mental health.

GLOSSARY OF KEY TERMS

Anti-psychiatry – a label applied to a range of radical critics of psychiatry from the 1960s and 1970s. These critics argued that mental illness is a myth, that psychiatry illegitimately coerces individuals and labels those who are different as mad.

Biopower – a concept of power that focuses on the way in which power produces and enables the production of forms of life – particularly focussing on biological notions of birth, death, fertility and sexuality. This concept is taken from the work of Michel Foucault.

Co-production – the sharing of power between professionals, service users and carers to plan and deliver mental health services.

Governmental power – power that is diffused through the organisations and institutions of society –for example, the power embedded within the many institutions that comprise the welfare state.

Ideology – a set of ideas that serve particular interests, usually those in a dominant position of power, whilst claiming to be value-neutral.

Liberalism – the belief that political systems should be organised to respect the autonomous rights of individuals to live their lives free from interference, other than for public safety and protection.

Marxism- a range of political theories that derive from Karl Marx's critique of capitalism. Marxists argue that all societies based on capitalist exchange principles are fundamentally exploitative and unequal.

Communicative power - a positive notion of power that separates power from notions of coercion and violence, and focuses on empowerment and collective, democratic action.

Sovereign power – power that is dominating and rests with a narrow group or singular person (namely, the sovereign).

FURTHER READING

Good books on the power of psychiatry include the following;

Bentall, R.P. (2009) *Doctoring the Mind. Is Our Current Treatment of Mental Illness Really Any Good?* New York: New York University Press.

Double, D. (ed.) (2006) *Critical Psychiatry. The Limits of Madness.* Basingstoke: MacMillan.

Greenberg, G. (2013) *The Book of Woe: DSM and the Unmaking of Psychiatry,* Melbourne/London: Scribe.

Ingleby, D. (2004) *Critical Psychiatry. The Politics of Mental Health.* London: Free Association Books.

INTERNET RESOURCES

The critical psychiatry website hosts a range of resources from psychiatrists critical of mainstream practice and can be found at: http://www.criticalpsychiatry.co.uk/

The magazine *Asylum* is the oldest magazine in the UK developing the critical psychiatry perspective in an explicitly political approach, and can be found at: http://www.asylumonline.net/

REFERENCES

Adorno, T.W. (1990) *Negative Dialectics,* translated by E.B. Ashton. London and New York: Routledge.

Agamben, G. (2005) *State of Exception.* Chicago and London: University of Chicago Press.

APA (American Psychiatric Association) (2013) "Major depressive disorder and the bereavement exclusion". Available at: http://www.dsm5.org/Documents/Bereavement%20Exclusion%20Fact%20Sheet. pdf (accessed 10 April 2014).

Anderson, S., "Coercion", *The Stanford Encyclopaedia of Philosophy* (2014) spring edn, Edward N. Zalta (ed.). Available at: http://plato.stanford.edu/archives/spr2014/entries/coercion/ (accessed 10 April 2014).

Arendt, H. (1970) *On Violence.* San Diego, New York, London: Harcourt Publishers.

Arendt, H. (1986) "Communicative Power" in Lukes, S. (ed.) *Power.* Cambridge: Blackwell.

Basaglia, F. (2004) "Breaking the Circuit of Control", in Ingleby, D. (ed.) *Critical Psychiatry. The Politics of Mental Health.* London: Free Association Books.

Bentall, R.P. (2009) *Doctoring the Mind. Is Our Current Treatment of Mental Illness Really Any Good?* New York: New York University Press.

Bracken, P. and Thomas, P. (2005) *Postpsychiatry. Mental Health in a Postmodern World.* Oxford: Oxford University Press.

Bracken, P. and Thomas, P. (2010) "From Szasz to Foucault: On the role of critical psychiatry", *Philosophy, Psychiatry, & Psychology,* 17(3): 219–28.

Brecher, B. (2011) "Which values? And whose? A reply to Fulford", *Journal of Evaluation in Clinical Practice,* 17: 996–8.

Buchanan-Barker, P. and Barker, P. (2009) "The convenient myth of Thomas Szasz", *Journal of Psychiatric and Mental Health Nursing,* 16: 87–95.

Cromby, J. (2011) "The greatest gift: Happiness, governance and psychology", *Social and Psychology Personality Compass,* 5(11): 840–52.

Crossley, N. (1998) "R.D. Laing and the British anti-psychiatry movement: A socio-historical analysis", *Social Science and Medicine,* 47(7): 877–89.

Davies, J. (2013) *Cracked – Why Psychiatry is doing More Harm than Good.* London: Icon Books.

Donnelly, M. (1992) *The Politics of Mental Health in Italy.* London and New York: Routledge.

Eagleton, T. (2007) *Ideology. An Introduction.* London: Verso.

Escobar, J. (2012) "Diagnostic bias: Racial and cultural issues", *Psychiatric Services,* September, 63(9): 847.

Foucault, M. (1986) *The History of Sexuality,* Volume 1. London: Penguin.

Foucault, M. (1991) *Discipline and Punish. The Birth of the Prison.* London: Penguin.

Foucault, M. (1993) *Madness and Civilization. A History of Insanity in the Age of Reason,* translated by R. Howard. London: Routledge.

Foucault, M. (2002) "Truth and Power" in Faubion, J. (ed.) *Power – Essential Works of Foucault – 1954–1984,* Volume 3. London: Penguin.

Frances, A. (2013) *Saving Normal.* New York: William Morrow.

Gert, B., Culver, C. and Clouser, K. (2006) *Bioethics: A Systematic Approach.* Oxford: Oxford University Press.

Gramsci, A. (1999) *The Gramsci Reader,* edited by D. Forgacs. London: Lawrence & Wishart.

Habermas, J. (1986) "Hannah Arendt's Communications Concept of Power" in Lukes, S. (ed.) *Power.* Cambridge: Blackwell.

Hobbes, T. (2008) *Leviathan.* Oxford: Oxford University Press.

Horkheimer, M. (1973) *Critical Theory – Selected Essays.* London and New York: Continuum.

Klerman, G.L. (1978) "The evolution of a scientific nosology" in Shershow, J.C. (ed.) *Schizophrenia, Science and Practice.* Cambridge, MA: Harvard University Press.

Kupfer, D., First, M. and Regier, D. (eds) (2002) *A Research Agenda for DSM-V.* Washington, DC: American Psychiatric Association.

Laing, R.D. (1967) *The Politics of Experience and the Bird of Paradise.* London: Penguin.

Laing, R.D. (1990) *The Divided Self.* London: Penguin.

Layard, R. (2011) *Happiness: Lessons from a New Science* (2nd edn). London: Penguin.

Lukács, G. (1971) *History and Class Consciousness,* translated by R. Livingstone. London: Merlin Press.

Lukes, S. (1986) *Power. A Radical View.* Basingstoke: Palgrave Macmillan.

Lupton, D. (1997) "Foucault and the medicalisation critique" in Petersen, A. and Bunton, R. (eds) (1997) *Foucault, Health and Medicine.* London and New York: Routledge.

Marx, K. (1988) *Selected Writings,* edited by D. McLellan. Oxford: Oxford University Press.

Mill, J.S. (2006) *On Liberty.* London: Penguin Classics.

Miller, P. and Rose, N. (1986) (eds) *The Power of Psychiatry.* Cambridge, UK: Polity Press.

NEF (New Economics Foundation) – Slay, J. and Stephens, L. (2013) *Co-production in Mental Health: A Literature Review.* Available at: http://s.bsd.net/nefoundation/default/page/file/ca0975b7cd88125c3e_ywm6bp3l1.pdf (accessed 10 April 2014).

Parker, I., Georgaca, E., Harper, D., McLaughlin, T. and Stowell-Smith, M. (eds) (1995) *Deconstructing Psychopathology.* London: SAGE.

Rose, N. (2006) *The Politics of Life Itself: Biomedicine, Power and Subjectivity in the 21st Century*. Princeton: Princeton University Press.

Rose, N. (2007) "Beyond medicalisation", *Lancet*, 369(9562): 700–2.

Rose, N. and Abi-Rached, J.M. (2013) *Neuro. The New Brain Sciences and the Management of the Mind*. Princeton: Princeton University Press.

Scott, J. (2001) *Power*. Cambridge: Polity Press.

Sedgwick, P. (1982) *Psycho Politics*. London: Pluto Press.

Showalter, E. (1987) *The Female Malady: Women, Madness and English Culture, 1830–1980*. London: Virago Press.

Szasz, T. (1972) *The Myth of Mental Illness: Foundations of a Theory of Personal Conduct*. St Albans: Paladin.

Szasz, T. (1976) *Schizophrenia: The Sacred Symbol of Psychiatry*. New York: Basic Books.

Szasz, T. (2010) "Psychiatry, anti-psychiatry, critical psychiatry: What do these terms mean?", *Philosophy, Psychiatry, & Psychology*, 17: 229–32.

Treffert, D.A. (1973) "Dying with their rights on", *American Journal of Psychiatry*, 130: 1041.

Whitaker, R. (2010) *Anatomy of an Epidemic – Magic Bullets, Psychiatric Drugs and the Astonishing Rise of Mental Illness in America*. New York: Broadway Paperbacks.

Woodbridge, K. and Fulford, K.W.M. (2004) *Whose Values? A Workbook for Values-based Practice in Mental Health Care*. London: Sainsbury Centre for Mental Health.

6 | Power, knowledge and personal narratives

Chapter Summary

This chapter will:

- Introduce the reader to concepts of power and narratives in knowledge production.
- Introduce the reader to personal narratives of mental distress, including a brief summary of their presence in the history of psychiatry, and an overview of their variety in terms of scope and objectives.
- Critically appraise how they have been engaged with in mental health theory and practice.
- Address methodological and ethical questions in working with personal narratives within values-based practice.

Power and knowledge production

"Who we are and what we do are influenced by the stories that we tell about ourselves," writes narrative therapist David Denbrough (2014: 3). Our lives are also influenced by the stories others tell about us, and while we may not always be able to change the stories others tell about us, as Denbrough also suggests, "we can influence the stories we tell about ourselves and those we care about. And we can, with care, rework or rewrite storylines of identity" (2014: 3).

Knowledge is produced through story telling or narrative. As sociologist Arthur Frank has written, "stories told about categories of persons can injure those persons. But silences can be equally injurious, implying that there is no story to tell about lives such as these" (Frank, 2010: 75). What is held up as "true" knowledge depends on a variety of factors influenced by the power relations in our societies and culture. Power, as we saw in Chapter 5, results from interpersonal relationships in a variety of ways. These relationships can be one of dominance and subjugation, restriction of liberties, control of knowledge, and, importantly, also the ability and capacity to carry out actions as political citizens who are empowered. In this chapter, we will examine how power operates in knowledge production and discourses about the experience of madness and mental distress, and the challenges posed to the power of psychiatric narratives by the personal narratives of those who have experienced mental distress.

In *Madness and Civilisation*, the French philosopher Michel Foucault (introduced in Chapter 5) writes that the history of psychiatry is a "monologue of reason about unreason" (1971, xii–xiii). What Foucault means by this is that, in psychiatry, the "dominant discourse" – the narratives, rules, definitions, ways of understanding, and institutions that are considered to be of more value than any other – is one that has been shaped by the need to organise and manage society by those who could lay claim to "reason". Psychiatrists and philosophers Pat Bracken and Phil Thomas draw our attention to the narratives that psychiatry employs in developing a "modernist" framework for itself: that mental distress can be understood and classified in terms of "symptoms"; that it can be investigated scientifically, and measured and evaluated using special tools and techniques; that specific expertise, language and vocabulary is needed to intervene, manage and treat it; that progress in our understanding is made by new discoveries in scientific disciplines within laboratories and academic institutions (Bracken and Thomas, 2013: 124).

This dominant discourse, however, has had to contend with the personal narratives of madness and mental distress, dealing with the spiritual, moral, cultural, personal and philosophical aspects of mental distress – in essence, the "lived" experience of it. Psychiatric narratives became the "dominant discourse" by privileging the "technical" aspects of understanding madness and mental distress over these other aspects.

The power of narratives

At its simplest, a narrative is a sequence of connected events, communicated through written, spoken or visual form. The word "story" is sometimes used synonymously with "narrative"; at other times, a narrative may refer to the structure of events in a story. Narratives are important to all cultures; indeed, it is how we, as human beings, make sense of our lives, our identities and our worlds. The philosopher and neurobiologist Owen Flanagan suggests that: "humans in all cultures come to cast their own identity in some sort of narrative form. We are inveterate storytellers" (1992: 198). Similarly, the psychoanalyst Roy Schafer says that: "we are forever telling stories about ourselves" (1981: 31).

However, we also know that some narratives often take on the form of "universal" truths, to the detriment of all other narratives. This is especially true of knowledge systems where one type of knowledge comes to be considered "expert" knowledge. There have always been several different types of knowledge available to us about madness and mental distress across disciplines, and the theory and practice of mental health across cultures. But "universally true" knowledge of psychiatry and mental health is often considered to be based on the expertise of professionals and practitioners, and not on the experiential expertise of the people who have lived with mental distress. In this chapter, we will see how this expertise is constituted, the challenges posed to it, and how they connect to our understanding and reading of personal narratives.

Exercise 6.1

The following is an excerpt from an interview with the African writer Chinua Achebe (1994). Achebe is describing the predominance, in colonial literature, of stories about Africa and its people written by Europeans from a position of cultural and racial dominance (an example would be Joseph Conrad's *Heart of Darkness*). Read the passage and reflect on the questions below.

> When I began going to school and learned to read, I encountered stories of other people and other lands. In one of my essays, I remember the kind of things that fascinated me. Weird things, even, about a wizard who lived in Africa and went to China to find a lamp. ... Fascinating to me because they were about things remote, and almost ethereal.
>
> Then I grew older and began to read about adventures in which I didn't know that I was supposed to be on the side of those savages who were encountered by the good white man. I instinctively took sides with the white people. They were fine! They were excellent. They were intelligent. The others were not. ... they were stupid and ugly. That was the way I was introduced to the danger of not having your own stories. There is that great proverb – that until the lions have their own historians, the history of the hunt will always glorify the hunter. That did not come to me until much later. Once I realized that, I had to be a writer. I had to be that historian. It's not one man's job. It's not one person's job. But it is something we have to do, so that the story of the hunt will also reflect the agony, the travail – the bravery, even, of the lions.

QUESTIONS:

- What is Achebe trying to say about the difference between a lion's story of the hunt and that of the hunter's?
- Think about your own life (identity, values, society, and so on) to see if there are instances that will illustrate "the dangers of not having your own story".

Personal narratives of mental distress: A historical overview

Narratives about life events and experiences that are often described as madness, mental illness or disorder have existed as long as human cultures have discussed human experiences. Our concern here is narratives that are personal or autobiographical, and mainly in the written form. While it will be impossible to review the entire history of such narratives within the confines of a chapter, we will attempt a quick overview, highlighting some key moments in this history.

The work credited as the oldest known autobiography in the English language, *The Book of Marjory Kempe*, written in 1436, describes the life of a woman possessed by spirits and confined in a store room until she was venerated within the Church. While the book does not speak of "madness" or "mental illness" as we know it today, it describes a spiritual journey which challenges the social orthodoxies of the day and provides an alternative morality of social life. In 1677, Christoph Haizmann, a Bavarian painter, recorded his experiences in the form of diaries, written in Latin and German, accompanied by paintings (Peterson, 1982). Several such narratives exist which record "extraordinary" experiences incongruent with prevalent views on "normal" life. However, it is not until the mid-seventeenth century and the establishment of institutions to separate people deemed mad, along with the other "undesirables" in society – what Foucault calls the "Great Confinement" – that personal narratives of madness and mental distress as we understand them today started emerging. From this time on, the management of madness became more organised, with the development of private madhouses and, later, of state-run asylums under the supervision of medical doctors, and personal narratives started being published as independent pamphlets and books, and as part of professional journals.

Stories from the inside

Experiential narratives written by people confined in madhouses and asylums exposed the terrible conditions and inhuman treatment within many of these institutions. For example, Alexander Cruden (1739) and Samuel Bruckshaw (1774) both wrote pamphlets about their unjust confinement and treatment in private madhouses as part of their plea for justice. Louisa Lowe published several pamphlets describing wrongful practices by "government servants" (1872). Elizabeth Parsons Ware Packard, a woman who was confined in an asylum on her husband's orders, wrote several narratives both about her own experience and about the broader conditions of nineteenth-century asylum care in the USA which resulted in the passing of "personal liberty" laws in many of the states (see, for example, 1866, 1874). Identified only as "Inmate, Ward 8" at the time of publication, Marion Marle Woodson wrote one of the few accounts of the passing of the Eugenics-based sterilisation laws from the point of view of those against whom it was directed (1994 [1932]). This account forms an important part of the history of psychiatry as it is one of the few accounts, from the point of view of those against whom it was directed, of a law that sterilised over 60,000 people with diagnoses of mental illness between 1907 and 1963 in the United States (Lombardo, 1985).

This theme of "bearing witness" to the living conditions within institutions and the values governing psychiatric practice continued into the twentieth century and is still one of the main themes of personal narratives. The Testimony Project by the Mental Health Media in the UK, for example, recorded twentieth-century psychiatric institutional care through audio-visual narratives of people who had lived in these institutions. These narratives are now part of the British Library's Life Story Collection, ensuring that they remain a part of the human history we all share (see Resources at the end of this chapter).

Socio-political criticism

Many personal narratives throughout history, while giving voice to personal experiences of mental distress, and interpretations and analyses of madness, also raised questions about existing power structures in society and the medical/psychiatric establishment's role in perpetuating these structures. For example, intertwined with feminist critiques of patriarchal power structures, women's narratives throughout the twentieth century challenged society's and psychiatry's view of women's madness as deviance from "normal" feminine behaviour. A good example is the writings of novelist Charlotte Perkins Gilman. The best known exposition of Gilman's views on women's madness is her novel *The Yellow Wallpaper* (1973 [1892]), but her posthumous autobiography (1935) provides the wider context within which her views about women's rights and roles, and mental distress developed. Gilman was diagnosed with "neurasthenia" and treated by Dr Silas Weir Mitchell, the proponent of the "rest cure", which involved enforced domesticity and a ban on intellectual activity. Gilman's narrative is an insightful critique of the patriarchal assumptions involved both in the understanding of women's madness as deviance from domesticity and femininity and in its cure as a return to accepted norms of womanhood.

Several of the best-known personal narratives written by women continued to develop these themes of resistance and challenge to the socio-cultural hegemony of patriarchal values in psychiatry. While some writers – for example, Susanna Kaysen (1995) and Jill Johnston (1985) – used their narratives to critique madness as social constructs based on dominant ideologies of womanhood, sexuality, and so on; others – for example, Joanne Greenberg (1964) – challenged the values and ethics of psychiatric practice and its treatment of women while accepting psychiatric definitions of their experiences.

Clearly, there are differences in perceptions of madness and mental distress, pointing to the fact that the lived experience of it is wide and varied. It could be argued that the psychiatric discourse fails because it prioritises a technical narrative set within a bio-medical model and seeks to "fix" multiple meanings and experiences. The personal narratives discussed so far remind us, as the cultural theorist Homi Bhabha does, that:

> "it is from those who have suffered the sentence of history – subjugation, domination, diaspora, displacement – that we learn our most enduring lessons for living and thinking. ... that the affective experience of social marginality – as it appears in non-canonical cultural forms – transforms our critical strategies" (1994: 246).

Narratives from the mental health user/survivor movements

In the latter part of the twentieth century, mental health service user/survivor movements and organisations started emerging in those parts of the world where bio-medical models of psychiatry were the primary form of mental health care. Validating people's right to their voice and stories, enabling people to tell their stories, became a central part of these movements. There are several excellent narratives by individuals identifying as part of the user/

survivor movement published in print, audio-visual and online formats, focussing on various aspects of the experiences of madness and mental distress. These include encounters with psychiatry and mental health systems, alternative perspectives and theories on what constitutes madness, diagnostic categories, treatment options, healing and recovery, and challenging mental health discrimination and stigma.

A significant development in the history of personal narratives is the emergence of efforts to articulate a collective politics and theories of madness and mental distress. In fact, the use of personal experience and narrative in a collective way can be dated back to the seventeenth-century pamphlet issued by inmates of Bethlem Hospital and their petition to the House of Lords about the conditions within the hospital (1620). And, in the mid- nineteenth century, the inmates of the Utica State Lunatic Asylum wrote and edited a 10-volume journal, *The Opal*, discussing various issues of interest to them including their lives, politics and government, art and culture, religion and spirituality, psychological theory and practice, rights and the liberation movement (Tenney, 2006).

A more recent example of how a collective voice and theory is presented through personal narratives is *Self-Harm: Perspectives from Personal Experience* (Pembroke, 1994). The accepted psychiatric perspective on self-harm is that it is "inappropriate behaviour" and a valid category in determining several diagnoses. By focusing on personal history and experience, the narratives in this collection propose that self-harm is an entirely understandable response to some life events; what is "inappropriate" is the response to it from the psychiatric profession and its attempt to categorise it as deviant, and control it without addressing the personal, cultural and moral issues behind it. Similarly, *Navigating the Space between Brilliance and Madness* is a reader produced by the Icarus Project in the USA, bringing together narratives, experimental visual elements, "community narratives" from the project's website and other innovative modes of narration to provide "an atlas of alternative maps" and to create "a reasonable language to talk about 'madness'" (McNamara and du Brul, 2004). The aim here is as much to support each other as to challenge dominant understandings of "bipolar disorder" and other mental illness categories.

Similar works have come out of collective activism, as have calls for resistance and radical change both in the understandings of madness and mental distress, and in psychiatric and mental health practices. The Canadian collection from Burstow and Weitz (1998) presented the personal narratives, journals, interviews, poetry and art of over 40 psychiatric survivors, aiming to inform the public of "the truth about psychiatry" in the tradition of speak-outs and consciousness-raising that characterised other rights-based campaigns such as the feminist and anti-racism movements. The anthology, published by the Mad Pride movement in the UK, proclaimed to be "the first great civil liberties movement of the new millennium" and celebrates defiance, direct action, the refusal of a "victim" status and an assertion of the "mad" identity by reclaiming and re-articulating that experience (Curtis et. al., 2000). An international collection of narratives of forced treatment was published (Minkowitz and Dhanda, 2006) at a time when negotiations concerning the UN Convention on the Rights of Persons with Disability were under way, with the aim of influencing its content.

"Race", racialisation and personal narratives

While narratives from the mental health user/survivor movements have played an important role in providing alternative ways of understanding and theorising mental distress and madness, they have also been criticised for retaining a white, Euro-centric reading of the experience of madness in society. A key aspect of this criticism is that these counter-narratives and critical positions have not sufficiently engaged with the origins of psychiatric discourse in the social construction of people into categories of "race". For example, in a critical reading of *Navigating the Space between Brilliance and Madness*, Louise Tam discusses how these narratives from the mainstream mental health user/survivor movement, while appropriating metaphors and practices from indigenous cultures and drawing parallels between anti-racism struggles and the civil rights movement, does not sufficiently intervene against psychiatric discourse "as a knowledge and institution that has everything to do with race in the origins and constitution of pathology" (2013: 295). Tam suggests that the narrative process that seeks to authenticate personal identities and experiences needs to begin with locating the source of its unease with psychiatric knowledge: "We must ask ourselves: How might my story differentiate from other people's histories within the psy complex?" (2014: 296).

There is also a methodological issue to encounter. The personal narratives, individual and collective, we have discussed so far presuppose an individual "self" that narrates itself, an idea that is rooted in the concept of Western individualism. However, many narratives, especially from the margins of organised movements and society itself, challenge this notion of an individualised self by doing so using methods that challenge conventions in first-person narratives. Indeed, for many people, the very act of telling their story involves breaking away from cultural taboos around public telling of personal stories, and requires supportive forums and frameworks (Kalathil et. al., 2011: 76). And, for others, the personal is always collective and telling of stories is a communal act. This is demonstrated by *Lifting Barriers*, one of the very few books of survivor narratives that address the personal experiences of people from minority ethnic communities living in the UK (Atkinson et. al., 2008). The narratives in this book were developed within a storytelling group and address not only the experience of mental distress and its treatment, but also the struggles of living in the UK as members of communities for whom the experience of intolerance, racism and discrimination are everyday realities. By choosing to present the narratives in thematic groups, rather than as self-contained individual narratives, the narrators point to the collective nature of their experiences, identities and personhood, and their experiences with psychiatry as part of the institutionalisation of both "race" and madness.

A similar departure from conventional ways of telling stories and presenting narratives is offered in a work about African American experiences of mental health systems (Jackson, 2001). The stories in this work were collected and presented using an oral history methodology and the use of this methodology was a conscious political one:

> "The telling of stories has been an integral part of the history of people of African descent. From the griots of ancient Africa to the sometimes painful lyrics of hip-hop artists, people of African descent have known that our lives and our stories must be spoken, over and over again, so that the people will know our truth" (Jackson, 2001: 2).

Challenges have also been posed to the language and metaphors used within personal narratives to describe the negative aspects of mental distress. For example, depression, in Western societies, and especially in the English language, is often spoken of using metaphors of "blackness" or "darkness" – the most famous example being Winston Churchill's description of depression as a "black dog" (Foley, n.d.). Meri Nana-Ama Danquah addresses the difficulties involved in talking about depression as a black woman:

> "You've heard descriptions of depression before: A black hole; an enveloping darkness; a dismal existence through which no light shines; the black dog; darkness, and more darkness. But what does darkness mean to me, a woman who has spent her life surrounded by it? The blackness of my skin; the darkness of my friends and family. I have never been afraid of darkness. It poses no harm to me. What is the color of my depression? (1998: 22).

By pointing to the "oppressive nature of the existing language surrounding depression" Danquah exposes the double pathologisation that black people face, both in terms of their disability and in terms of their "race".

Exercise 6.2

Choose a difficult time in your life and create a personal narrative about that time. Reflect on the following:

- What do you need in order to be able to tell your story?
- Does your narrative present congruence or conflicts (moral, cultural, philosophical, spiritual, material, even factual) with other narratives about the same incident/time?
- What do you feel about these congruencies or conflicts? How would you use them to help you understand and articulate your experience?

Engaging with personal narratives: Ethical and methodological issues

Given the long history of and variety within personal narratives of mental distress and madness, why is it that the technical, professional-led narrative of psychiatry has become and remains, the dominant discourse in mental health? Why are diagnostic categories, treatments, and the organisation of mental health practices still thought of as the domain of professionals, despite recent calls for co-production of knowledge? Why are personal narratives, and the theories and conceptualisations arising from them, not a regular part of the curricula for mental health professionals? The answer to these questions is to be found in examining the limitations of current professional engagement with them.

The process of telling a story is a process of meaning making, a process which is essentially as temporal and in flux as the worlds and lives they represent. They contain their own interpretations and insights into moral, cultural, philosophical, spiritual and material worlds. Listening to and understanding stories is also a process of meaning making. Beyond the level of the personal, a narrative's potential for making meaning is borne out in the interaction between the story teller and the reader/listener/viewer. In a broad sense, the assertion of the moral worth of individuals – the idea of individualism – promises a person's right to their story. However, shared norms, values and moralities of the cultures and contexts we live in have control over the "right" kind of story, the stories others tell about us and about how our stories are interpreted. This is the idea of "normality". Straying too far from the accepted and shared norms, values and behaviour of our context and society is often defined as "abnormality". In this sense, a narrative of difference from the norm carries with it a risk of being labelled mad.

Narratives in clinical practice

For people encountering a provider-user/consumer relationship through introduction into mental health services as a "patient", "telling our stories" is both a routine experience and an impossibility. This may seem contradictory at first glance. But let us think about it. As "patients" seeking help, or forced into accepting the need for help, we are invited to tell our stories to psychiatric professionals: the psychiatric interview, assessments, therapy sessions, care plan reviews are all occasions where we tell our stories. The psychiatric interview uses "a priori systems of meanings" (Mishler, 1986). Simply put, this means that assessment protocols and diagnostic categories – the "technical" framework of psychiatry we discussed earlier – are already fixed. Our stories are mediated and interpreted through this "technical" framework. Little space is to be found here for engaging with personal meaning making and the contexts from which these meanings are made.

Let us consider an example. In 1966, Susanna Kaysen was diagnosed with Borderline Personality Disorder (BDP) and admitted as an in-patient at McLean hospital. In a chapter entitled 'My Diagnosis' in her autobiography, Kaysen says that she is tempted to refute the diagnosis but, fearing that she would be "open to further charges of 'defensiveness' and 'resistance'", she proceeds instead to present a personal annotation of the diagnosis (Kaysen, 1995: 150–9). The excerpt here deals with her interpretation of one of the markers that described BPD at the time: "The person often experiences this instability of self-image as chronic feelings of emptiness or boredom." Here is Kaysen's analysis:

> "My chronic feelings of emptiness and boredom came from the fact that I was living a life based on my incapacities, which were numerous. A partial list follows. I could not and did not want to: ski, play tennis, or go to gym class; attend to any subject in school other than English and biology; write papers on any assigned topics (I wrote poems instead of papers for English, I got Fs); plan to go or apply to college; give any reasonable explanation for these refusals.

> My self-image was not unstable. I saw myself, quite correctly, as unfit for the educational and social systems.

> But my parents and teachers did not share my self-image. Their image of me was unstable, since it was out of kilter with reality and based on their needs and wishes. They did not put much value on my capacities, which were admittedly few, but genuine.

> ...

> As far as I could see, life demanded skills I didn't have. The result was chronic emptiness and boredom" (Kaysen, 1995: 155–6).

The passage illustrates the dissonance between Kaysen's self-image and the accepted norm for a young American middle-class woman of the time, reflected in the diagnostic criterion. It also illustrates the clear insight she has of herself. But the incongruence between this personal meaning and the technical framework required of psychiatric process results in her personality being defined as having a "disorder" rather than self-awareness.

Another example where our narratives are interpreted through technical frameworks of psychiatry is a case study, the origin of which – as we know and use them today – is to be found in the idea of "pathography". Pathography was originally defined as "a description of disease" in the nineteenth-century *Medical Lexicon* by Robley Dunglison. Its definition was expanded later in the *Psychiatric Dictionary* as "the study of the effects of any illness on the writer's (or other artist's) life or art, or the effects of an artist's life and personality development on his creative work" (Campbell, 1989). Used extensively in mental health practice, service delivery and knowledge production (including in this book), a case study is often presented as "patient's story". However, in reality, a case study is a professional's interpretation of a patient's/person's story, or a story about a hypothetical person, made out of several narratives. We have already noted the issue of how people's stories are represented as case studies and case examples in the introduction to this book, and how this represents a distinct power imbalance in mental health care.

In both the psychiatric interview and in the case study, our stories enter a relational realm where they go through interpretations. This is, in one sense, inevitable. However, this relational realm is also one of power imbalances, where the "dominant discourse" of psychiatry may be the prism through which the meaning of the story is arrived at. For many people entering the provider-user/consumer relationship as a "patient", the experience has been one where their stories go through a process of "de-narrativisation" – a process by which a narrative is interpreted and re-presented, removing elements of *personal* meaning making and the *contexts* that the narrator brings to it. So, while we spend a lot of time telling our stories, the process of de-narrativisation makes it also an "impossibility" to narrate our stories in the context of mental health practice.

Exercise 6.3

The following is an extract from 'Two Accounts of Mental Distress' by Mary O'Hagan (1996). O'Hagan kept a journal during her last stay in the hospital and later, after gaining access to her in-patient files, she put together this narrative juxtaposing her own and the psychiatric professionals' versions of the same story. The text in italics is O'Hagan's narrative, which is followed by excerpts about the same incident from her case files. Read the extract and reflect on the questions below:

> *Every morning the night nurses pull off my blankets. They are rough. I can't fight back. Even their softest touches bruise me.*
>
> *A nurse said to me "Face the world". But I am facing all the pain inside me. I cannot face both ways at once.*
>
>> Mary is not to hide away in her bed. She is to be encouraged to get up for breakfast and engage in ward activities.
>
> *Sometimes a speck of light gets into my black hole. The speck is a thought that has come back into focus.*

> *I am coming up a bit but I feel all weak and wobbly from being on my bed for days. Before, I looked up. This took courage. It was like coming out of a cocoon; the light was strong; it was strange. The next thing I did was walk around and say hello to people. It feels good to be halfway back and looking up.*

Is beginning to interact. Says she is feeling much better. Asked permission to go out which was refused. Accepted this well. Enjoyed a game of Scrabble, giggling at times but this was mostly appropriate e.g. at mildly humorous antics of other patients.

Mary is to be discharged. The family have intimated that they would be glad if I continued to manage Mary. I will be ready to step in if she has any further psychotic breaks and needs the control of this ward.

QUESTIONS:

- In what ways do Mary's perspectives and understandings of her situation differ from those of the professionals?
- What are the processes of meaning making through which Mary's story is being de-narrativised?
- What could the professionals do differently to retain the meanings of and engage with Mary's perspectives and understandings of her experience?

Personal narratives in knowledge production

There has been a certain amount of professional interest in personal narratives of "insanity" right from the time when psychiatry was being established as a separate discipline tasked with the management and treatment of madness and distress. The first psychiatric journal, the *American Journal of Insanity*, was published in 1844 by the American Psychiatric Association. Subsequent issues of the journal published personal experiences of people treated within asylums and hospitals in the form of letters. These were annotated by psychiatrists and, by and large, focused on the origins, nature and subsequent "cure" of insanity. The *Journal of Psychological Medicine and Mental Pathology* published such narratives in the 1850s under the title "Autobiography of the Insane". Many of these were written in response to invitations from psychiatrists by their former patients. The editorial introduction to one such article states:

> "We cannot conceive anything more deeply interesting to the practical physician, so touchingly affecting to the philanthropist, or instructive to the speculative metaphysician and medical psychologist, than the account given by those who have recovered from attacks of insanity, of the workings of the mind, and state of their feelings and sensations, during the existence of mental derangement" (Winslow, 1855: 338).

This introduction is followed by substantial excerpts from a narrative, identified in a footnote as *Scenes from the Life of a Sufferer: being the Narrative of a Residence in Morningside*

Asylum, interspersed with short editorial annotations. The concluding editorial remarks state that although the pamphlet has its "faults and exaggerations", the editors were "anxious to select those portions of the pamphlet that are likely to amuse and instruct our readers" (Winslow, 1855: 353). Such editorial "frames" that pre-define the value and purpose of personal narratives – in this case, amusement and instruction of professionals – is evident in other professional journals too. Analysing the editorial statement launching "first-person accounts" in the *Schizophrenia Bulletin* in 1979, Angela Woods writes:

> "Particularly striking is the insistence upon clarity, originality and clinically relevant 'take-home' messages. This is at once an invitation for future contributors to adopt a style congruent with the conventions of academic writing, and ... a caution against the submission of anything which could be classed as 'mad' writing" (2013: 41).

The interest in personal narratives continues to be, as expressed in an 1854 edition of the *Journal of Psychological Medicine and Mental Pathology*, as "data ... invaluable in the hands of those competent, by psychological study and practical knowledge, to appreciate the phenomena of healthy and morbid mind" (Winslow, 1854: 356–57). The experience of madness or distress, and the conceptualisations or theoretical positions arising out of this experience, are often disregarded in favour of reading personal narratives as "recovery stories" that provide some sort of clinical evidence (Woods, 2013: 46).

This interest in personal narratives as "data" or clinical evidence to be interpreted and re-presented is evident in much of the academic research engagement with these narratives as well. Louise Pembroke writes about how her cartoons from *Self-harm: Perspectives from Personal Narratives* (1994) were subjected to a "mental state analysis" in an academic work (2007: 768). Pembroke sees this as a "pathologisation" of her narrative, through an academic exercise that seeks to re-interpret her meaning, rather than reflect on the possible alternative conceptualisation of self-harm and the response to it from an experiential perspective. A further example of re-pathologising personal narratives is the recent anthology, *First Person Accounts of Mental Illness and Recovery* (LeCroy and Holschuh, 2012). Despite an introduction, entitled "More than just a diagnosis", discussing the importance of engaging with personal narratives, the editors nevertheless chose to arrange the narratives under section and sub-section headings that follow the DSM classification of disorders, thereby asserting the primacy of engagement as one defined by the technical narrative of psychiatry.

In a review of *Agnes' Jacket* (Hornstein, 2009), Jasna Russo calls our attention to damages that can be caused by "the academic re-telling and packaging of individual and collective survivor stories" (2012: 28). Hornstein's book is based on her observations of and reflections on survivor testimonies and user/survivor groups in the UK. Hornstein uses the concept of "history of the present" as described by Timothy Garton Ash in his work about the Revolution of 1989 (Garton Ash, 1999) and writes in the introduction that "[i]n witnessing madness from the inside, I've tried to write from much the same place" (Hornstein, 2009: xxv).

Russo contends that, in her effort to engage with survivor experiences as an opportunity to "witness madness from the inside" and re-interpret it for others outside of the experience, Hornstein perpetuates the "'subtle forms of silencing' preventing 'patients' from producing knowledge about madness on equal terms" that she seeks to critique:

"The reality is that there is very little of our own, survivor-authored analysis of our individual and collective histories, and that we face massive barriers when seeking scholarly recognition and resources gives a bitter flavour to the expanding genre of narrative inquiry about madness by non-survivor academics ... By her insistence on the 'patient' identity, by gathering and 'explaining' our experiences, and taking on the role of the bridge-builder between survivors and academia, Hornstein inevitably contributes to the very same process of silencing which she says she aims to combat" (Russo, 2012: 29).

Russo's critique bears significance in the light that Hornstein's book has been hailed as "a psychological adventure story" in the world of "the truly mad" (Hornstein, 2009, back cover).

A further issue is how certain narratives are prioritised and valued over others in some contexts. In the UK, the anti-stigma campaign Time to Change actively encourages service users to tell their "stories of recovery" in an attempt to promote the idea that mental health problems are a common experience. The use of "celebrity disclosures" of the experience of mental distress is a key part of the programme. The telling of "positive" stories has also become part of "recovery orientation" within mental health services. This interest in a particular kind of narrative – a narrative that follows a linear path from illness to wellness where both illness and recovery are re-articulated in terms of bio-medical and social constructions of normality – is being widely criticised for limiting the scope and validity of personal narratives in contributing to our knowledge about psychiatry and mental health (Crepaz-Keay and Kalathil, 2013) and for sanitising them by absorbing resistance to dominant practices (Costa et. al., 2012).

The problem of the dominance of psychiatric discourse, then, is not to do with the existence of experiential knowledge through personal narratives, or their validity in contributing to developing and changing our understanding of madness and mental distress, and mental health practices. It is about how we engage with them in ways that do not reduce them into another set of data to be analysed and interpreted using existing hierarchical values and criteria, or as commodities for marketing institutional or organisational agendas. We will now look at some enabling ways of engaging with narratives.

Exercise 6.4

Choose a narrative from the Icarus Project Reader (see Resources list for link). Write down your reflections after reading this narrative. Keep in mind the problems discussed so far in interpreting narratives. Then refer to the next section and re-analyse your reflections, this time keeping in mind the four points discussed below: thinking about the context of storytelling, complexities around authenticity and truth, considering narratives as valid knowledge, and entering into a dialogue with narratives.

Values and ethics in engaging with personal narratives

As discussed in Chapters 3 and 4, values-based practice is not a mechanical way of finding concrete answers but, rather, a process that helps us find the answers through engaging and reflecting on complex, conflicting and, sometimes, complimentary values. It would be impossible, and counter-productive, to prescribe set ways of engaging with personal narratives because the meaning making process inescapably brings together the world of the narrator with the world of the reader/listener/viewer. But there are some principles that we can keep in mind: the importance of "context"; confronting the question of authenticity and truth; narratives as expert knowledge, not "data"; and letting stories breathe.

The importance of "context"   Academic and clinical research and practice is often considered to be objective and, hence, devoid of subjective interpretations. The subjective nature of personal narratives is often seen as reason enough to invalidate them as scholarship. Despite the claim to objectivity, professional interactions with personal narratives take place within the inter-relational space influenced by our moral, ethical, social and political values and contexts. It is important to acknowledge, as the cultural theorist and sociologist, Stuart Hall, reminds us: "We all write and speak from a particular place and time, from a history and a culture which is specific. What we say is always 'in context', *positioned*" (Hall, 1990: 223).

These contexts and positions are influenced by hierarchies of power and it is important to reflect on how they affect our engagement with narratives and knowledge that are different to ours. Keeping the contexts from which personal narratives convey their particular perspectives and the contexts we as readers/listeners/viewers bring into the meaning making process in mind helps us work in ways that value diverse human experiences. While many personal narratives focus on the loss of power inherent in the experience of mental distress and its treatment and management within psychiatric settings, they also point to a different kind of power – a power that allows for self-determination through narrating one's own story. It points to the possibility of "communicative power" (Arendt, 1970), the human ability to act in concert. As discussed in Chapter 5, the idea of "communicative power" is fundamental to co-production. What is important is to be vigilant about the existing inequalities and hierarchies that may affect co-production of meaning and knowledge. Reflexive practice that validates personal narratives and takes into account the contexts and positions from which meaning is made helps us become mindful of these inequalities and hierarchies.

Confronting the question of authenticity and truth   A key question that the engagement with personal narratives raises is about the authenticity of the story and the truth about the experience and/or events that story unveils. On the one hand, the "personal" aspect of the narrative already lays claim to the authenticity and "truth" contained in the narrative from the point of view of the writer. And this claim is a valid one: it is our story as told by us. On the other hand, as we have seen, dominant discourses and power relations in society challenge the claims of authenticity and "truth" of personal narratives in relation to the technical knowledge of psychiatry. Arthur Frank, the sociologist who has written extensively about story telling in the context of illness, suggests that authenticity is always in negotiation, "always being a dialogue, and sometimes a contest, between storyteller and listener" (2010: 12). In that sense, rather than looking for direct access to fixed notions of authenticity and "truth", and disclaiming it if it does not provide these, a values-based approach allows for the authenticity and "truth" of the narrative to be revealed through the meaning making process of dialogue and interaction with the narrative.

Narratives as expert knowledge, not "data"   A values-based understanding of human experience allows us to think of knowledge and expertise as inherent in the experiential narrative. As we have seen from the discussion, personal narratives are expressions of that experiential expertise, containing within them interpretations and insights into the moral, cultural, spiritual, material and philosophical aspects of madness and mental distress. Applying pre-fixed frames of analysis without acknowledging their contextual nature and personal meaning making processes runs the risk of losing the unique insights they bring to our collective understanding of the worlds of which they speak. As Fred Newman says in the context of narrative therapy, "Stories do not need theories any more than works of fiction do: we do not ask which is the truer story, *Moby Dick* or *Les Miserables*, although surely there is much to say about these two creative masterpieces" (2000: 259).

The idea that those who use mental health services are "experts by experience" is an accepted part of UK mental health policy. However, in academic and professional engagement, personal narratives, as we have seen, are still only included as "data" or information to be interpreted and analysed. Acknowledging that personal narratives offer their own theories and concepts of distress and madness is the first step towards deconstructing the dominance of psychiatric discourse and accepting that the psychiatric discourse is only one of many viable discourses about "problems of living" that we experience.

Letting stories breathe   Arthur Frank reminds us that narratives have a value beyond the information they provide; that the "witness offers testimony to a truth that is generally unrecognised or suppressed" and that our engagement with this testimony is a "moral responsibility" (1997: 137). The moral responsibility we have as readers/listeners/viewers of narratives is to enter into a "dialogical relationship" – a relationship that opens a dialogue, forms a relationship and is reflexive of, as highlighted earlier, our own pre-dispositions and contexts. Frank suggests that, "there is not, nor should there be, any method of narrative analysis, if *method* is understood as a prescribed set of steps that the analyst should follow" (2010: 72). Instead, he proposes the idea of a "dialogical relationship" between the narrative and its reader/listener/viewer. Dialogue allows us to avoid "finalisation" of meaning. Analyses and interpretations based on a dialogical relationship have "little interest in excluding – it welcomes a proliferation of possibilities" (Frank, 2010: 110). In essence, they "let stories breathe".

GLOSSARY OF KEY TERMS

Dominant discourse: The accepted way of understanding and talking about any subject; usually determined by those stories, people and institutions in power.

Narrative: A narrative is a sequence of connected events, sometimes thought of as a story, or at other times thought of as the events within a story. A narrative can be fictional or factual, and in any form including written, oral or visual.

De-narrativisation: A process of interpreting or re-telling the story in such a way that the meaning given by the initial narrator and the context in which the narrative is set is removed from it.

Pathologisation : Interpreting an incident, behaviour or experience as if it was a medical or an organic condition that requires treatment.

(Mental health) User/Survivor movement: Rights-based coming together of people who have had personal experience of mental distress or of being diagnosed as 'mentally ill'. There is more than one user/survivor movement around the world, but all share a fundamental interest in the welfare and rights of people who are prone to be discriminated against in society because of their (perceived) mental health status.

FURTHER READING

Personal Narratives of Madness (annotated bibliography). Available at:
http://global.oup.com/booksites/content/9780199579563/narratives/

The Mental Health Testimony Archive (Audio and video recordings): British Library catalogue no: C905. Available at: http://cadensa.bl.uk/uhtbin/cgisirsi/x/0/0/5?searchdata1=CKE Y5542415&library=ALL

The Icarus Project Reader. Available at: http://www.theicarusproject.net/files/navigating_the_space.pdf

REFERENCES

Achebe, C. (1994) "The art of fiction". Interview by J. Brooks, *Paris Review*, 133, winter. Available at http:// www.theparisreview.org/interviews/1720/the-art-of-fiction-no-139-chinua-achebe (accessed 2 April 2014).

Anonymous (1620) *The Petition of the Poor Distracted People in the House of Bedlam*. London.

Anonymous (1855) "Autobiography of the insane", *Journal of Psychological Medicine and Mental Pathology*, 11, July: 338–53.

Arendt, H. (1986) "Communicative power" in Lukes, S. (ed.) *Power*. Cambridge: Blackwell.

Ash, T.G. (1999) *We the People: The Revolution of '89 Witnessed in Warsaw, Budapest, Berlin and Prague*. London: Penguin Books.

Atkinson, A., Douglas, C., Francis, D., Laville, M., Millin, S., Pamfield, J., Smith, P. and Smith, R. (2008) *Lifting Barriers: African and Caribbean People Tell Stories of Struggle, Strength and Achieving Mental Health*. London: Mellow, SAFH, THACMHO, East London NHS Trust.

Bhabha, H. (1994) *The Location of Culture*. New York: Routledge.

Bracken, P. and Thomas, P. (2013) "Challenges to the modernist identity of psychiatry: User empowerment and recovery", in Fulford, K.W.M, Davies, M, Gipps, R.G.T., Graham, G., Sadler, J., Stanghellini, G. and Thornton, T. (eds) *The Oxford Handbook of Philosophy and Psychiatry*. Oxford: Oxford University Press.

Bruckshaw, S. (1774) *The Case, Petition, and Address of Samuel Bruckshaw, who Suffered a Most Severe Imprisonment, for Very Near the Whole Year, Loaded with Irons, without Being Heard in his Defense, Nay Even without Being Accused, and at Last Denied an Appeal to a Jury. Humbly Offered to the Perusal and Consideration of the Public*. London: The Author.

Burstow, B. and Weitz, D. (eds) (1998) *Shrink Resistant*. Vancouver: New Start Books.

Campbell, R.J. (1989) *Psychiatric Dictionary* (6th edn). Oxford: Oxford University Press.

Costa, L., Voronka, J., Landry, D., Reid, J., McFarlane, B., Reville, D. and Church, K. (2012) "Recovering our stories: A small act of resistance", *Studies in Social Justice*, 6(1): 85–101.

Crepaz-Keay, D. and Kalathil, J. (2013) "Introduction", *Personal Narratives of Madness* (annotated bibliography). Available at: http://global.oup.com/booksites/content/9780199579563/narratives/ (accessed 29 May 2015).

Cruden, A. (1739) *The London-Citizen Exceedingly Injured; or, a British Inquisition Display'd, in an Account of the Unparallel'd Case of a Citizen of London, Bookseller to the Late Queen, Who Was in a Most Unjust and Arbitrary Manner Sent on the 23rd of March Last, 1738, by One Robert Wightman, a Mere Stranger, to a Private Madhouse.* London: T. Cooper.

Curtis, T., Dellar, R., Lestie, E. and Watson, B. (eds) (2000) *Mad Pride: A Celebration of Mad Culture.* London: Spare Change Books.

Danquah, M.N.-A. (1998) *Willow Weep for Me: A Black Woman's Journey through Depression.* New York: Ballentine.

Denbrough, D. (2014) *Retelling the Stories of Our Lives: Everyday Narrative Therapy to Draw Inspiration and Transform Experience.* New York and London: Norton.

Flanagan, O. (1992) *Consciousness Reconsidered.* Cambridge, MA: MIT Press.

Foley, P. (n.d.) "'Black dog' as a metaphor for depression: A brief history". Available at: http://www.blackdoginstitute.org.au/docs/foley.pdf (accessed on 5 April 2013).

Foucault, M. (1971) *Madness and Civilisation: A History of Insanity in the Age of Reason.* London: Tavistock.

Frank, A.W. (1997) *Letting Stories Breathe: A Socio-Narratology.* Chicago: University of Chicago Press.

Frank, A.W. (2010) *Letting Stories Breathe: A Socio-Narratology.* Chicago: University of Chicago Press.

Gilman, C.P. (1935) *The Living of Charlotte Perkins Gilman: An Autobiography.* New York and London: Appleton-Century.

Gilman, C.P. (1973 [1892]) *The Yellow Wallpaper.* New York: Feminist Press.

Greenberg, J. (1964) *I Never Promised You a Rose Garden.* London: Signet.

Hall, S. (1990) "Cultural identity and diaspora", in Rutherford, J. (ed.) *Identity: Community, Culture, Difference.* London: Lawrence & Wishart.

Hornstein, G. (2009) *Agnes's Jacket: A Psychologist's Search for the Meaning of Madness.* New York: Rodale.

Jackson, V. (2001) *In Our Own Voice: African-American Stories of Oppression, Survival and Recovery in Mental Health Systems.* Massachusetts: National Empowerment Center.

Johnston, J. (1985) *Paper Daughter.* New York: Knopf.

Kalathil, J., Collier, B., Bhakta, R., Daniel, O., Joseph, D. and Trivedi, P. (2011) *Recovery and Resilience: African, African Caribbean and South Asian Women's Narratives of Recovering from Mental Distress.* London: Mental Health Foundation and Survivor Research.

Kaysen, S. (1995) *Girl, Interrupted.* London: Virago.

Kempe, M. (1985 [1436]) *The Book of Marjory Kempe*, translated by B.A. Windeatt. New York: Penguin.

LeCroy, C. and Holschuh, J. (2012) *First Person Accounts of Mental Illness and Recovery.* Chichester: Wiley.

Lombardo, P.A. (1985) "Three generations, no imbeciles: New light on Buck v. Bell", *New York University Law Review*, 60: 30–62.

Lowe, L. (1872) *Gagging in Madhouses as Practised by Government Servants in a Letter to the People, by One of the Gagged.* London: Burns.

McNamara, A. and du Brul, S. (eds) (2004) *Navigating the Space between Brilliance and Madness: A Reader and Roadmap of Bipolar Worlds.* New York: Icarus Project.

Minkowitz, T. and Dhanda, A. (eds) (2006) *First Person Stories on Forced Interventions and Being Deprived of Legal Capacity.* Pune: WNUSP and BAPU Trust.

Mishler, E.G. (1986) *Research Interviewing: Context and Narrative.* Cambridge, MA: Harvard University Press.

Newman, F. (2000) "Does a story need a theory? Understanding the Methodology of Narrative Therapy" in Fee, D. (ed.) *Pathology and the Postmodern: Mental Illness as Discourse and Experience*. London and New York: Sage.

O'Hagan, M. (1996) "Two accounts of mental distress" in Read, J. and Reynolds, J, (eds) *Speaking Our Minds: An Anthology*. Basingstoke: Palgrave Macmillan.

Packard, E.P.W (1874) *Modern Persecutions, or Insane Asylums Unveiled, As Demonstrated by the Report of the Investigating Committee of the Legislature of Illinois*, Volumes I and II. Hartford, CT: Case, Lockwood & Brainard.

Packard, E.P.W. (1866) *Marital Power Exemplified in Mrs. Packard's Trial and Self-Defense from the Charge of Insanity; or, Three Years Imprisonment for Religious Belief, by the Arbitrary Will of a Husband, with an Appeal to the Government to so Change the Laws as to Afford Legal Protection to Married Women*. Hartford, CT: Case, Lockwood.

Pembroke, L. (2007) "Recovery and arts as activism", *Journal of Psychiatric and Mental Health Nursing*, 14: 768–70.

Pembroke, L. (ed.) (1994) *Self-harm: Perspectives from Personal Experience*. London: Survivors Speak Out.

Peterson, D. (ed.) (1982) *A Mad People's History of Madness*. Pittsburgh: University of Pittsburgh.

Russo, J. (2012) "'Give me your story and I will take care of the rest?" *The case of Agnes's jacket: A psychologist's search for the meaning of madness'*, *Asylum*, winter: 28–30.

Schafer, R. (1981) "Narration in the psychoanalytic dialogue" in Mitchell, W.J.T. (ed.) *On Narrative*. Chicago: Chicago University Press.

Tam, L. (2013) "Whither indigenizing the mad movement? Theorising the social relations of race and madness through conviviality" in LeFrancois, B., Menzies, R. and Reumme, G. (eds) *Mad Matters: A Critical Reader in Canadian Mad Studies*. Toronto: Canadian Scholars' Press Inc.

Tenney, L. (2006) "Who fancies a revolution here? *The Opal* revisited", *Radical Psychology*, vol 5.

Winslow, F. (1854) "Spiritual pathology; or, the autobiography of the insane", *Journal of Psychological Medicine and Mental Pathology*, 7, July 1: 356–85.

Winslow, F. (1855) "Autobiography of the insane", *Journal of Psychological Medicine and Mental Pathology*, 1, July 1: 338–53.

Woods, A. (2013) "Rethinking 'patient testimony' in the medical humanities: The case of *Schizophrenia Bulletin*'s first person accounts", *Journal of Literature and Science*, 6(1): 38–54.

Woodson, M. (1994 [1932]) *Behind the Door of Delusion*. New York: Macmillan.

7 | Coercion and autonomy

Chapter Summary

This chapter will:

- Explore the potential tensions in mental health practice when promoting autonomy and choice.
- Examine the use of coercive interventions in mental health practice using the example of community treatment orders.
- Consider how the concepts of informed consent and capacity influence decision making.
- Outline therapeutic approaches which facilitate autonomy and choice.

Introduction

Recovery involves self-determination, the opportunity to make choices and take back control within your own life (Repper and Perkins, 2003). As citizens within contemporary society, we are all subject to norms and laws which may restrict opportunities for choice. This is a necessary aspect of a functioning society. However, the opportunities for people with mental health problems to exercise choice may be further restricted by the very systems that aim to provide support and care, which creates a challenge for facilitating recovery.

Since the development of centralised institutional care in the 1800s, there has been debate regarding the true function of mental health services. On the one hand, mental health services aim to provide care for people who are distressed and may be vulnerable. Focus is maintained on the importance of the therapeutic relationship, person-centred approaches and recovery. Alternatively, mental health services have been identified as a mechanism of social control governing a population constructed as risky, dangerous and different (Morrall and Hazelton, 2000; Paterson and Stark, 2001). From this perspective, systems such as the care programme approach and risk assessment are seen as instruments of surveillance. These dual agendas create the potential to be pulled in different directions when making decisions that may impact on a person's autonomy.

People with experience of mental health problems have identified that recovery is inhibited where choices are restricted by services (Gosling, 2010). Yet, equally, there are times where people may not have the capacity to make decisions and feel that they need support. For mental health professionals, these debates can mean they feel caught in a process of trying to strike a balance between promoting a person's choice and exerting control (Hopton, 1996; Morrall and Hazleton, 2000; Davis, 2002).

The notion of choice for people with mental health problems is clearly a complex one. This chapter explores some of the tensions surrounding how people's choices are enabled or restricted within mental health practice. In order to do so, it will use examples of interventions that highlight these tensions. It will also critically examine the use of coercion in mental health practice.

Exercise 7.1

The following questions aim to help you reflect on your values and beliefs regarding mental health legislation.

- What role do you think the Mental Health Act serves?
- What are the benefits of mental health legislation? Who benefits?
- What are the potential costs of mental health legislation? Who may experience these costs?
- What arguments are you aware of that may be used to weigh up these costs and benefits?

The issues raised by coercion and compulsion are, clearly, deeply value laden. Correspondingly, therefore, as we saw in Chapters 3 and 4, it may be useful to be aware of your own values, as this chapter examines different positions in relation to the role and justification of mental health law. We give examples of further reading on values and values-based practice in this difficult area at the end of the chapter.

Coercion

Ordinarily, within health care, respecting a person's wishes is afforded priority, reinforced by the dominance of a principles-based approach to ethical decision making (see Chapter 2, for further details) (Beauchamp and Childress, 2001; Olsen, 2003). In these circumstances, a person is viewed as competent, able to exercise autonomy and to make decisions free from pressure or influence. However, exceptions to this principle are deemed to be justified in certain scenarios.

Within mental health care, the compromise of an individual's autonomy is legally sanctioned through the use of mental health legislation. Here, a person experiencing mental distress becomes exposed to coercive practices. Coercion involves subjecting a person to the will of another. It is identified as undermining autonomy and freedom – usually involving an expression of power (Arnold, 2001). The Mental Health Act permits the use of legalised coercion. A person can therefore be forced to act – such as stay in hospital, or take medication – based on the will of another; namely, the mental health staff and services providing support for that person. However, one could argue that the notions of support and coercion here conflict with each other. Indeed, international conventions such as the UN Convention on Rights of People with Disabilities points out that the use of "force" is not congruent with the notion of "providing support" (UN, 2006). Exceptions to the need to respect a person's wishes are justified on the basis of two arguments. The first argument is that the person has a defined mental disorder. This is taken as indication that competence to make informed rational decisions is impaired (Olsen, 2003). The second argument is that there is the potential for the person to cause harm, either to themselves or to others (Department of Health, 2008). Compulsion and treatment is therefore rationalised on the basis that this is in the person's "best interests".

Both of these arguments used to justify legal coercion have been viewed as problematic. Having a diagnosed mental disorder in relation to the Mental Health Act implies that mental disorder automatically impairs decision making abilities (Szmukler and Holloway, 1998). Being able to assimilate information and think through the implications of action is an important part of decision making. However, capacity can be fluid and variable (Chan, 2002). A diagnosis of mental disorder does not, therefore, automatically impact on decision making capabilities, and these capabilities are not static. Additionally, despite recommendations to the contrary in the last revision of the Mental Health Act, capacity is not specifically judged as part of the Act. Consequently, a person may have the capacity to make a decision regarding treatment and yet still be forced to undergo it under the powers of mental health legislation (Szmukler and Holloway, 1998). It could be argued this undermines the position of impaired competence used to justify coercion and compromises autonomy.

There are also weaknesses in the argument that coercion can be justified on the basis that it serves a person's best interests. Treatment without consent is generally viewed as in the person's best interests, if it can be shown to help regain health (Szmukler and Holloway, 2000). Compulsory treatment in psychiatric practice often involves medication. Pharmacological interventions may have limited benefits for people with mental health problems who have been defined as "treatment resistant". Those diagnosed with "treatment resistant disorders" tend to be sectioned for the longest period (Szmukler and Holloway, 2000). The potential of treatment to regain health can be questioned here as undermining the statement of best interests (this is examined in more depth in the discussion of community treatment orders). Chan (2002) highlights that there is an inherent risk that best interest arguments actually serve the interests of people other than the service users (such as the government) and, as such, can promote a policing role for mental health professionals. This is further emphasised by the disproportionate use of the Mental Health Act in relation to some socio-cultural and racialised groups – in particular, African-Caribbean men – underlining the potential for mental health legislation to reflect social prejudice, consequently serving interests other than therapeutic goals (this issue will be further discussed in Chapter 8).

These concerns are evidenced in the final justification for coercion in mental health legislation: that of the potential for harm to self or others. Unlike the majority of other laws governing harm, the Mental Health Act is predicated on the basis of anticipated, rather than actual, acts. Predicting the likelihood of harm has been shown to be notoriously difficult and some would argue impossible (Goldacre, 2006; Fazel et al., 2012). As a result, mental health legislation has been criticised for unfairly targeting people with mental health problems. They become subject to coercion based on their perceived dangerousness in ways that others who may pose more of a danger and be equally "treatable" (such as drink drivers) are not, (Szasz, 1963; Szmukler and Holloway, 2000; Pilgrim, 2007).

The use of coercion as a result of invoking the Mental Health Act has caused much debate. This may be because it involves a departure from prioritising the principles of autonomy and self-determination that underpin both UK law and good practice in health care decision making (Richardson, 2008). It can be distressing for service users and for the staff implementing it. However, Olsen (2003) argues that part of the problem lies in the frameworks used for judging the ethics of the Act, which inevitably pit one principle against another. Consequently, coercion is judged as either right or wrong. This ignores the conceptual problems in defining and understanding coercion and the limitations of a principles-based approach to ethics. Instead, Olsen (2003) argues that relational approaches offer a more useful way of understanding influence and power in mental health. Here, coercion is recognised at the point that it creates "moral discomfort" which, according to Olsen (2003), provides a stronger position to challenge its use in mental health care. The Mental Health Act includes safeguards such as the right to appeal and to independent advocacy (Department of Health, 2008), which it could be argued offer greater protection against coercion than those receiving treatment voluntarily.

Community treatment orders (CTOs)

In the amendments made in 2007 to the Mental Health Act 1983 in England and Wales, powers were extended to cover involuntary treatment within the community. Such changes, at the time of their introduction, were controversial – raising further questions regarding coercion and the role of mental health services in promoting social control. This section examines arguments for and against their use, exploring ethical implications for choice and autonomy.

A community treatment order is a form of legally mandated supervised community treatment. Under a community treatment order (CTO), a person can be required to meet certain conditions that aim to:

- Ensure that they undertake treatment.
- Prevent harm to the person.
- Protect others.

They can be tailored to the individual and, in order to ensure the above aims are met, can specify other conditions – such as where treatment in the community can take place, where the person lives and what situations defined as high risk they should avoid (Department of Health, 2008). A person subject to a CTO can be recalled to hospital for a period of 72 hours before either the order must be revoked, or the person must be admitted for treatment. Internationally, a form of supervised community treatment for people with mental health problems has existed for a number of years in jurisdictions including the USA, Canada, New Zealand, Australia and Israel. They were introduced in Scotland in 2005 (Churchill et al., 2007)

CTOs: A necessary modernisation of mental health law?

The succession of a Labour government in the late 1990s in the UK heralded a renewed focus on modernising health services (Lester and Glasby, 2006). Underpinning the commitment to change was a concern that care in the community had failed, which contributed to a need to seek to improve support for individuals with mental health problems in the wider community (Szmukler and Holloway, 2000). Under this backdrop, current legislative frameworks were perceived by the government as being outmoded and failing to ensure public safety (Department of Health, 1998). This provided the foundation to introduce legislative reform to the Mental Health Act. The 1983 Mental Health Act also focussed on compulsory detention to hospital, yet the majority of contemporary mental health services are delivered in the community. Legislation which identified institutional care as the cornerstone of mental health services was recognised as being in need of change. The introduction of community treatment orders in the amendments to the Mental Health Act was an important attempt to address these concerns.

Mandatory community treatment is employed on the basis of two main concerns: to ensure treatment is undertaken, and to prevent harm to the person and others.

CTOs and treatment

CTOs were seen as a mechanism to ensure that a person experiencing mental health problems undertakes treatment. They were introduced, in part, to target people defined as so called "revolving door patients" (Churchill et al., 2007). These persons were frequently admitted to hospital on compulsion – often, on a section under the Mental Health Act – and once discharged would stop taking medication. Stopping medication is often seen as being "non-compliant" with treatment and professional decisions, and this often results in further admissions (Segal and Burgess, 2008). Mental health policy and legislation promises the delivery of care within "the least restrictive environment" (Department of Health, 1999; 2008), and treatment (however coerced) within the community setting is often seen as the least restrictive option compared with hospital admission. Within this situation, some commentators have argued that a person's autonomy is actually increased, in comparison with hospital admission (O'Brien et al., 2009). For example, proponents of CTOs have argued that service users may be unable to choose to stop taking medication without risking admission. However, the person still has liberty and some freedom to exercise choice as they are not contained within a hospital. In this scenario, CTOs are justified on the basis that they provide a less restrictive environment for treatment than hospital. As we will see later in this chapter, when we consider the issue of CTOs in more detail, these arguments are widely contested and the evidence base for CTOs is weak.

There have been arguments that untreated mental health problems and frequent relapses may cause damage to a person. This damage may be as a result of loss of relationships, increased stigma and exclusion that could impact on a person's long-term health and quality of life. It may also be as a result of the mental health problems themselves. For example, Gleeson et al. (2013) estimate that, in service users experiencing first episode psychosis, up to 70 per cent are adversely effected by relapse; they highlight an increased risk that this can lead to further periods of crisis, as well as inhibiting recovery. The aim of CTOs is to promote adherence to treatment on the basis that this leads to improvements in a person's mental health problems. It could therefore be argued that CTOs improve health outcomes and the use of CTOs becomes a paternalistic act. Paternalism involves an action or omission with the aim of avoiding harm and doing good on behalf of the person, and can involve overriding their wishes (Beauchamp and Childress, 2001). The argument that advocates for CTOs put forward is that improving health through adherence to treatment avoids the harm of frequent relapse and achieves good in the potential impact on wellbeing.

Prevention of harm to the self and others

Introduction of plans to amend the 1983 Mental Health Act made explicit that the aim was to ensure "patients who might be a danger to themselves or others can no longer refuse treatment" (Department of Health, 1998: 2). The justification for a compromise to autonomy is made here on the basis of prevention of harm and promoting the public good.

During the 1990s, there was a small number of high-profile homicides committed by people with mental health problems which drew attention in the media. This fuelled fears that the public was threatened by people with mental health problems now living in the community (Cutcliffe and Hannigan, 2001; Freshwater and Westwood, 2006). In Munro and Rumgay's (2000) analysis of homicides committed by people with mental health problems, relapse is identified consistently in the cases reviewed. Maden's (2006) analysis also concluded that homicides were associated with non-compliance with medication. Compulsory treatment in the community is identified as a mechanism to manage this non-compliance, reduce dangerousness (Coid, 1996), and is therefore justified on the basis of an action to prevent harm.

CTOs: An infringement on rights and mechanism of social control?

The introduction of CTOs attracted opposition from both service users and mental health professionals. Some of these groups combined to create the Mental Health Alliance, who campaigned for the proposal to introduce enforced CTOs to be rejected. Concerns were raised that enforced treatment would drive people away from mental health services and further infringe the rights of people with mental health problems (Parker, 2001; Laurence, 2003; Mental Health Alliance, 2005).

In order to explore the problems with CTOs, it is important to examine how the justification for their use can be challenged, and the problems that they can create for promoting choice and recovery.

CTOs: Treatment and recovery

The use of CTOs has been justified on the basis that it enables care to be delivered in the least restrictive environment. However, international research on the use of enforced community treatment has demonstrated that this is not necessarily the case; hospital admission stays the same and, in some studies, even increases for those on CTOs (Kisely et al., 2005; Burgess et al., 2006; Churchill et al., 2007). A recent clinical trial conducted in England found no evidence of CTOs reducing hospital admission for people experiencing psychosis and concluded that this meant there was no justification for the restrictions placed on people's liberty (Burns et al., 2013). These findings suggest that service users are not only exposed to higher restrictions within hospital, but also that their autonomy is further violated through the enforcement of treatment in the community.

A CTO may include conditions governing where a person may live, what they should do and who they should see. This suggests that the perception of "least restrictive" is problematic, given that CTOs effectively extend the powers restricting peoples choices once discharged from hospital and living in their own homes. This creates a false sense that these individuals being supported in the community have greater freedom.

A person's opportunity for self-determination can therefore become inhibited. Self-determination entails the ability to act with free will and can be an important aspect of a person's recovery. It has significance for underlining personal power and reinforcing the internal locus of control. Deegan (1995) highlights that people's self-determination should be an outcome for recovery orientated mental health services. Conversely, in the same work, Deegan proposes that compliance is not a desired outcome and that it maintains an external locus of control reinforcing a cycle of learned helplessness for people using services.

Compliance is an issue arising consistently in Mancini's (2007) exploration of turning points in the recovery process. Participants reported that resisting treatment perceived to be oppressive was important in initiating and sustaining a recovery process, and non-compliance was often how participants achieved this. It included not taking prescribed medication and exercising choice not to participate in treatment regimes that they found unhelpful.

Medication is often the main form of treatment in hospital and, as seen here, non-compliance with medication has been used in arguments for the implementation of CTOs. However, the idea that mental health problems are easily treatable with medication is an oversimplification. Some people diagnosed with "psychosis" do not respond to pharmacological treatments (the very people CTOs claim to target) and continue to experience relapse (Moncrieff, 2003). Not being part of the decision making process in relation to medication is what many service users perceive as problematic. Instead, engaging people in this process enables them to use medication as part of self-management, rather than just taking it because they have to (Deegan, 1995; Deegan and Drake, 2006).

Alternative approaches enabling people to manage their mental health problems – such as talking therapies, assertive outreach and strengths working – all have empirical evidence to show health outcomes have been improved. For many of these approaches, research has also demonstrated improvement in social outcomes and service users' satisfaction. Churchill et al. (2007) highlight that this is an important gap in studies on the effectiveness of CTOs,as many lack any measures that are meaningful to service users and their families. It is also necessary to recognise the complexity of health and social needs of people with mental health problems that are not easily resolved with the prescribed treatment and compliance that CTOs promote (Snow and Austin, 2009). The claim that CTOs are justified on the basis of benefits to health outcomes can therefore be questioned. Instead, they may be detrimental to a person's recovery.

Risk and the prevention of harm to self and others

Homicides committed by people with mental health problems are a very rare event. The government and media response to those homicides that do occur have been presented as a "moral panic" resulting from stigma and the growth of de-institutionalisation (Paterson and Stark 2001). The vast majority of murders in the UK are perpetrated by those without mental health problems – (about 85 per cent, according to Laurence (2003)). The rate of homicides committed by people in touch with mental health services has been in steady decline despite the murder rate, as a whole, increasing (Laurence, 2003; Appleby et al., 2013). Statistical analysis looking at population data has found correlation of violence with characteristics independent of a diagnosed mental health problem (such as misusing certain drugs, being male and young). Maden's (2006) conclusion that, of the homicides he reviewed, the main issue was non-compliance could be inaccurate. Substance misuse and being abused as a child were more common experiences for the perpetrators in the cases he studied.

Predicting the likelihood that harm will occur is inherently problematic. Yet, the rationale for using a CTO is based on the notion of prevention and protection. Goldacre (2006) highlights that the most sensitive risk assessment tools are inaccurate 86 times out of 100, which rises to 97 times out of 100 when predicting serious violence because it is so rare. This situation is compounded by the claim that mental health professionals are more likely to predict false positives (Buchanan, 1999; Morgan, 2007) – that is, over-estimate the potential for harm, meaning there are no grounds for coercive interventions. It is estimated that 85 orders for community treatment would be needed to prevent one hospital admission and 238 to prevent one arrest (Kisely et al., 2012). The change in the law to introduce CTOs was believed to have the potential to prevent 32 suicides (from around 1,500) of people with mental health problems (Laurence, 2003). The suicide rate for people in touch with mental health services, however, is actually increasing (Appleby et al., 2013).

It is estimated that, in 2012, people who were subject to a CTO in England numbered 22, 267, a figure that has risen between 5 per cent and 10 per cent annually since 2010 (Health and Social Care Information Centre, 2012). Nearly half of this number, in 2012, ended with the person's section being reinstated (further undermining the idea of "least restrictive"). African and African-Caribbean minorities are also over-represented in CTO use. These figures suggest not only that the argument that CTOs can be ethically justified on the basis of prevention of harm is flawed, but also that not using them would actually benefit the most people. Exercise 7.2 is a case study which encourages you to explore these arguments using an example from practice.

Exercise 7.2

Ashna and Tom work in a community mental health team and have arranged to meet for supervision. Tom is concerned about one of the service users he is supporting and brings this to supervision to reflect on. He discusses the current situation with Ashna and seeks her advice.

"Jamal's been living in temporary housing since he left hospital. He lost his rented flat when he became unwell, fell behind on payment and damaged the flat ... though Jamal explains that this was because he believed he was building defences against government agencies ... he'd stopped taking his medication at that point too ... but then he has never seen his experiences in the same way as the psychiatrists ... he sees himself as having special powers and in need of protection so medication isn't important to him, he feels it just makes him so tired ... though in the 20 years that he has been part of services the diagnosis he has been given is of treatment resistant schizophrenia.

He misses his son Leon a lot ... he's 5 now but access to him was stopped after the threats he made to his ex-partner just before he was admitted ....
He sees it as our fault that he can't see Leon ... which is difficult ... it's been hard for me to build up that trust. Jamal was placed subject to a CTO on his discharge from hospital. He is prescribed anti-psychotic medication via depot injection but I am just not sure if this is right, it means he is taking his medication and things are settling but I don't know what that might mean for the long term."

- What do you think would be the potential benefits for Jamal of being subject to a CTO?
- What do you think the costs of being subject to a CTO would be?
- How do these relate to the arguments in this chapter?

To answer these questions it might be helpful to think not only about his health, but also his social situation alongside his relationship with mental health services.

The introduction of CTOs has focussed attention on concerns regarding increased coercion and the role of mental health professionals as enforcers of social control. Practices such as forced treatment have been identified by service users as a barrier to accessing care (Snow and Austin, 2009). This may be exacerbated for minority groups who are more likely to be the subject of these compulsory powers. This concern is not only confined to those under the Mental Health Act. There is evidence that service users have experienced voluntary admission to hospital as coercion (Laurence, 2003; Bindman et al., 2005). Service developments, such as locked wards, have also been identified as inherently coercive (Bentall, 2013). In order to understand these experiences in more detail, the following section will examine the different pressures that can be applied in relation to treatment and care decisions.

Within the mental health literature, coercion has been identified as the use of physical force (such as restraint) or, more broadly, as incorporating a range of interpersonal interactions resulting in influencing service users decision making and action (O'Brien and Golding, 2003). These authors support a broad definition of coercion that includes manipulation of service users' wishes and restricting access to information. Szmukler and Appelbaum (2008) divide such pressures into five types: persuasion, interpersonal leverage, inducements, threats and compulsion or compulsory treatment.

Persuasion The risks and benefits of different options are explored to encourage a reasoned discussion. The person's perspective of their situation is examined. This influence is most closely related to negotiated decision making and is described as the least problematic by Szmukler and Appelbaum (2008), though this still involves an attempt to influence the decision outcome.

Interpersonal leverage The worker exploits their relationship with the person to demonstrate disapproval, either verbally or non-verbally. This is dependent on the closeness established within the therapeutic relationship, and may make use of a person's emotional dependence on that relationship and fear of rejection.

Inducements Rewards for a course of action may be offered, enticing a person to follow that option. It is a conditional proposal in that, if the specified action happens, there will be a response from the worker.

Threats A threat is also a conditional proposal as it suggests that there will be a specified response from the worker. This is closely related to inducement but can be distinguished in that, with a threat, the response leaves the person in a worse off position as a result. Threats can be determined as a form of coercion.

Compulsion or compulsory treatment These are supported by legislation, using this to ensure that a course of action is followed by the person. As highlighted in this chapter, admission to hospital on a section of the Mental Health Act and Community Treatment Orders is a form of compulsory treatment. They have also been determined as a form of coercion.

Consider Case study 7.1 about Josie and her mental health worker. Read the statements at the bottom outlining the possible responses of her mental health worker. Identify which type of treatment pressure the worker is using in each statement. The answers can be found at the end of the chapter

---

❏ Case Study 7.1

Josie has been referred to a substance misuse counsellor by her mental health worker, Nathan. Josie has been struggling with alcohol addiction alongside her mental health problems. When Josie drinks heavily, she can feel very hopeless and low. Before seeing the counsellor, Josie made two attempts to kill herself when drunk. However, Josie has said she does not want to continue seeing the substance misuse counsellor as she does not find it helps her.

Josie and her worker discuss this. Nathan responds by:

(a) Folding his arms and tutting when Josie tells him she wants to stop counselling. He says he would have expected more from her.

(b) He tells Josie that the team have had some cinema passes donated to them and proposes to Josie that, if she continues to attend substance misuse counselling for the next two months, then he will ensure she has one of the passes.

(c) Exploring with Josie the reasons why she wants to give up the counselling and what she may gain by continuing to attend. He says he understands her reluctance to go and wonders whether other models of support with her addiction might be helpful instead, such as going to a group.

(d) Getting the Multidisciplinary Team to agree to add that Josie needs to see a substance misuse counsellor as part of the conditions of her CTO.

(e) Informing Josie that he will not complete a reference for her housing application if she does not continue seeing the counsellor. He emphasises that she is unlikely to secure the tenancy unless she has a good reference.

It appears that service users are exposed to a range of pressures, both within in-patient settings and within the community, to make certain choices. This challenge the opportunities people have to take back control in their own lives and progress their recovery journey. Contributing to this concern is the tendency for these pressures to become an accepted part of decision making and even be justified on the basis of recovery (Morgan and Felton, 2013).

In order to further understand how service users can be supported within decision making, the following section considers consent, capacity and how a person's preferences can be respected at times when these may be compromised.

Informed consent

The ethical principle that each person has a right to self-determination and is entitled to have their autonomy respected finds its expression in law through the notion of informed consent. For consent to be valid, it must be "real" – that is, certain criteria must be met. The service user must:

- Have the capacity to give consent.
- Know, in broad terms, to what they are consenting.
- Give their consent freely without being misled, placed under duress or subject to undue influence.

If an adult person meets the criteria to be able to consent to treatment. then they also have the right to refuse treatment – both at the time it is offered and in the future. Such a refusal of treatment must be respected, even if it may lead to the death of the service user. This issue is particularly important in light of the exploration of treatment pressures. Informed consent recognises that service users have a right to make decisions free from influence (including coercion). However, the Mental Health Act 2007 can be used to override a person's competent refusal of treatment for a mental disorder in certain circumstances.

Capacity

Competence is a pivotal concept in decision making about medical treatment. Competent decisions about accepting or rejecting proposed treatment are respected. Incompetent service user's choices, on the other hand, are put to one side, and alternative mechanisms for deciding about their care are sought (Grisso and Applebaum, 1998). The legal mechanism for making decisions about the care and treatment of people who lack capacity to make decisions has been governed by statute law since 1 October 2007 due to the Mental Capacity Act 2005.

This Act provides a statutory framework to empower and protect people who lack the capacity to make some decisions for themselves. It generally applies only to people aged 16 or over. It also brings in legal mechanisms that a person with capacity can use to make preparations for a time when they may lack capacity in the future.

The whole Act is underpinned by a set of five key principles set out in Section 1 of the Act:

(1) A presumption of capacity: every adult has the right to make his or her own decisions and must be assumed to have capacity to do so unless it is proved otherwise;
(2) Individuals being supported to make their own decisions: a person must be given all practicable help before anyone treats them as not being able to make their own decisions;
(3) Unwise decisions: just because an individual makes what might be seen as an unwise decision, they should not be treated as lacking capacity to make that decision;
(4) Best interests: an act done or decision made under the Act for or on behalf of a person who lacks capacity must be done in their best interests; and
(5) Least restrictive option: anything done for or on behalf of a person who lacks capacity should consider options that are less restrictive of their basic rights and freedoms if they are as effective as the proposed option.

The Act sets out a single clear test for assessing whether a person lacks capacity to take a particular decision at a particular time. It is a "decision specific" and time specific test. No one can be labelled 'incapable' simply as a result of a particular medical condition or diagnosis. Section 2 of the Act makes it clear that a lack of capacity cannot be established merely by reference to a person's age, appearance, or any condition or aspect of a person's behaviour that might lead others to make unjustified assumptions about capacity. If a doctor or health care professional proposes treatment or an examination, they must assess the person's capacity to consent. In settings such as a hospital, this can involve the multi-disciplinary team but; ultimately, it is up to the professional responsible for the person's treatment to make sure that capacity has been assessed. A person's capacity must be assessed specifically in terms of their capacity to make a particular decision at the time it needs to be made.

How to assess capacity

Capacity is assessed by asking the following questions:

- Does the person have an impairment of the mind or brain, or is there some sort of disturbance affecting the way their mind or brain works?
- If so, does that impairment or disturbance mean that the person is unable to make the decision in question at the time it needs to be made?

A person is unable to make a decision if they cannot:

- Understand information about the decision to be made.
- Retain that information in their mind.
- Use or weigh that information as part of the decision making process.
- Communicate their decision (by talking, using sign language or any other means)

The first three points above need to be applied together. If a person cannot do any of these three things, they will be treated as unable to make the decision.

An act done or decision made for or on behalf of a person who lacks capacity must be in that person's best interests. A person can put his/her wishes and feelings into a written statement if they so wish, which the person making the determination must consider. In addition, people involved in caring for the person lacking capacity have to be consulted concerning a person's best interests.

Advance decision

One way in which a person can make their wishes known during a time when they are considered as lacking capacity would be to create an advance decision (also known as an advance directive). This can be an important tool to support recovery and enable a person to have an influence on choices that affect their lives when they may struggle with capacity. This is made when the person still has capacity and is used if they are not able to make the decision themselves at the time of the proposed medical treatment. It is legally binding and cannot be overridden by a medical professional.

An advance decision can be made verbally, or in writing. The code of practice in the Mental Capacity Act (2005) provides a checklist of information to be included in any written statement. The statement should show:

- Full details of the person you act for and who is making the statement.
- The name and address of their general practitioner (GP).
- Whether the GP has a copy of the statement.
- That the decision is intended to have effect if the person you are looking after lacks the capacity to make treatment decisions.
- A clear statement of the decision, specifying the treatment to be refused and the circumstances in which the decision should be used or which will trigger a particular course of action.
- The date the document was written and, if appropriate, the date it was reviewed.
- The person's signature. If the person cannot write, they must give authority to somebody else to sign on their behalf in their presence.
- A signature from a witness to the above.

The development of an advance decision encourages the person to think about what they would like to happen to them in a period of crisis and enables them to maintain autonomy. It ensures that the person's voice is at the heart of treatment decisions, even when they are not able to be present within the decision making forum. The principles underpinning an advance statement can also be applied to the development of other directives – such as crisis and recovery plans which, while not legally binding, can be an important part of working towards recovery. This would entail discussing with individuals their plans and wishes when they may experience a crisis or increase in their distress.

Outlined here is an activity that aims to enable you to explore how advance decisions may impact on mental health practice. A digital story (available at http://www.patientvoices. org.uk/flv/0365pv384.htm) demonstrates some of the challenges of advocating for a person's wishes when they are not able to communicate for themselves. Watch the digital story and consider the following:

- How might an advance decision help or hinder the communication between Susanna and the established nurse?
- How might an advance decision influence the care of Aimee while admitted to the ward?
- What information might be helpful to include in an advance decision for Aimee?

CONCLUSION

Compromise to autonomy is enshrined within mental health law; consequently, coercion is a reality of mental health practice. Protective mechanisms are built into legislation to provide safeguards against unnecessary loss of autonomy – such as the concepts of consent and capacity. Yet, this chapter has highlighted that coercion is not confined to the Mental Health Act. The justification for the use of coercive practices both within and outside mental health law has been questioned. What these debates highlight is a need for all mental health practitioners to examine practice in a critical way to prevent unquestioningly accepting increases in control and coercion that undermine recovery.

ANSWERS TO CASE EXAMPLE ACTIVITY IN CASE STUDY 7.1

(a) Interpersonal leverage.
(b) Inducement.
(c) Persuasion.
(d) Compulsory treatment.
(e) Threat.

KEY TERMS

Autonomy: Self-Rule, the right to make our own decisions

Coercion: Subjecting a person to the will of another. However, precise definitions are debated leading to some disagreement over what may or may not be considered coercive.

Community Treatment Order: Form of supervised community treatment used in England and Wales outlined under the requirements of the Mental health Act. CTO means a person can be mandated to accept treatment outside of the hospital setting.

Treatment pressures: A hierarchy of techniques that may be used by organisations or workers with the aim of influencing a service users decisions.

Non-adherence to medication: A person does not consistently take their prescribed medication. Term sometimes used interchangeably with compliance and concordance.

FURTHER READING

The UN Convention on the Rights of People with Disabilities (UNCRPD) is a landmark document enshrining the rights of people who experience mental distress in international law. You can find the document at: http://www.un.org/disabilities/convention/conventionfull.shtml

In the drafting of this convention, service user/survivor voices were key in drafting the UNCRPD. Much of this work stems from contributions from the Center for the Human Rights of Users and Survivors of Psychiatry, particularly the work of Tina Minkowitz. For further information and documents, see: http://www.chrusp.org/home/about_us

Laurence, J. (2003) *Pure Madness: How Fear Drives the Mental Health System.* London: Routledge.

> Jeremy Laurence is a journalist and uses this style to investigate the state of mental health care in Britain. His focuses, in particular, is the issues of risk, dangerousness and the responses of the state and mental health services to this. Chapters 3 and 5 consider coercion and the Mental Health Act.

For some personal perspectives on being sectioned, see;

Henderson, J. (2009) "Experiences of 'care' in mental health" in Reynolds, J., Muston, R., Heller, T., Leach, J., McCormick, M., Wallcraft, J. and Walsh, M. (eds) *Mental Health Still Matters.* Palgrave: Milton Keynes.

Snow, N. and Austin, W. (2009) "Community treatment orders: The ethical balancing act in community mental health", *Journal of Psychiatric and Mental Health Nursing,* 16, 177–86.

> This paper provides a good overview of the ethical issues of enforced community treatment examining the issues from both a national and international perspective. It has broad application as it considers the implications for community workers.

Szmukler, G. and Holloway, F. (2001) *Mental Health Law: Discrimination or Protection?,* Maudsley Discussion Paper No 10, Kings College. London. Available at http://www.kcl.ac.uk/iop/mentalhealth/publications/discussion-papers/index.aspx

> Critical perspective on the ethics of the Mental Health Act (written prior to the 2007 amendments)

A debate between service users and providers about values and capacity is reported in Woodbridge et al. (2005). For research on the values driving decision making under the Mental Capacity Act, see Shah, Banner et al., 2009 and Shah, Heginbotham et al., 2009. We return to the role of values-based practice in the contested area of coercion and involuntary treatment in Chapter 12.

REFERENCES

Appleby, L., Kapur, N., Shaw, J., Hunt, I., While, D., Flynn, S., Windfuhr, K. and Williams, A. (2013) *The National Confidential Inquiry into Suicide and Homicide by People with Mental Illness.* Manchester: University of Manchester.

Arnold, D. (2001) "Coercion and moral responsibility", *American Philosophical Quarterly,* 38(1): 53–67.

Beauchamp, T. and Childress, J. (2001) *Principles of Biomedical Ethics* (5th edn). Oxford: Oxford University Press.

Bentall, R. (2013) "Too much coercion in mental health services", *The Guardian*, 1 February. Available at: http://www.theguardian.com/commentisfree/2013/feb/01/mental-health-services-coercion (accessed 29 June 2014).

Bindman, J., Reid, Y., Szmukler, G., Tiller, J., Thornicroft, G. and Leese, M. (2005) "Perceived coercion at admission to psychiatric hospital and engagement to follow-up", *Social Psychiatry Psychiatric Epidemiology*, 40: 160–6.

Buchanan, A. (1999) "Risk and dangerousness", *Psychological Medicine*, 29: 465–3.

Burgess, P., Bindma, J., Leese, M., Henderson, C. and Szmukler, G. (2006) "Do community treatment orders for mental illness reduce admission to hospital", *Social Psychiatry and Psychiatric Epidemiology*, 41: 574–9.

Burns, T., Rugaska, J., Molodynski, A., Dawson, J., Yeeles, K., Vazquez-Montes, M., Voysey, M., Sinclair, J. and Priebe, S. (2013) "Compulsory treatment orders for patients with psychosis (OCTET): A randomised control trial", *The Lancet*, 381(9878): 1627–33.

Chan, P. (2002) "In whose best interests? An examination of the ethics of the UK government's White Paper 'Reforming the Mental Health Act'", *Journal of Psychiatric and Mental Health Nursing*, 9: 399–404.

Churchill, R., Owen, G., Singh, S. and Hotopf, M. (2007) *International Experiences of Using Community Treatment Orders*. London: Institute of Psychiatry.

Coid, J. (1996) "Dangerous patients with mental illness; Increased risks warrant new policies, adequate resources and appropriate legislation", *BMJ*, 312: 965–6.

Cutliffe, J. and Hannigan, B. (2001) "Mass media, monsters and mental health clients: The need to increased lobbying", *Journal of Psychiatric Mental Health Nursing*, 8(4): 315–21.

Davis, S. (2002) "Autonomy versus coercion: Reconciling competing perspectives in community mental health", *Community Mental Health Journal*, 38(3): 239–51.

Deegan, P. (1995) "Principles of a recovery model including medication", Available at: http://www.power2u.org/downloads/MedicationMeetingPacket.pdf (accessed January 2014).

Deegan, P. and Drake, R. (2006) "Shared decision making and medication management in the recovery process", *Psychiatric Services*, 57(11): 1636–9.

Department of Health (1998) *Mental Health Services Safe, Sound and Supportive*. London: TSO.

Department of Health (1999) *National Service Framework for Mental Health, Modern Standards and Service Models*. London: TSO.

Department of Health (2008) *Code of Practice, Mental Health Act 1983*. Norwich: TSO.

Fazel, S., Singh, J., Doll, H. and Grann, M. (2012) "Use of risk assessment instruments to predict violence and antisocial behaviour in 72 samples involving 24,827 people: A systematic review and meta-analysis", *BMJ*, 345: 1–12.

Freshwater, D. and Westwood, T. (2006) "Risk, detention and evidence: Humanizing mental health reform", Editorial, *Journal of Psychiatric and Mental Health Nursing*, 13: 257–9.

Gleeson, J., Cotton, S., Alvarez-Jimenez, M., Wade, D., Gee, D., Crisp, K., Pearce, T., Spiliotacopoulos, D., Newman, B. and McGorry, P. (2013) "A randomized controlled trial of relapse prevention therapy for first-episode psychosis patients: Outcome at 30-month follow-up", *Schizophrenia Bulletin*, 39(2): 436–48.

Goldacre, B. (2006) "It's not easy to predict murder – Do the maths". Available at: www.guardian.co.uk/science/2006/dec/09/badscience.uknews (accessed 29 May 2015).

Gosling, J. (2010) "The ethos of involvement as the route to recovery" in Weinstein, J. (ed.) *Mental Health Service User Involvement and Recovery*. London: Jessica Kingsley.

Grisso, T. and Appelbaum, P. (1998) *Assessing Competence to Consent to Treatment: A Guide for Physicians and Other Health Care Professionals*. New York: Oxford University Press. ISBN 0195103726, 9780195103724.

Health and Social Care Information Centre (2012) *Inpatients Formally Detained in Hospitals Under the Mental Health Act 1983 and Patients Subject to Supervised Community Treatment – England, 2011–2012, Annual figures*, 24 October. Available at: http://www.hscic.gov.uk/catalogue/PUB08085 (accessed January 2014).

Hopton, J. (1996) "Towards a critical theory of mental health nursing", *Journal of Advanced Nursing*, 25: 492–500.

Kisely, S., Campbell, L.A. and Preston, N. (2005) "Compulsory community and involuntary outpatient treatment for people with severe mental disorders", *Cochrane Database of Systematic Reviews 2005*, 20.

Laurence, J. (2003) *Pure Madness: How Fear Drives the Mental Health System*. London: Routledge.

Lester, H. and Glasby, J. (2006) *Mental Health Policy and Practice*. New York: Palgrave Macmillan.

Maden, T. (2006) *Review of Homicides by Patients with Serious Mental Illness*. London: Imperial College.

Mancini, M. (2007) "A qualitative analysis of turning points in the recovery process", *American Journal of Psychiatric Rehabilitation*, 10: 223–44.

Mental Health Alliance (2005) "Towards a Better Mental Health Act: The Mental Health Alliance Policy Agenda", Mental Health Alliance. Available at: http://www.mentalhealthalliance.org.uk/pre2007/documents/AGENDA2.pdf (accessed 29 May 2015)

Moncrieff, J. (2003) *Is Psychiatry for Sale? An Examination of the Influence of the Pharmaceutical Industry on Academic and Practical Psychiatry*, Maudsley Discussion Paper. London: Institute of Psychiatry.

Morgan, A. and Felton, A. (2013) "From constructive engagement to coerced recovery" in Coles, S., Keenan, S. and Diamond, B. (eds) *Madness Contested: Power and Practice*. Ross-on-Wye: PCCS Books.

Morgan, J. (2007) *Giving Up Culture of Blame, Risk Assessment and Risk Management in Psychiatric Practice*. London: Royal College of Psychiatrists.

Morrall, P. and Hazleton, M. (2000) "Architecture signifying social control: The restoration of asylumdom in mental health care?", *International Journal of Mental Health Nursing*, 9(2): 89–96.

Munro, E. and Rumgay, J. (2000) "Role of risk assessment in reducing homicides by people with mental illness", *British Journal of Psychiatry*, 176: 116–20.

Nozick, R. (1969) "Coercion" in *Philosophy, Science and Method: Essays in Honour of Ernest Nagel*, Morgenbesser, S., Suppes, P. and White, M. (eds). New York: St Martin's Press.

O'Brien, A.J., McKenna, B. and Kydd, R. (2009) "Compulsory community mental health treatment: Literature review", *International Journal of Nursing Studies*, 46: 1245–55.

O'Brien, A.J. and Golding, C.G. (2003) "Coercion in mental healthcare: The principle of least restrictive", *Journal of Psychiatric and Mental Health Nursing*, 10: 167–73.

Olsen, D.P. (2003) "Influence and coercion: Relational and rights-based ethical approaches to forced psychiatric treatment", *Journal of Psychiatric and Mental Health Nursing*, 10(6): 705–12.

Parker, C. (2001) *Review of Mental Health Legislation in the UK, Updates*, Volume 4(5). London: Mental Health Foundation.

Paterson, B. and Stark, C. (2001) "Social policy and mental illness in England in the 1990s: Violence, moral panic and critical discourse", *Journal of Psychiatric and Mental Health Nursing*, 8: 257–67.

Pilgrim, D. (2007) "New 'mental health' legislation for England and Wales: Some aspects of consensus and conflict", *Journal of Social Policy*, 36(1): 79–95.

Priebe, S., Burton, A., Asby, D., Ashcroft, R., Burns, T., David, A., Eldridge, S., Firn, M., Knapp, M. and McCabe, R. (2009) "Financial incentives to improve adherence to anti-psychotic maintenance medication and non-adherent patients: A cluster randomised controlled trial (PACT)", *BMC Psychiatry*, 9: 61.

Repper, J. and Perkins, R. (2003) *Social Inclusion and Recovery*. Edinburgh: Balliere Tindhall.

Richardson, G. (2008) "Coercion and human rights: A European perspective", *Journal of Mental Health*, 17(3): 245–54.

Segal, S. and Burgess, P. (2008) "Use of community treatment orders to prevent psychiatric hospitalisation", *Australian and New Zealand Journal of Psychiatry*, 42: 732–9.

Shah, A.K., Banner, N., Heginbotham, C. and Fulford, K.W.M. (2009) "The application of the Mental Capacity Act 2005 among geriatric psychiatry patients: A pilot study", *International Psychogeriatrics*, 21(5): 922–30.

Shah, A., Heginbotham, C., Fulford, K.W.M., Banner, N. and Newbiggin, K. (2009) "The early experience of old age psychiatrists in application of the Mental Capacity Act: Issues for black and minority individuals", *Ethnicity and Inequalities in Health and Social Care*, 2(2): 4–10.

Snow, N. and Austin, W. (2009) "Community treatment orders: The ethical balancing act in community mental health", *Journal of Psychiatric and Mental Health Nursing*, 16: 177–86.

Symonds, B. (1998) "The philosophical and sociological context of mental health care legislation", *Journal of Advanced Nursing*, 27(5): 946–54.

Szasz, T. (1963) *Law, Liberty, and Psychiatry: An Inquiry into the Social Uses of Mental Health Practices*. New York: Macmillan.

Szmukler, G. and Appelbaum, P. (2008) "Treatment pressures, leverage, coercion and compulsion in mental health care", *Journal of Mental Health*, 17(3): 233–44.

Szmukler, G. and Holloway, F. (1998) "Mental health legislation is now a harmful anachronism", *Psychiatric Bulletin*, 22: 662–5.

Szmukler, G. and Holloway, F. (2000) "Reform of the Mental Health Act. Health or safety?", *British Journal of Psychiatry*, 177: 196–200.

United Nations (2006) Convention on the Rights of Persons with Disabilities. Available at http://www.un.org/disabilities/default.asp?id=259 (accessed 21 February).

Wall, S., Churchill, R., Hotopf, M., Buchanan, A. and Wesseley, S. (1999) *A Systematic Review of Research Relating to the Mental Health Act* (1983). London: Department of Health.

Woodbridge, K., Williamson, T., Allott, P., Fleming, B. and Fulford, K.W.M. (2005) "Values, mental health and mental capacity: Debates in cyberspace", *Mental Health Review*, 10(4): 25–9.

8 | Diagnosis as an ethical question in psychiatry

Chapter Summary

This chapter will:

- Explore why diagnosing mental distress is both an ethical issue and value-laden.
- Analyse the debate around one contemporary contested diagnosis: schizophrenia.
- Introduce the reader to debates about the usefulness and validity of diagnostic categories used in mental health care.
- Explore ethical issues in the global mental health agenda, and the "exporting" of psychiatric categories to the majority world.
- Analyse possible alternative conceptualisations of mental distress.

Diagnosis, ethics and values

It may seem intuitively odd to think of diagnosing illness as an ethical issue, or even a value-laden issue. Most traditional bioethical concerns around diagnosis are preoccupations with the context of a diagnosis, rather than the diagnostic act itself. For example, there are debates around informed consent, or the capacity to understand the implications of treatment. However, the act of diagnosis itself is not contested in most of medical practice. It is rare for someone to contest that they have cancer once a diagnosis is given whereas, in mental health settings, service users may often dispute, negotiate or reject their diagnoses.

The reason for this divergence is due to the historical creation of categories of mental distress in psychiatry. The classifications of all major mental illnesses occurred in the absence of any identification of underlying pathology. Depression, bi-polar disorder and schizophrenia were all classified as illnesses at the beginning of the twentieth century, but the classification occurred through a process of observation and description of behaviours as abnormal, rather than a scientific identification of physical alterations in the brain or other causal factors (Porter, 2002). In medicine, too, a descriptive approach dominated its early development: the careful observations of the great seventeenth-century physician Thomas Sydenham and many others laid the foundation for modern scientific theories of disease. But in mental health, as many psychiatrists and neuroscientists openly acknowledge (Kupfer et al., 2002, introduction; Insel, 2013), there has been no corresponding development of disease theory. The descriptive approach in psychiatry led to what is known as the Kraepelinian paradigm in diagnosis, named after the German psychiatrist Emil Kraepelin (1856–1926). Kraepelin divided severe mental illnesses into a range of classifications based on the observations of patient populations in asylums. Famously, he divided so-called major mental illness between schizophrenia (he had termed it "dementia praecox") and manic depression (later termed "bi-polar disorder") (Bentall, 2004). This approach to classifying discrete conditions based on observation, grouping of symptoms and treatment approaches has dominated psychiatry through the twentieth century and into the twenty-first century, and has produced progressively more classifications of conditions, nearly all of which are based on observation and clinical judgement, rather than specific knowledge about any underlying biological causation (Greenberg, 2013).

Diagnosis in mental health care has thus always been an inherently value-laden approach because the classification of disease categories occurred through the observation of "abnormal" behaviours. The definition of abnormality here was laden with the values and beliefs of the observers. This meant that abnormality often equated to behaviours that were not culturally acceptable, such as supposed sexual promiscuity in women or homosexuality in men. Homosexuality was classified as a mental illness by the American Psychiatric Association until the early 1970s, and it only removed the classification due to demonstrations by gay and lesbian activists (Kutchins and Kirk, 1997). The value-laden nature of diagnosis meant that the definition of abnormality could easily lead to oppression and long-term incarceration in a period where the labelling of someone with a mental illness often meant long stays in institutional asylums.

One of the most terrible incidences of this association of values, oppression and diagnosis occurred in Nazi Germany where those people diagnosed with mental health problems were first sterilised and then put to death, due to the Nazi belief that they were "polluting" the racial heritage of the German nation (Torrey and Yolken, 2010). Less dramatic, but no less terrible, have been the many situations in which the values driving the use of psychiatric "treatment" for political and social purposes have remained implicit. These "background values", as we called them in Chapter 3, were the basis of widespread abuses in the former Soviet Union (Fulford et al., 1993) and similar abuses have been reported in many other parts of the world (Voren, 2002). It is vitally important to be aware of the influence of implicit values for our own practice. Remember here, from Chapter 3, how it was our own implicit values that led us to neglect the values of Sally Coombs in what we called "her" story (see the section "Your values matter too", p. 33). We will see later, in Chapter 9, just how close losing sight of our own values brought the team working with Sally Coombs to well-intentioned but deeply mistaken interventions.

With these issues in mind, Moncrieff (2010) has written of diagnosis in psychiatry as an inherently "political" approach. A psychiatric diagnosis enables a social situation to be framed within "medical contexts", and this medicalisation of the diagnosis obscures the value-laden nature of psychiatric judgement and interpretation (Moncrieff, 2010). Szmukler (2014) has written of the drastic implications of a psychiatric diagnosis, rather than a medical diagnosis, and, particularly, the possibility of involuntary detention and coercion that follows from a psychiatric diagnosis. He argues that a psychiatric diagnosis is often construed in global contexts as a judgement on the "status" of a person, rather than a judgement on "functioning", and that a diagnosis of mental disorder thus often results in a loss of a range of civil, economic and cultural rights. Drew et al. (2011) conducted a study of participants globally from a range of low- and middle-income countries, and uncovered a catalogue of losses of civil, economic and individual rights that followed the diagnosis of mental health problems.

One of the most controversial ways in which diagnosis is value-laden is when psychiatric practice encounters other forms of institutional discrimination and racism. In fact, the history of psychiatry shows that diagnostic categories and the practice of psychiatry had its roots in the social construction of "race". For example, in 1851, Samuel L. Cartwright joined the disease category drapetomania, defined as a condition "that induces the negro to run away from services" (Caplan et al., 1981). More recently, Jonathan Metzl (2010) has presented historical evidence on how "schizophrenia" went through conceptual revisions – from changes in personality into "masculine belligerence" and, during the mid-1970s civil rights movements in the USA, into a diagnosis given disproportionately to black men. "Race" and culture, and differences in human behaviours attributed to these, continue to impact on psychiatric practice to this day. Fernando (2010) has written of how mental health assessments are treated as free of bias and objective, and thus ignore possible prejudices that might ascribe particular behaviours that are representative of diverse, cultural experiences as pathological instances of mental disorder. In the UK, the Care Quality Commission (2014) continues to report disproportionate numbers of people from particular ethnic backgrounds – especially African and African-Caribbean backgrounds – who are overrepresented in in-patient mental health services and more likely to be subjected to coercive measures under the Mental Health Act.

These debates demonstrate the intrinsic problems and value-laden nature of psychiatric diagnosis. This has led some critics of psychiatry to call for an end to diagnosis (Timimi,

2013), or for a radical shift in classifications towards more user-led models (Bentall, 2009) Callard (2014) has pointed out the "muddy" aspects of psychiatric diagnosis that are not often discussed in the polarised debates around whether diagnosis is good or bad. She writes that diagnosis is a "process" and that service users "live with, through, against and beyond" their diagnoses (Callard, 2014: 530). She argues for a more open and dialogic approach to understanding mental distress that takes the process of diagnosis as the beginning of a dialogue that will explore meaning, rather than result in the ascription of a medical fact (Callard, 2014).

One of the main concerns around diagnosing mental illness is the manner in which it has traditionally cut off any debate around the meaning of people's experiences. Karl Jaspers (1997) famously argued that there were some mental illnesses so severe that they were "un-understandable" but could only be explained biologically. Whilst Jaspers was grappling with the complexity of attempting to understand experiences that are at the limits of comprehension, his work was misinterpreted as an approach to mental distress that could just label disorders and dispense with any attempt to explore the subjective meaning and context within which those experiences arose. In recent years, even traditional psychiatrists have bemoaned the dominance of a "checklist" approach within psychiatry that ignores the meaning of experiences and an understanding of the whole person. For example, Allen Frances, who was previously in charge of the creation of an edition of the Diagnostic Manual of Mental Disorders (in this case, DSM-IV), has written recently that modern psychiatry has often been reduced to "filling out a checklist" and the art of understanding the "narrative arc of the patient's life and the contextual factors" has been lost (Frances 2013: 67).

Diagnostic systems

There are two classification manuals within psychiatry that determine the symptom groupings of various mental disorders and the mechanisms for diagnosing those disorders. In the USA, there is the Diagnostic and Statistical Manual of Mental Disorders (DSM). In May, 2013 the fifth edition of this manual was published by the American Psychiatric Association and is referred to as the DSM-5 (APA, 2013). In the rest of the world, there is a section of the International Classification of Diseases that is devoted to mental illness, and is developed and published by the World Health Organization. This is currently being revised for its eleventh edition, which is referred to as the ICD-11.

The fact that we have two manuals for classifying mental disorder and multiple versions of those manuals demonstrates the manner in which classification in psychiatry is often subject to revision, dispute and contestation (Greenberg, 2013). The debates leading up to the publication of DSM-5 were interesting when considering the ethical issues surrounding diagnosis.

First, there was an internal debate within official US psychiatry about the efficacy and validity of current constructs of mental disorder. There were several working groups set up to study diagnoses such as schizophrenia, and to think through whether these diagnostic labels were still valid and useful (Pierre, 2008). In the preface to the document laying out the research task ahead of official psychiatry for DSM-5, Kupfer et al. (2002: xviii) wrote that existing psychiatric categories have no objective validity, in that "not one laboratory marker has been found to be specific in identifying any of the DSM-defined syndromes". There is also a lack of reliability due to an inability to distinguish amongst major Kraepelinian syndromes, leading to "extremely high rates of comorbidities" and "short-term diagnostic instability" (Kupfer et al., 2002: xviii). Finally, they write that there is a lack of treatment specificity, and that this lack is the "rule rather than the exception" (Kupfer et al., 2002: xviii-xvix). This was an acknowledgement that there are no objective markers for constructs such as schizophrenia, bi-polar disorder and schizoaffective disorder, and an acceptance of an inability to police the boundaries of these disorders adequately, and accurately and clearly diagnose on first presentation, or match pharmacology to disorder in a straightforward manner.

This led the authors to conclude that the current categories of mental disorder are no more than constructs that have been "reified" to the extent that they are "considered to be equivalent to diseases", when they are just ways of trying to order and capture varieties of mental distress (Kupfer et al., 2002: xix). Not only is there an acceptance of mental disorders as constructs, not diseases, the authors of the research agenda believe they are no longer useful constructs as they are "more likely to obscure than to elucidate research findings" (Kupfer et al., 2002: xix). This was a radical acknowledgement of the instability of current diagnostic categories although, when DSM-5 was eventually published, these categories all remained in place. However, interestingly, the research arm of psychiatry in the USA, the National Institute for Mental Health, announced that it would re-orient its research endeavour away from categories such as schizophrenia and towards a range of behaviours and presentations that did not fit a Kraepelinian paradigm (Pickersgill, 2014).

Second, there was a debate around "diagnostic inflation" and "medicalising normality" (Frances, 2013; Greenberg, 2013). Critics of the diagnostic classification system argued that it was creating more and more disorders, which led to more and more people coming into the orbit of mental health services and specifically being targeted by pharmacological intervention. As we saw in Chapter 4 a particular area of contention here was the issue of medicalising sadness through the removal of the "bereavement exclusion" in the diagnosis of depression (Greenberg, 2013).

This debate is value laden and depends on attitudes towards what is normal, and the role of suffering in life, which invoke larger philosophical, cultural and ethical commitments (Davies, 2013). In the controversies surrounding DSM-5, we can see how diagnosis in mental illness tends to invoke larger questions of what sorts of people we want to be and how we want to live in society.

Exercise 8.1

- Write down your thoughts on psychiatric classifications? Do you think they are useful or a hindrance to working in mental health care?
- Would it be possible to work in your area of mental health without a classification system, and would that change your relationship with people using services?
- What do you think of the Kraepelinian paradigm in psychiatry? Does it make sense to distinguish between schizophrenia and bi-polar disorder?

Should we abolish the schizophrenia label?

A major source of contention within psychiatric diagnosis in recent years has been the debate about the label of schizophrenia and whether it is a useful label, or whether it should be abolished (Boyle, 2002; Bentall, 2009; Timimi, 2013). There has been a recent independent commission looking into schizophrenia. The commission was established by Rethink Mental Illness and produced a report looking at the problems consequent on a diagnosis of schizophrenia, and the reported stigma and discrimination faced by the majority of people with a diagnosis of schizophrenia (Schizophrenia Commission/Rethink, 2012). There is also an ongoing independent Inquiry into the Schizophrenia Label (ISL) that takes a service user/survivor/experts perspective and is gathering evidence from people who have been diagnosed with schizophrenia. Initial findings from the inquiry demonstrate that 80 per cent of people felt the label of schizophrenia is damaging and dangerous (see Thomas et al., 2013)

Current diagnostic classifications of schizophrenia define the "illness" through a range of "first rank" symptoms such as delusions, hallucinations and interference with thoughts, alongside a range of so-called "negative" symptoms such as breakdown in forms of thinking and speech, problems in emotional responses and social withdrawal (APA, 2013). The controversy over the label consists of three areas of concern. First, there is the issue of stigma, and that receiving a diagnosis of schizophrenia is extremely damaging to those to whom it is applied. Second, there is a debate about the validity of the diagnosis of schizophrenia, and an argument that the label is too broad and does not scientifically identify a disease or a syndrome. Third, there is concern about how the label is affected by discriminatory judgements based on "race" and "ethnicity".

Stigma and schizophrenia

Erving Goffman (1990) developed the concept of stigma as a form of "spoiled identity" within society. Stigma thus refers to the way in which designations and attributions that are assigned to a person serve as a means of discrediting them within society. Ben-Zeev et al. (2010) have discussed three elements within stigma as it applies to people diagnosed with a mental illness. First, there is the notion of "public stigma" where large groups in society endorse and uphold discrediting attributions about minority groups, and may even act out these attributions, thus discriminating against people with mental illness. Second, there are forms of "self-stigma" where individuals take on negative connotations of labels of mental illness that then affect their self-esteem and self-efficacy. Finally, there is "label avoidance" where people avoid help to avoid the negative connotations of labels of mental illness (Ben-Zeev et al., 2010; 319).

All three of these types of stigma apply in the case of schizophrenia. The term "schizophrenia" is poorly understood in the wider culture and often misused to refer to a type of "split personality", when its initial formulation by Eugen Bleuler was meant to connote a fragmentation of the mind, rather than a splitting into two personalities (Bleuler, 1950). There is a popular association of schizophrenia with violence that leads to stigmatising attitudes. The ISL found that 88 per cent of respondents to the inquiry felt that schizophrenia was associated with violence in the public mind. Furthermore, cross-global studies have consistently shown correlations between stigma and a diagnosis of schizophrenia. Thornicroft et al. (2009) found that following a diagnosis of schizophrenia service users faced problems in applying for jobs, discrimination from family members and problems in forming new relations (particularly sexual relationships). A damning finding from their study was that 72 per cent felt the need to hide their diagnosis from colleagues and friends (Thornicroft et al., 2009).

An interesting development in recent years has been the changing of the schizophrenia label across a number of countries in East Asia (Sato, 2006; Sartorius et al., 2014). Japan changed the schizophrenia name in 2002 due to the particularly stigmatising connotations of the notion of "split mind" within Japanese culture (Sato, 2006). They developed a new term of "integration" disorder which also involved a re-conceptualisation of problems of schizophrenia and a move towards frameworks that emphasised possibilities of recovery for those diagnosed and a lessening of an emphasis on a chronic disease process (Sartorius et al., 2014). Sartorius et al. (2014) report on a web-based survey of people who only know the new term for schizophrenia in Japan and find that they felt more likely to seek help, more positive about possible recovery outcomes and more able to disclose their diagnosis than those people who were labelled with the old diagnosis of schizophrenia. The label has also been changed in Korea to an "attunement disorder" and, in Hong Kong, a new name has been developed which roughly translates as "dysfunction of thought and perception" (Sartorius et al., 2014: 2). These changes indicate the specific cultural issues of a diagnosis of "schizophrenia" in East Asia and the possibilities of change through both a change of name and a re-conceptualisation of the mental health issues associated with schizophrenia away from chronicity towards recovery.

Exercise 8.2

- Do you think that changing the label of schizophrenia will change the stigma associated with the term?
- Will the stigma inevitably attach itself to new names? For example, there is an increasing tendency to refer to "psychosis" but this is also a stigmatised term, with associations to violence.

Schizophrenia is not a scientific diagnosis

Critics of the schizophrenia label do not target their critique only on the issues of stigma, but also focus on questions of the validity and usefulness of the schizophrenia label. In the absence of any identifiable organic cause of the purported disease, how can we claim that schizophrenia exists as a disease? There are various biological hypotheses for the causation of schizophrenia but these are all only hypotheses and are all subject to contestation. Differences in brain volume of those people diagnosed with schizophrenia have been found but recent studies have suggested that these differences may be due to prolonged use of anti-psychotic medication (Ho et al., 2011). There was a longstanding belief that over-activity of the dopamine system causes schizophrenia but this ignores the multiple and diverse experiential causes of excesses of dopamine in the system, and the effect of anti-psychotic medication (Moncrieff, 2009). Genetic studies have shown rates of diagnosed schizophrenia of 22.4 per cent for identical twins and 4.6 per cent for non-identical twins, which suggests some limited biological vulnerability that is complicated by psychological and environmental factors (Joseph, 2003). Therefore, at the very least, there is still debate about the possible biological causes of schizophrenia.

However, one problem is that many researchers have argued that schizophrenia names too many different processes to map it easily on to a single biological cause (Bullmore et al., 2009; Hyman, 2010). There is a growing consensus that the concept of schizophrenia is too broad and encompasses too many features to enable the accurate identification of a straightforward aetiology. Service user/survivor conceptualisations have focussed on specific experiential phenomena such as auditory/verbal hallucinations and paranoia, and their relationship to trauma and, particularly, child abuse (Read et al., 2014). Many of those who experience voices and visions do not see them as "hallucinations" or "delusions" but as experiences that are perhaps not in consensual or shared reality (see, for example, Shingler, 2008). Woods (2013) has argued that survivor narratives and conceptualisations of the experience of voice hearing have created a new identity of "voice hearer" that separates itself from notions of schizophrenia. The notion of the "voice hearer" became prominent through the work of Marius Romme and Sandra Escher in Holland (Romme and Escher, 2000). In 1987, Romme appeared on television with Patsy Hague, who was working with him around her voices and had persuaded Romme, as her psychiatrist, to accept that her voices were real and had meaning for her (Woods, 2013). Romme and Hague asked people to phone in if they, too, heard voices and had not had contact with the psychiatric system. They were surprised at the volume of responses they received and, particularly, with the numbers of people who had "made sense" of their voices and integrated them with their life (Romme and Escher, 1993). This led to an understanding of how the experience of being a "voice hearer" was not intrinsically a disease process; neither was it without meaning. In fact, it was only through making sense of the voices that people were able to integrate their experience and remain healthy (Romme and Escher, 2000).

This work was ground-breaking in empowering survivors of the psychiatric system to assert the meaning of their mental distress and led to the setting up of Hearing Voices groups and networks, where service users were able to share their experiences and the methods of coping and working with voices without being subject to disease interpretations (Romme et al., 2009). The focus on particular experiences, rather than a global concept such as schizophrenia, is now becoming increasingly central not only in practice and research led by survivors of mental health services, but also in clinical research efforts which are moving away from focussing on concepts such as schizophrenia and towards a focus on hearing voices or experiences of paranoia (Badcock and Hugdahl, 2014).

Richard Bentall has famously argued that we should replace diagnosis based on grand concepts such as schizophrenia with an approach that he terms "complaint-oriented" (Bentall, 2006). We should work with the issues that people present with and understand those issues, rather than trying to frame them in terms of an overarching diagnosis. Therefore, if a person presents with issues and distressing experiences from hearing voices, then we discuss the meaning that they ascribe to those voices, and help them to cope and structure the voices in a way that is manageable, rather than simply diagnosing and prescribing medication.

Schizophrenia, culture and racism

A central controversy about the diagnosis of schizophrenia has been the way in which judgements about race and ethnicity coalesce to produce a particular constellation of concerns around the label schizophrenia. The ISL has published initial findings which demonstrated that 60 per cent of respondents to the inquiry felt that issues of race and ethnicity affected the diagnosis of schizophrenia in multiple ways. A central controversy has been around the consistent finding in epidemiological studies that, amongst certain minority ethnic populations, there is a markedly raised incidence of diagnosis of schizophrenia (Van Os et al., 2010). In the UK, there has been particular concern around the raised incidence of a diagnosis of schizophrenia in the African-Caribbean population, and a number of studies have shown rates of schizophrenia in this population ranging from twice to eighteen times greater than other groups in the population (Morgan et al., 2006). There are three core theories that attempt to explain this epidemiological finding, all of which demonstrate the impact of social factors and value judgements on diagnosis.

First, there has been a range of work carried out which has argued that cultural bias and ascriptions by psychiatrists have entered into the way that a diagnosis of schizophrenia takes place in an encounter between a minority ethnic group and institutional power (Littlewood and Lipsedge, 1997; Ingleby, 2008; Fernando, 2010). Particular cultural experiences and religious experiences that are not easily understood from a Western perspective become labelled and re-described as experiences of mental illness, and this can particularly be the case when spiritual and religious experiences are re-described in terms of psychosis. Kleinman (1977) has argued that the use of diagnostic categories developed within Western systems and then applied as though cultural differences are irrelevant is a "category mistake". This mistake is compounded when discriminatory judgements around risk and violence enter the picture when diagnosing schizophrenia. A number of reports and documents have considered the issues of how labels of "risk" and "dangerousness" are applied to young Black men and lead to the overuse of coercive measures and restraint in in-patient and community settings (Bhui, 2003; NIMHE, 2003). The independent inquiry into the death of David "Rocky" Bennett while in an in-patient facility catalogued numerous issues of stereotyping, and failures in engaging with the person, their family and carers, that contributed to a diagnosis of schizophrenia, compulsory admissions and the eventual restraint and death of the person (Norfolk, Suffolk and Cambridgeshire Strategic Health Authority, 2003).

The second area of concern has focussed on the issue of migration itself and the impact of migration on a person's mental health. Cantor-Graee and Selten (2005) conducted a synthesis of findings from a range of studies to demonstrate that the experience of migration was a risk-factor for a diagnosis of schizophrenia. Selten and Cantor-Graee (2007) postulate a range of reasons for these risk factors increasing for first- and second-generation migrants, including racial discrimination, poor social position within society, and increased vulnerability and feelings of threat. In a study of narratives of recovery and resilience by African, African-Caribbean and South Asian women, Kalathil et al. (2011) writes of the importance of minority communities joining together to develop a communal cultural identity in defiance of experiences of discrimination and social injustice. This points to the importance of a notion of communal recovery, rather than simply thinking of recovery in individualised terms (Kalathil et al., 2011).

The third area of concern around the high incidence of diagnosed schizophrenia amongst Black and minority ethnic populations relates to this issue of community solidarity versus isolation. In recent years, a number of research efforts have shown a correlation between raised rates of diagnoses of schizophrenia and the "ethnic density" of the area in which a person is living; this has been termed the "ethnic density hypothesis" (Van Os et al., 2010). The hypothesis is that people from minority ethnic groups are more vulnerable to developing experiences of "paranoia" if they are living in areas with fewer people from the same background as themselves, as they are more liable to threat, attack, and being hypervigilant and aware of threats (Shaw et al., 2012). In a review of studies, Shaw et al. (2012) did find that there was a greater risk of developing psychosis for certain minority ethnic groups if people lived in communities where they were more isolated, and where there were fewer people living of the same ethnic origin. This goes some way to explaining the finding that there is a raised incidence of a diagnosis of schizophrenia not only in first-generation migrants, but also in their sons and daughters, and in the third-generation following. This suggests that it is not merely an experience of migration that makes people feel threatened and more vulnerable to developing experiences of mental distress, but more the threat and reality of racist attitudes, behaviours and attacks, particularly when people feel isolated and vulnerable.

The global mental health agenda

It is an irony that, at the point when psychiatric categories are subject to renewed debate and contestation within Western countries, there is, at the same time, an effort to "scale up" psychiatric treatments and interventions within low- and middle-income countries (Mills, 2014). The World Health Organization launched the Mental Health Gap Action Programme in 2008 (mhGAP) to address the lack of care and access to psychiatric interventions in low- and middle-income countries (WHO, 2010). The programme frames interventions for mental health issues in the same way as for physical health issues, and writers have made a moral argument for the need for parity of access to psychiatric treatments across the globe. Patel et al. (2006) argue that it is "unethical" to deny treatment that is evidence-based to people across the world in dire need of care. As Mills (2014) has pointed out, though, this global effort is far from unproblematic. There is little attention to the way that notions of a "burden of disease" and "debilitating illnesses" frame notions of mental illness as chronic and disabling, particularly in a context where recovery approaches are challenging such paradigms in Western countries. Watters (2010) has written of how this movement for global mental health could ride roughshod over local and non-psychiatric ways of conceptualising and working with mental distress.

This is a particularly significant issue, as the World Health Organization itself had coordinated a research effort into recovery from mental illness globally that had shown better recovery rates in some low- and middle-income countries than in Western countries. This was particularly the case in rural areas where access to pharmacological treatment was lower (Hopper and Wanderling, 2000). The danger is that these cultural factors and the significance of alternative approaches may be ignored in the rush to what Mills (2014) has termed the "psychiatrization of the majority world".

The "Grand Challenges in Global Mental Health" (GCMH) programme supported by the National Institute of Mental Health (NIMH) was launched in an article in *Nature* in 2011

(Collins et al., 2011). A consortium of researchers, advocates and clinicians launched the initiative to reduce the so-called "burden" of untreated mental illness in low- and middle-income countries. This initiative is highly controversial. A group of concerned activists and practitioners (including Jayasree Kalathil, a co-author of this book) from a range of international organisations wrote a response to this initiative in the form of a letter to *Nature*, but the journal did not publish this response. It was later published in the *Indian Journal of Medical Ethics* (see Abhay et al., 2012). The authors of the letter listed six key critiques of the global mental health effort as currently constituted. They stated these as follows:

- The lack of active collaboration with local communities and those people in those communities with personal experience of mental health problems.
- The focus on biologically reductionist notions of "molecular and cellular" structures at the level of the brain, while ignoring the situations and context in which mental distress occurs.
- The imposition of a "global norm" of mental health, regardless of cultural differences.
- The concern over the involvement of pharmaceutical companies in the global mental health agenda.
- The notion that human rights violations of those with mental health problems are more prevalent in the non-Western world. A lack of acknowledgment that human rights violations and coercion exist internationally, in Western and non-Western countries. (See Abhay et al., 2012, see also Summerfield, 2012).

CONCLUSION

This chapter has introduced the reader to the critique of psychiatric diagnosis. By concentrating on the schizophrenia label, we have explored the value-laden nature of diagnosis, problems with stigma and problems with the scientific validity of diagnosis in psychiatry. The chapter has discussed issues of culture and racism in diagnosis, and in exporting Western psychiatry to the majority world.

In Chapter 9, we will explore in a more positive way how recognising the values in mental health assessment in an explicit fashion and working with them in a collaborative way can produce a new direction for working in mental health practice.

GLOSSARY OF KEY TERMS

DSM – refers to the *Diagnostic and Statistical Manual* of mental disorders that is the classification system for mental illnesses that is published by the American Psychiatric Association. The latest edition was published in May 2013 and is known as DSM-5.

Ethnic density hypothesis – the hypothesis that members of minority ethnic groups may have better mental health when they live in areas with higher proportions of people with the same ethnicity.

ICD – refers to the International Classification of Diseases, which contains a chapter on mental illnesses and is published by the World Health Organization. The current edition is being revised with a view to a new edition appearing in the next two years, which will be ICD-11.

Kraepelinian paradigm – refers to the structuring of mental illnesses into psychoses and neuroses, and the division of psychoses into schizophrenia and bi-polar disorder, based around the work of the psychiatrist Emil Kraepelin (1856-1926).

FURTHER READING

For an interesting report on the care of people with schizophrenia, see Schizophrenia Commission/Rethink (2012) "Schizophrenia – The Abandoned Illness". Available at: http://www.rethink.org/media/514093/TSC_main_report_14_nov.pdf

For the Inquiry into the Schizophrenia Label, see Inquiry into the Schizophrenia Label (2014) "Preliminary findings". Available at: http://www.schizophreniainquiry.org/news/isl-releases-preliminary-findings

For a debate on schizophrenia and diagnosis, see http://www.kcl.ac.uk/iop/news/debates/podcast-archive.aspx and look for debates 18 and 30.

For a discussion of the urgent need to develop co-productive approaches to understanding mental distress as the basis of more effective translation of research into practice, see Fulford et al. (2014). We give further reading on values in mental health assessment in Chapter 9.

REFERENCES

Abhay, S. et al. (2012) "Critical perspectives on the NIMH initiative 'grand challenges to global mental health'", *Indian Journal of Medical Ethics*, 4.

APA (American Psychiatric Association) (2013) *DSM-5 – Diagnostic and Statistical Manual of Mental Disorders* (5th edn). Washington, DC: American Psychiatric Association.

Badcock, J.C. and Hugdahl, K. (2014) "A synthesis of evidence on inhibitory control and auditory hallucinations based on the Research Domain Criteria (RDoC) framework", *Frontiers in Human Neuroscience*, 8(180). doi: 10.3389/fnhum.2014.00180

Bentall, R. (2004) *Madness Explained: Psychosis and Human Nature*. London: Penguin.

Bentall, R. (2006) "Madness explained: Why we must reject the Kraepelinian Paradigm and replace it with a 'complaint-orientated' approach to understanding mental illness", *Medical Hypotheses*, 66: 220–33.

Bentall, R.P. (2009) *Doctoring the Mind. Is Our Current Treatment of Mental Illness Really Any Good?* New York: New York University Press.

Ben-Zeev, D., Young, M. and Corrigan, P. (2010) "DSM-5 and the stigma of mental illness", *Journal of Mental Health*, 19(4): 318–27.

Bhui, K. (2003) "Cultural identity and mental health", *International Journal of Social Psychiatry*, 49(4): 243–6.

Bleuler, E. (1950) *Dementia Praecox or the Group of Schizophrenias*, translated by J. Zinkin. New York: International Universities Press.

Boyle, M. (2002) *Schizophrenia: A Scientific Delusion?* London and New York: Routledge.

Bullmore, E., Fletcher, P. and Jones, P. (2009) "Why psychiatry can't afford to be neurophobic?", *British Journal of Psychiatry*, 194: 293–5.

Callard, F. (2014) "Psychiatric diagnosis: The indispensability of ambivalence", *Journal of Medical Ethics*, 40(8): 526–30.

Cantor-Graee, E. and Selten, J. (2005) "Schizophrenia and migration: A meta-analysis and review", *American Journal of Psychiatry*, 162(1): 12–24.

Caplan, A.L., Engelhardt, H.T. and McCartney, J.J. (eds) (1981) *Concepts of Health and Disease*. Reading: Addison-Wesley.

Care Quality Commission (2014) "Monitoring the Mental Health Act in 2012/2013". Available at: http://www.cqc.org.uk/sites/default/files/media/documents/cqc_mentalhealth_2012_13_07_update.pdf (accessed 14 April 2014).

Collins, P.Y., Patel, V., Joestl, S.S., March, D., Insel, T.R., Daar, A.S. (2011) "Grand Challenges to Global Mental Health", *Nature*, 475: 27–30.

Davies, J. (2013) *Cracked. Why Psychiatry is doing More Harm than Good*. London: Icon Books.

Drew, N., Funk, M., Tang, S., Lamichane, J., Chavez, E., Katontoka, S., Pathare, S., Lewis, O., Gostin, L. and Saraceno, B. (2011) "Human rights violations of people with mental and psychosocial disabilities: An unresolved global crisis", *Lancet*, 378: 1664–75.

Fernando, S. (2010) *Mental Health, Race and Culture*. Basingstoke: Palgrave Macmillan.

Frances, A. (2013) *Saving Normal*. New York: William Morrow.

Fulford, K. W. M., Bortolotti, L. and Broome, M. (2014) "Taking the long view: An emerging framework for translational psychiatric science", Special Article for *World Psychiatry*, 13/2: 10817. Also available on the World Psychiatric Association website (www.wpanet.org) and on the Wiley Online Library(http://onlinelibrary.wiley.com/journal/10.1002/%28ISSN%292051-5545).

Fulford, K.W.M., Smirnov, A.Y.U. and Snow, E. (1993) "Concepts of disease and the abuse of psychiatry in the USSR", *British Journal of Psychiatry*, 162: 801–10.

Goffman, E. (1990) *Stigma: Notes on the Management of Spoiled Identity*. London: Penguin.

Greenberg, G. (2013) *The Book of Woe. The DSM and the Unmaking of Psychiatry*. London and Melbourne: Scribe Press.

Ho, B.-C., Andreasen, N., Ziebell, S., Pierson, R. and Magnotta, V. (2011) "Long-term antipsychotic treatment and brain volumes: A longitudinal study of first-episode schizophrenia", *Archives of General Psychiatry*, 68(2): 128–37.

Hopper, K. and Wanderling, J. (2000) "Revisiting the developed versus developing country distinction in course and outcome in schizophrenia: Results from ISoS, the WHO collaborative follow-up project", *Schizophrenia Bulletin*, 26(4): 835–46.

Hyman, S. (2010) "The diagnosis of mental disorders: the problem of reification", *Annual Review of Clinical Psychology*, 6: 155–79.

Ingleby, D. (2008) *New Perspectives on Migration, Ethnicity and Schizophrenia*. Malmo: Malmo University.

Inquiry into the Schizophrenia Label (2014) "Preliminary findings", International Universities Press. Available at: http://www.schizophreniainquiry.org/news/isl-releases-preliminary-findings (accessed 29 May 2015).

Insel, T.R. (2013) "Transforming Diagnosis". Available at: www.nimh.nih,gov (accessed 29 May 2015).

Jaspers, K. (1997) *General Psychopathology*, Volume 2, translated by J. Hoeing and M. Hamilton. Baltimore: Johns Hopkins University Press.

Joseph, J. (2003) *The Gene Illusion: Genetic Research in Psychiatry and Psychology under the Microscope*. Ross-on-Wye: PCCS Books.

Kalathil, J., Collier, B., Bhakta, R., Daniel, O., Joseph, D. and Trivedi, P. (2011) *Recovery and Resilience: African, African-Caribbean and South Asian Narratives of Recovering from Mental Distress*. London: Mental Health Foundation.

Kleinman, A. (1977) "Depression, somatization and the 'new cross-cultural psychiatry'", *Social Science and Medicine*, 11: 3–10.

Kupfer, D., First, M. and Regier, D. (eds) (2002) *A Research Agenda for DSM-V*. Washington, DC: American Psychiatric Association.

Kutchins, H. and Kirk, S. (1997) *Making Us Crazy: DSM: The Psychiatric Bible and the Creation of Mental Disorders.* New York: Free Press.

Littlewood, R. and Lipsedge, M. (1997) *Aliens and Alienists: Ethnic Minorities and Psychiatry.* London: Routledge.

Metzl, J. (2010) *The Protest Psychosis: How Schizophrenia became a Black Disease.* Boston: Beacon Press.

Mills, C. (2014) *Decolonising Global Mental Health: The Psychiatrisation of the Majority World.* London: Routledge.

Moncrieff, J. (2009) "A critique of the dopamine hypothesis of schizophrenia and psychosis", *Harvard Review of Psychiatry*, 17(3): 214–25.

Moncrieff, J. (2010) "Psychiatric diagnosis as a political device", *Social Theory and Health*, 8: 370–82.

Morgan, C., Dazzan, P., Morgan, K., Jones, P., Harrison, G., Leff, J., Murray, R. and Fearon, P. (2006) "First episode psychosis and ethnicity: Initial findings from the AESOP study", *World Psychiatry*, 5(1): 40–6.

NIMHE (2003) *Inside Outside. Improving Mental Health Services for Black and Minority Ethnic Communities in England.* Available at: http://webarchive.nationalarchives.gov.uk/20130107105354/http://www.dh.gov.uk/prod_consum_dh/groups/dh_digitalassets/@dh/@en/documents/digitalasset/dh_4019452.pdf (accessed 29 May 2015).

Norfolk, Suffolk and Cambridgeshire Strategic Health Authority (2003) "Independent Inquiry into the Death of David Bennett". Norfolk, Suffolk and Cambridgeshire Strategic Health Authority.

Patel, V., Boardman, J., Prince, M. and Bhugra, D. (2006) "Returning the debt: How rich countries can invest in mental health capacity in developing countries", *World Psychiatry*, 5(2): 67–70.

Pickersgill, M. (2014) "Debating DSM-5: Diagnosis and the sociology of critique", *Journal of Medical Ethics*, 40(8): 521–5.

Pierre, M.P. (2008) "Deconstructing schizophrenia for DSM-V: Challenges for clinical and research agendas", *Clinical Schizophrenia and Related Psychoses*, 2(2): 166–74.

Porter, R. (2002) *Madness: A Brief History.* Oxford: Oxford University Press.

Read, J., Dillon, J. and Lampshire, D. (2014) "How much evidence is required for a paradigm shift in mental health?", *Acta Psychiatrica Scandinavica*, 129: 477–81.

Romme, M. and Escher, S. (1993) *Accepting Voices.* London: MIND.

Romme, M. and Escher, S. (2000) *Making Sense of Voices.* London: MIND.

Romme, M., Escher, S., Dillon, J., Corstens, D. and Morris, M. (2009) *Living with Voices: 50 Stories of Recovery.* Ross-on-Wye: PCCS Books.

Sartorious, N., Chiu, H., Heok, K., Lee, M.-S., Ouyang, W.-C., Sato, M., Yang, Y. and Yu, X. (2014) "Name change for schizophrenia", *Schizophrenia Bulletin*, first published online January 2014.

Sato, M. (2006) "Renaming schizophrenia: A Japanese perspective", *World Psychiatry*, 5(1): 53–5.

Schizophrenia Commission/Rethink (2012) "Schizophrenia the abandoned illness", Available at: http://www.rethink.org/media/514093/TSC_main_report_14_nov.pdf (accessed 29 May 2015).

Seltan, J. and Cantor-Graee, E. (2007) "Hypothesis: Social defeat a risk factor for schizophrenia?", *British Journal of Psychiatry*, 191: s9–s12.

Shaw, R., Atkin, K., Becares, L., Albor, C., Stafford, M., Kiernan, K., Nazroo, J., Wilkinson, R. and Pickett, K. (2012) "Impact of ethnic density on adult mental disorders: Narrative review", *British Journal of Psychiatry*, 201: 11–19.

Shingler, A. (2008) *One in a Hundred.* Oregon: Thorntree Press.

Summerfield, D. (2012) "Afterword: Against 'global mental health'", *Transcultural Psychiatry*, 49 (3): 1–12.

Szmukler, G. (2014) "When psychiatric diagnosis becomes an overworked tool", *Journal of Medical Ethics*, 40(8): 517–20.

Thomas, P., Seebohm, P., Wallcraft, J., Kalathil, J. and Fernando, S. (2013) "Personal consequences of the diagnosis of schizophrenia: A preliminary report from the Inquiry into the 'schizophrenia' label", *Mental Health and Social Inclusion*, 17(3): 135–9.

Thornicroft, G., Brohan, E., Rose, D., Sartorius, N. and Leese, M. (2009) "Global pattern of experienced and anticipated discrimination against people with schizophrenia: A cross-sectional survey", *Lancet*, 373: 408–15.

Timimi, S. (2013) "No more psychiatric labels: Campaign to abolish psychiatric diagnostic systems such as ICD and DSM (CAPSID)", *Self and Society*, 40(4): 6–14.

Torrey, E. and Yolken, R. (2010) "Psychiatric genocide: Nazi attempts to eradicate schizophrenia", *Schizophrenia Bulletin*, January, 36(10): 26–32.

Van Os, J., Kenis, G. and Rutten, B. (2010) "The environment and schizophrenia", *Nature*, 468: 203–12.

Voren, R. van (2002) "Editorial: The WPA World Congress in Yokohama and the issue of political abuse of psychiatry in China", *Mental Health Reforms-1*, vol. 7.

Watters, E. (2010). *Crazy Like Us: The Globalization of the American Psyche*. New York: Free Press.

Woods, A. (2013) "The voice hearer", *Journal of Mental Health*, 22(3): 263–70.

WHO (World Health Organization) (2010) *mhGAP Intervention Guide for mental, neurological and substance use disorders in non-specialised health settings*. World Health Organization.

9 | Values-based assessment

Chapter Summary

This chapter will:

- Present the 3 Keys Programme: a shared approach to assessment in mental health.
- Discuss the 3 Keys and values-based practice.
- Present examples of the First Key: person-centred assessment.
- Present examples of the Second Key: multidisciplinary assessment.
- Present examples of the Third Key: strengths based assessment.
- Present an overview of the 3 Keys, co-production and recovery.

In this chapter, we look at the importance of values in mental health assessment and how working with them in a positive and collaborative way can play a key role in recovery practice. We have seen in Chapter 8 that the issue of diagnosis in psychiatry has always been controversial in raising a whole series of values issues, social, political and, indeed, personal. We have also seen how values cannot – and, indeed, should not – be excluded from assessment in mental health care. Yet, a values-excluding approach to diagnosis and assessment is the norm in much biomedicine. Biomedical ethics, too, has often been complicit in this values-excluding approach. It has tended to focus downstream, as it were, on how issues are managed, while neglecting the first and essential step of understanding how the issues in question are actually comprehended.

Values-based practice, by contrast, takes a strongly *values-including* approach to assessment. This is a cross-cutting approach. Assessment in mental health comes in a wide variety of forms. Medical diagnosis of specific disorders (as in the *DSM*) is just one of these; other examples include needs-based assessment and risk assessment. There are also important approaches to assessment that avoid the language of problems ("disorder", "needs", "risk", and so on). We will explore more recovery oriented approaches in further detail in Chapter 10. Values-based practice shows that values are important across the *full range* of assessments, including the most "high tech" forms of medical diagnosis. This is partly a matter of theory (see Further Reading). But it is also a matter of practice. Recall here (from Chapter 4) the importance in values-based practice of keeping a sharp eye on the values in play in *all* areas of health care decision making.

This chapter describes the 3 Keys Programme as an example of what keeping a sharp eye on the values in mental health assessment means in practice. We start with a brief overview of the Programme and how this reflects the elements of values-based practice described in Chapter 4. We then explore each of the 3 Keys individually as illustrated by examples of good practice identified by the Programme. A further episode from Sally Coombs' story (as told in Chapters 3 and 4) will indicate the significance of these examples of good practice for recovery.

Implementing the 3 Keys has proved, in some respects, challenging. But, as we indicate in our conclusion, there is much to learn from this. For the challenges faced by the 3 Keys are essentially the challenges faced by co-production in any area of recovery practice. It is with these challenges that the remaining three chapters of the book are concerned.

The 3 Keys Programme

The 3 Keys Programme has included a national consultation on good practice in mental health assessment and a pilot implementation project. The consultation was organised as part of a series of initiatives in values-based practice in the UK's Department of Health (National Institute for Mental Health in England (NIMHE) and the Care Services Improvement Partnership, 2008). It was co-produced by service users, carers and service providers, and took in a wide range of stakeholders, including service user/survivor and carer groups, nurses, social workers, psychologists, psychiatrists, occupational therapists and pharmacists. Voluntary as well as statutory sector organisations were included.

The "3 Keys" that emerged from the programme represent three aspects of assessment that all these different stakeholder groups agreed were important. The 3 Keys, in other words, are three shared values. Each group of stakeholders had its own assessment methods. But they all agreed that assessment, however it is carried out and wherever it occurs, should be *person-centred, multidisciplinary* and *strengths-based.*

Key 1: Person-centred assessment: There should be *active participation* of *the service user concerned* in an assessment process aimed at mutual understanding with his or her service providers and, where appropriate, with their carers. (In the original report this first key was actually *called* "active participation" to emphasise the importance of this in a person-centred approach to assessment. We have renamed it here to reflect the fact that the Programme as a whole was part of the Department of Health's personalisation agenda.

Key 2: Multidisciplinary assessment: Wherever possible, assessment should include input from different provider perspectives within a *multidisciplinary approach.*

Key 3: Strengths-based assessment: assessment should focus on the *strengths, aspirations and resiliencies* of the individual service user concerned as well as identifying his or her needs and challenges.

A further more general point of agreement was about how assessment should be understood. Assessment is widely thought of as a one-off event. But it should be thought of, rather, as a holistic and ongoing process through which mutual understanding develops. We will see later that an ongoing process of assessment was important in Sally Coombs' story.

More difficult than it looks

The 3 Keys may seem obvious enough. Who could disagree with the importance of active participation and multi-disciplinary team work in a strengths-based approach to person-centred assessment? As aspects of assessment, these are all directly relevant to promoting recovery and development of self-management skills

What the consultation showed, however, was that (as is so often the case with "obvious" values) there was wide variation in the extent to which the 3 Keys were actually being carried out in everyday practice. Everyone *said* this was how assessment should be done. But much of the time this was not how assessment was actually *being done*. Carers described being inappropriately excluded. Service users recounted endless processes of assessment ("assessed to death!") that seemed often pointless ("So what!") and incomprehensible ("all Greek to me!"). Within teams, similarly, instead of multidisciplinary assessment, the norm was for one or other (usually a medical) perspective to have the dominant voice.

It was clear, therefore, that there was a good deal of work to do if we are to translate 3 Keys "talk" into 3 Keys "walk". In support of this, the 3 Keys report included a series of examples of good practice. We return to these examples later in the chapter. As we will see, they illustrate some of the many innovative ways individuals and groups have found for implementing the 3 Keys in often challenging circumstances. The urgent need, though, was to find ways of spreading good practice more widely and it is with this that the current pilot project is concerned.

The pilot implementation project

Where the original consultation was carried out nationally, the pilot implementation project has deliberately been focussed locally. Various small-scale pilots have been attempted. In the latest and most extensive, a small group of service users/survivors, carers, service providers and academics, with the support of the Avon and Wiltshire Mental Health Partnership NHS

Trust, has been exploring ways of implementing the 3 Keys with local teams (Fulford et al., forthcoming, 2015; Hicks et al., forthcoming, 2015).

The approach from the start, as with the original consultation, has been based on co-production. The "Bristol Group", as it has come to be called, is representative of the range of stakeholders concerned in assessment (we list the members of the Group in full in the Acknowledgements). But the methodology, too, has been based on co-production. Thus, a key stage in implementation locally has been for local stakeholders (service providers, as well as service users/survivors and carers) to agree their own outputs – what they would like to improve in their assessment processes and how this might be done. Thus far, as we will indicate further, this has proved challenging. But an important outcome from the process to date has been the experience of Group members from very different backgrounds in coming together in an increasingly effective way. We return to the importance of this for co-production later in the chapter.

The 3 Keys and values-based practice

We have described the 3 Keys here as being a values-based approach to assessment. But "values", you will recall from Chapter 3, means many different things. Before we come to the details of the 3 Keys, therefore, it will be worth pausing for a moment to reflect on exactly how and in what ways the 3 Keys really are values-based.

Exercise 9.1

The 3 Keys and values–based practice

For this exercise, you may find it helpful to go back to the table of values-based practice we built up as we worked through Chapter 4. Look through the table again and, from what you have read thus far about the 3 Keys, see how many of the elements of values-based practice you can spot.

We give our own summary of this in Table 9.1 but, as with all our other exercises, you will derive a great deal more from this chapter if you spend a few minutes trying this for yourself before reading on.

Mutual respect

Taking Table 9.1 from the top, we can see that, without the starting point of values-based practice in mutual respect, the Programme could not have got off the ground at all. Had one or other constituent group claimed "the right", there could have been no possibility of a shared approach. Mutual respect, moreover, has characterised the way the Programme itself has been carried out. The consultation was marked by sharing, rather than shouting. And the success of the pilot implementation project in creating an effective co-production group directly reflects the mutual respect of group members for each others' knowledge, experience and skills.

The skills for values-based practice

The four areas of clinical skills important for values-based practice are clearly important for implementation of the 3 Keys: a participatory person-centred approach (Key 1) and multi-disciplinary team work (Key 2) both depend (in the ways described in Chapter 4) on the full

Elements of values-based practice	The 3 Keys
Premise of mutual respect	The foundation for both the method adopted (co-production) and the output of the programme (a shared approach); also underpins co-production of implementation projects.
Skills areas	
1. Awareness	Important in the genesis of the programme; also to implementing all three keys.
2. Reasoning	Important to implementing all three keys.
3. Knowledge	Important to implementing all three keys.
4. Communication	Important to implementing all three keys.
Professional relationships	
5. Person-values-centred care	Directly reflected in Key 1 (person-centred assessment) and supported by Key 3 (strengths-based assessment).
6. Extended MDT	Directly reflected in Key 2 (multidisciplinary assessment) and vital to Key 1 (understood as person-*values*-centred assessment).
Values and evidence	
7. Two feet principle	Underpins the rationale of looking carefully at values in assessment.
8. Squeaky wheel principle	Emphasises that it is no less important to look equally carefully at the evidence.
9. Science-driven principle	Shows that values (meanings). as well as evidence. will remain important whatever future advances are made in "high tech" assessment methods such as brain imaging.
Partnership	
10. Dissensus within frameworks of shared values	3 Keys are a framework of shared values.
Balanced decisions in individual situations	

Table 9.1 The 3 Keys and values-based practice

range of these skills; and we return later in the chapter to their particular significance for strengths-based assessment as the basis of recovery.

These skills, though, have been important, too, in the way the Programme itself has been developed. Raised awareness of values, in particular, as elsewhere in values-based practice, has been foundational. Looking back on the consultation, the 3 Keys may seem, as we said earlier, obvious. But they were certainly not obvious from the start. This was why the Programme was launched in the first place. The focus of policy at the time had been directly on values-based approaches to person-centred care: as we described in Chapter 3, a values-based national framework of values had been produced that became the basis of a series of policies and service development initiatives, such as *The 10 Essential Shared Capabilities* (Department of Health, 2004), combining the twin resources of values-based and evidence-based practice. But the importance of assessment, let alone of the values guiding assessment, had been over-looked. This was spelled out by Ivan Lewis, the Minister with responsibility for mental health at the time, in his introduction to the report (Department of Health, 2004: 2). Assessment, he indicated, although the crucial first stage in person-centred care, had up to that point somehow been left off the personalisation agenda.

Professional relationships and values-based practice

It was raised awareness of values, then, that got the initial consultation going. Raised aware-ness, too, was directly connected with the first of the two aspects of professional relation-ships important in values-based practice, person-centred care: Ivan Lewis (Department of Health, 2004: 2) noted the importance of bringing the "needs and wishes" of the individual concerned fully into assessment. The second aspect, multidisciplinary assessment, emerged readily from the consultation itself. More surprisingly, perhaps, the third key – strengths-based assessment – almost failed to make it into the report. We come to the reasons for this later. But it was surprising, because understanding a person's strengths as well their needs and difficulties is vital to recovery. This is why strengths-based assessment is crucial to the person-*values*-centred assessment of values-based practice, to which, as we saw in Chapter 4, the *extended* multidisciplinary team is, in turn, crucial.

Values and evidence in values-based practice

The next group of elements of values-based practice are its three principles linking values with evidence. The first of these, the "two feet" principle, goes straight to the heart of values-based assessment. Assessments of all kinds are dependent on careful observations backed up by tests of one sort or another including, in some cases, laboratory tests. Assessment is, in this sense, strongly evidence-based (evidence, as we emphasised in Chapter 4, includes knowledge derived from experience). But it is precisely where decisions are strongly evidence-based that, the "two feet" principle reminds us, we must be careful not to lose sight of the values in play.

Equally important in assessment, though, is the second of the three principles: the "squeaky wheel" principle. This principle, you will recall, reminds us that just as we should not lose sight of the values in mental health assessment, so we should not go the other way and lose sight of the evidence.

> **Reflection point:** *What was the danger of losing sight of the evidence in Sally Coombs' story, as described in Chapter 4? Think back to Sally Coombs' story for a moment before reading on.*

The danger was that Sally Coombs might have been suffering from some undiagnosed medical condition such as diabetes. This was Dr Brown's concern, you will recall, in her disagreement with Nurse Matthews about what to do next. Nurse Matthews wanted Sally to be allowed to settle in with the least disturbance as a step towards establishing a trusting therapeutic relationship with the team. Dr Brown, on the other hand, was concerned that Sally might have some undiagnosed medical condition such as diabetes. This was unlikely but potentially dangerous, if missed; and there were signs (such as her apparent disorientation when she was first found by the police constables) that should not be ignored. The only way to exclude such a possibility, Dr Brown believed, was by doing an immediate "physical" and blood tests.

If the first and second principles are important, the third principle, the "science-driven" principle, is decisive. Some believe that, as we get ever more powerful brain imaging and other "high tech" methods of assessment, the need for understanding and empathic engagement will diminish. The "science-driven" principle denies this. It shows (as we described in Chapter 4) that progress in science and technology will actually increase, rather than diminish, the importance of values in health care. In assessment, this means that, whatever knowledge we may have in the future about underlying brain mechanisms, it will always remain important to understand the meaning of a mental health episode for the person concerned. We explored the importance of this in earlier chapters: through the limitations of overly narrow diagnostic concepts in Chapter 8; and through the importance of personal narratives in Chapter 6. The "science-driven" principle drives home the point once again from the perspective of values-based practice.

Partnership, dissensus and balanced decision making within shared framework values

We return later in the chapter to Sally's story and how things worked out in the event. As we will see, the outcome depended on partnership based on dissensus (Element 10 in the table of values-based practice). It was this that finally allowed Sally's own values to come fully into the frame. But partnership of this kind depends on what we called, in Chapter 4, "shared frameworks of values". And this is exactly what the 3 Keys provide. As three shared values guiding assessment in mental health, the 3 Keys provide a framework of shared values within which balanced decisions can be made according to the particular circumstances presented by an individual situation.

When we come back to Sally Coombs' story, we will revisit our table of the 3 Keys and values-based practice with some significant additions to make. First, though, we need to look at what the 3 Keys mean in practice.

Examples of the 3 Keys in practice

In the next three sections, we give examples of some of the innovative ways that different groups and individuals have found for implementing the 3 Keys. These examples are lightly edited but, otherwise, as they appeared in the original report. The examples are all based on real people's stories but with biographical and other details changed to ensure confidentiality. Taken together, therefore, they show just how practical the 3 Keys can be, as well as indicating some of the challenges that they present and how they can be overcome. The full 3 Keys report gives many further examples. If you want at look at these, there is a downloadable copy of the report on the VBP website – it makes a good read! (See Further Reading.)

As we look at each Key, we will be asking you to try thinking about how you would implement it in your own practice before reading about what others have done. This way you will be building up your own skills for values-based assessment. As with other areas of values-based practice, the 3 Keys are most effective if used together in a well-connected way (see Chapter 4).

Examples of Key 1: Person-centred assessment

> *Key 1: Person-centred assessment*: There should be active participation of the service user concerned in an assessment process aimed at mutual understanding with his or her service providers and where appropriate with their carers

The first Key came with an important caveat in the report: that "active participation" is not always what the person concerned wants. This may be so, for example, where they are in a crisis situation, or otherwise distressed. Person-centred assessment thus means being sensitive to and working with the individual's needs and wishes at the time. A person who, at one stage, is too distressed to participate could nonetheless very much wish to be actively involved later on when things have settled down.

With that caveat, we are now ready to look at how "active participation of the service user concerned" can be achieved in practice. This may seem straight forward enough with someone such as Sally Coombs (once she had settled down). But there are many other situations in mental health where there are potential barriers to participation. You can probably come up with a number of relevant situations. But, in the next Reflection point, we would like you to think particularly about people with severe learning difficulties.

> **Reflection point:** *How would you support active participation in someone with severe learning difficulties? You may or may not have personal or professional experience on which to draw in thinking about this. Either way, write down one or two ideas of your own before reading on.*

Key 1 (person-centred assessment): Example 1 – Group support and participation for people with severe learning difficulties   The psychotherapy service for people with learning difficulties at Springfield Hospital in London developed a group approach to empowering people with learning difficulties to play a full role in how their problems are understood. Sheila Hollins, the psychiatrist who set up the Springfield service and Co-Chair of the 3 Keys Steering Group, describes an example.

> A letter arrived for "Peter" following an assessment of his future housing needs. The psychologist leading the group said "We have a letter this week for Peter" and, with Peter's agreement, this was read to the group as a whole. The group came to a shared understanding of the letter. They drafted a reply using accessible language. This was typed up and edited further by the group before it was sent off. The reply had Peter's name on it together with the names of the others in the group.
>
> Working in this way has meant that group members felt fully engaged and that their problems were understood in their own terms. Professionals, including those from outside the service, began to relate to group members as people with their own views and a positive contribution to make to how their problems were understood and managed, instead of seeing them as people "for whom things need to be done".

As with all our examples, this is just one way of supporting active participation that worked in this particular context. It worked particularly well in that, as Sheila Hollins describes, it produced positive changes in the attitudes of people outside the service, as well as supporting people such as Peter. But it was very much a local solution, nonetheless. As with any aspect of values-based practice, there are no "off the shelf" solutions. People's values are so individual and context dependent that what works in one situation nearly always has to be carefully adapted for use in other situations. The context-sensitive nature of values-based practice is one of its strengths. but it is also among the challenges for implementation.

Key 1 (person-centred assessment): Example 2 – Involving carers   A particularly important group whose values are often excluded are carers. As one carer put it in the consultation (p. 7):

> "Things often go wrong right from the start because carers and families really
> can't understand how the person concerned thinks and behaves as they do.
> Having someone to help them understand at this early stage, even if they don't
> agree with it, gives a very different basis for subsequent engagement."

The other side to the engagement of carers is, of course, confidentiality. This is why the *balanced* approach of values-based practice is needed. We noted the conflict between carer engagement and confidentiality in Sally Coombs' story. If the service user (as an adult with capacity) refuses permission for their carers to be involved in the assessment process, this has to be respected. One way to respond to this is to arrange a carer's assessment separately with someone who is not directly involved with the service user concerned. An example of how this can work was given in the 3 Keys by Nathan Gregory and Gabby Mabbott from an early intervention team working in Gloucestershire.

> "It's a problem when the carer requires a carer's assessment but the service user
> refuses permission because they are worried we might say something they don't
> want us to. As service providers we are here primarily to work for the service user
> and have to be careful to avoid damaging a trust that we have worked hard to
> develop. But at the same time carers need our support and are often the ones that
> enable service users to live in the community.
>
> One member of our team was faced with this problem and so a different
> member of the team, Gabby, carried out the carer's assessment. The service user
> was happy Gabby was not going to disclose any information about them. The
> carer provided a great deal of support and was worried. Gabby gave her infor-
> mation about looking after her own mental health, made sure she knew who to
> contact if worried and put her in contact with a support organisation for carers.
> Gabby also arranged for her to spend a weekend at a locally organised carers'
> retreat."

This example, although about person-centred care (Key 1), also illustrates the importance of multidisciplinary working (Key 2) in values-based assessment. We noted earlier that the 3 Keys work best when used in a well-connected way.

Examples of Key 2: Multidisciplinary assessment

> *Key 2: Multidisciplinary assessment*: Wherever possible assessment should include
> input from different provider perspectives within a multidisciplinary approach.

In the above example, multidisciplinary practice involved a team who had been together for some time and who came from similar backgrounds in health care. But there are also roles for multidisciplinary team work understood more widely. The next example is of people from very *different* backgrounds coming together in cross-cultural care.

> **Reflection point:** *Where might you look for help in understanding the perspective of someone whose cultural background is very different from your own? Think about this in terms of the "extended" multidisciplinary team of values-based practice.*

Key 1 (multidisciplinary assessment): Example 1 – The "Listening Imam" The Listening Imam Project was set up by Sharing Voices, a voluntary sector mental health organisation in Bradford, a city in the North of England, in partnership with Imams from local mosques. They worked together, and with local statutory providers, on a wide range of issues. In the example that follows, an Imam had been asked for help by a psychiatrist from the local children's services.

> "A mother and father of Pakistani origin were concerned about their two and a half year old son who they believed had a number of behavioural problems. Physically the child seemed to be in perfect health and mentally he appeared to be acting his age.
>
> A *hakima*, a woman regarded by many within their culture as having religious knowledge of such things as *jinn* (evil spirits), had told them they had given their child the wrong name and should change it. The *hakima* said their son was abnormal because he had been affected by a spell possessed by a demon. The *hakima* came to this conclusion using "verse calculation" where the age, day and month of birth of the child is taken and then a search is done in the Holy Quran using the numbers only.
>
> The Imam explained that verse calculation is prohibited in Islam. He told them that their child was a normal two year old and acting his age. As a religious leader, he showed them how the Quran instead of causing distress was a source of strength, power and ability to heal. As a respected religious leader with authority, the Imam's reassurances were effective in helping this family where those of the child psychiatrist and other team members had failed."

This story illustrates many important points about values-based assessment. One general point it makes is that the mutual respect underpinning values-based practice is fully compatible with having deeply held personal beliefs, religious or otherwise. Mutual respect is not open-ended – it precludes the bigot, for instance (as we saw in Chapter 4). But all the major religions have included people and groups who have shown that, at least within the context of healing, it is entirely possible to combine deep personal convictions with complete openness to the beliefs of others (Atwell and Fulford, 2006).

In this instance, the role of the Imam as a religious leader within his community was the key to converting a problem (the misuse of the Holy Quran for "verse calculation") into a strength (the proper use of the Quran as a healing resource). In the terms of values-based practice, then, this was the *extended* multidisciplinary team at work. Values-based practice, you will recall from Chapter 4, extends the importance of multidisciplinary team work from providing a range of knowledge and skills to include also a range of values. It was values (as well as knowledge and skills) that the Imam brought to this story. The child psychiatrist involved and other team members may or may not have known about verse calculation and the Quran. But it was the authority of the Imam *as* an Imam, and all the values this carries with it within the culture of the family concerned, that was decisive.

Clearly, no team can include each and every cultural perspective. Neither will there be a Listening Imam project available everywhere. The point is, rather, that there are often resources and support available in the community beyond those of the team narrowly defined and it is important to be ready to draw on these as required. The 3 Keys gives other examples of wider team working in this way – for example, with services such as housing.

Examples of Key 3: Strengths-based assessment

> *Key 3: Strengths-based assessment*: Assessment should focus on the strengths, aspirations and resiliencies of the individual service user concerned as well as identifying his or her needs and challenges.

The third Key ties in explicitly with the emphasis on positives as well as negatives in values-based practice, specifically the StAR values of values-based communication skills. StAR values, as we saw in Chapter 4, add to the traditional ICE of communication skills training (focussing on Ideas, Concerns and Expectations) the positive values of Strengths, Aspirations and Resources. The "resiliencies" of the original 3 Keys, by the way, became converted into the "resources" of StAR values because the word "resilience" turned out to be prone to being misread as restricted to internal resources (such as "will power"), whereas many of our strengths are derived from external resources (including friends and family). The examples above of Keys 1 and 2 illustrate the role of three such external resources: respectively, peers, carers and religious leaders.

But what about the A in StAR values: "aspirations"? This may seem a less familiar strength. As we indicated earlier, it was the one area of the 3 Keys consultation that generated significant disagreement. This was essentially because some service providers were concerned that including personal aspirations would raise expectations that could not be met by health and social care services. On the other hand, though, it was recognised that personal aspirations may be the key of keys when it comes to recovery. So, aspirations, on balance, stayed in. But aspirations can only come into play in a given instance if someone takes the trouble to find out what they are. In the example that follows, "finding out" added yet another dimension to the importance of team work in values-based practice.

> **Reflection point:** *Which member of a multidisciplinary team do you think might be best placed to understand the personal aspirations of any particular service users?*

Key 3 (strengths-based assessment): Example 1 – Aspirations and non-professionally aligned workers

> "Jenny Correia, an STR worker (Support Time and Recovery worker) with the crisis intervention and home treatment team at Chase Farm Hospital, described how there is no obvious place on their CPA (Care Programme Approach) form to include the aspirations. Yet these are often low key and practical: '...just to go for

a walk in the park". The result was that many things that really mattered to her clients, and that she could help them with, often got overlooked by the team as a whole in the assessment process."

This example highlights the extent to which our identities as professionals may get in the way of understanding what matters to a given service user. This is unavoidable. It is our very knowledge and skills as professionals that give us a particular perspective on what is important and, hence, guide what we tend to focus on in assessment. Consider how Dr Brown and Nurse Matthews focussed on different aspects of Sally Coombs' presentation, reflecting their respective medical and nursing perspectives; and Colombo's work on models (Chapter 4) showing that, whatever our explicit commitment to a shared bio-psychosocial approach, when it comes to decision making for real we retain distinct professional perspectives.

This is why, in the consultation, we found that it was often the team member with the *least* specialist training, such as the STR worker in this example, who contributed most decisively to understanding people's aspirations. STR workers, as we described in Chapter 4, are people with minimal specialist training who were brought into multidisciplinary teams originally to free up time for trained professional team members to work in a more effective recovery-oriented way. This example, however, and others from the consultation, showed that, in focussing on aspirations, STR workers could make a crucial contribution to recovery in their own right. A similar role may now also be played by the growing number of peer support workers. "Non-professionals" such as these are sometimes viewed with suspicion by "professionals". Within a values-based model, however, they play a vital role in coming to a balanced person-*values*-centred assessment as the basis of effective recovery practice. This, as we will now see, was very much the case in Sally Coombs' story.

The 3 Keys, co-production and recovery

We have remarked at several points in this chapter on the importance of both co-production and recovery in the 3 Keys. In this section, we will bring these points together by returning for a final time to Sally Coombs' story.

We left Sally at the end of Chapter 4 in a "wait and watch" situation following her emergency admission under Section 136 to the Acute Care Ward of her local mental health hospital. This reflected Nurse Matthews' concerns that Sally should be allowed to settle in with a minimum of interference, thus allowing her to gain confidence in the team as the basis of an ongoing therapeutic relationship. But "wait *and watch*" was a balanced decision, in that it also reflected Dr Brown's concern about missing a possible underlying medical problem (such as a developing diabetic crisis). It was Jenny Khan, you will recall, the STR worker on the team, who offered to sit with Sally so that they could step in immediately if her mental state showed signs of deteriorating, or she developed new symptoms.

Exercise 9.2

The 3 Keys and Sally Coombs' story

From what you have read in this chapter, which of the 3 Keys might come decisively into play at this point in Sally's story? In thinking about this, go back to the end of Chapter 4 and remind yourself about what has been missing from Sally's story all along.

The missing link in Sally's story was Sally's values. We noted this initially in Chapter 3, when her story was first presented. The "case history" language used there positioned and framed Sally to the point that, reading the story as professionals, we were unlikely even to be aware that we had ended up with no idea what Sally's values really were. This remained true even by the end of Chapter 4, after we had been through all the elements of values-based practice, including the core concept of person-*values*-centred practice. We remained ignorant of just why Sally had "stormed out" of her art therapy group and why she had refused to go back. We might have made assumptions. As experienced professionals, we probably would have made assumptions. But, as we have seen, assumptions about other people's values are the last thing on which we should rely in values-based practice.

So, what happened in Sally's story? She continued to settle down and, with her agreement, the team talked with a range of people who had been involved previously in her care. A particular strength to which everyone who knew her kept returning was her skills as an artist. On the basis of this, the team (who were strongly recovery-oriented) started to formulate a care plan with returning to art college as a key longer-term objective.

But, when they came to discussing this in a team meeting, Jenny Khan pulled everyone up sharp. She alone knew that far from being a strength Sally's artistic skills were the *mainspring of her difficulties*. Sally was, indeed, a talented artist and for this reason had found herself after school at a top art college. And she enjoyed painting. But she absolutely did not want to make it her life's work. The heart of the problem, though, was that she had never felt able to admit this to anyone because her parents (of whom she was very fond) had given up many of their own ambitions in order to support her. She found herself unable to face going back to art college but unable, equally, to face letting her parents down. And the situation had been progressively worsened by a series of professionals assuming that she "wanted to do art" and "helping her" to get back to art college.

None of this came out initially, of course, when Jenny was sitting with Sally soon after her admission. But Jenny's calm and listening approach had struck a chord in Sally who felt that here at last was someone in whom she could safely confide. This she subsequently did on one of the walks that she and Jenny started to take together once things had settled down. At first Sally asked Jenny not to tell anyone else. But, as she gained confidence in the wider team, she agreed to this and, hence, Jenny was able to bring Sally's crucial aspirations (not to become an artist) into the care planning process. There was still a long road ahead, of course, and the care plan as a whole drew on the knowledge and skills of several other members of the team (all described more fully in the original; see Further Reading). But Sally's turning point towards recovery was when she shared with Jenny Khan her aspiration not to become an artist.

... And co-production?

Important as aspirations are for recovery, they would not have been included in the 3 Keys but for co-production. We have already noted this but it is a point worth emphasising. The concern, you will recall, from a number of workers was that including personal aspiration would raise expectations they could not meet. This was understandable at the time. But so too, was the importance of aspirations for recovery. Yet, it took the insistence of the service user and carer leads in the 3 Keys Project Group – respectively, Laurie Bryant and Lu Duhig – to ensure that aspirations were included in the final report. This was co-production in action then, at a pivotal point in the 3 Keys Programme. Had there not been an equality of voice in the Programme, aspirations, notwithstanding the availability of relevant evidence, would have been excluded.

We will come back to recovery in Chapter 10. As we will see, co-production remains a vital part of recovery practice. Co-production is a natural ally of values-based practice: the equality of voices of co-production equates closely both with the starting point of values-based practice in mutual respect and with its outputs based on partnership in decision making. Co-production is supported, too, in contemporary practice, by resources that were not available at the time of the 3 Keys consultation. Personal budgets, for one; and there are also new training resources. The National Occupational Standards for Mental Health have recently been revised to put co-production and values-based practice at the heart of recovery practice (Skills for Health, 2013). The Carer's Trust, too, has also recently published values-based work in *The Triangle of Care* (Worthington and Hannan, 2013).

Exercise 9.3

The 3 Keys, values-based practice and Sally Coombs' story

As a way of bringing together your ideas about values-based practice, please go back to Table 9.1 and try adding any points that were relevant to how Sally Coombs' story came out.

We have given our own additions in Table 9.2 in italics. You may have similar or different ideas. But we hope you included the central significance of (finally) finding out what Sally's values really were.

Elements of values-based practice	The 3 Keys and Sally Coombs
Premise of mutual respect	The foundation for both the method adopted (co-production) and the output of the programme (a shared approach); also underpins co-production of implementation projects.
Skills areas	
1. Awareness	Important in getting the programme off the ground in the first place; also to implementing all three keys. *Awareness of Sally's actual (not assumed) values (**Key 1**, person-centred assessment)*
2. Reasoning	Important to implementing all three keys.
3. Knowledge	Important to implementing all three keys.
4. Communication	Important to implementing all three keys. *StAR Values; in particular Sally's actual (not assumed) aspirations (not to become an artist) (**Key 3**, strengths)*
Professional relationships	
5. Person-values-centred care	Directly reflected in Key1 (person-centred assessment) and supported by Key 3 (strengths-based assessment). *(**Keys 1**, person-centred assessment and **Key 3**, strengths)*

Table 9.2 The 3 Keys, values-based practice and Sally Coombs' story

Elements of values–based practice	The 3 Keys and Sally Coombs
6. Extended MDT	Directly reflected in Key 2 (multidisciplinary assessment) and vital to Key 1 (understood as person-*values*-centred assessment). *Important balance between perspectives of Nurse Matthews and Dr Brown PLUS decisive insight from STR worker, Jenny Khan (all **Key 2**, multidisciplinary assessment)*
Values and evidence	
7. Two feet principle	Underpins the rationale of looking carefully at values in assessment. *Important to be sensitive to Sally's immediate needs for reassurance and support as basis for building therapeutic relationship (Nurse Matthews – **Key 2**, multidisciplinary assessment)*
8. Squeaky wheel principle	Emphasises that it is no less important to look equally carefully at the evidence. *Important not to lose sight of the evidence of possible undiagnosed medical problems (Dr Brown – **Key 2**, multidisciplinary assessment)*
9. Science-driven principle	Shows that values (meanings), as well as evidence, will remain important whatever future advances are made in "high tech" assessment methods such as brain imaging,
Partnership	
10. Dissensus within frameworks of shared values	3 Keys are a framework of shared values,
Balanced decisions in individual situations	*The dissensual "wait and watch" decision balanced the perspectives of Nurse Matthews and Dr Brown in the particular circumstances presented by Sally Combs at that time; it also provided space for Jenny Khan's decisive insight into Sally Coombs' real values (brings **all three Keys** together)*

Table 9.2 (Continued)

CONCLUSION

This chapter has described and illustrated a values-based approach to assessment in mental health called the 3 Keys. Derived as the 3 Keys were from an extensive consultation among stakeholders, they represent three shared values. Assessment, the 3 Keys says, should be:

- Person-centred in involving active participation of the person concerned,
- Multidisciplinary in reflecting a range of provider inputs, and

- Strengths-based in including as well as any needs and difficulties, the person's individual strengths, aspirations and resources.

These three shared values apply across the board to any mental health assessment including the most "high tech" of medical diagnoses.

We hope you will be able to find ways of using the 3 Keys in your own practice. This is not always easy. The Bristol 3 Keys Group (p. 135) has established a strong ethos of co-production which has produced some excellent initiatives (which can be viewed at the website listed in the additional resources for this chapter). But engaging more widely has proved challenging. Just why this should be so is currently being evaluated by the Group. But one clear reason is the challenge of co-production itself. The experience of local teams is of a barrage of new initiatives with the "equality of voices" demanded by co-production thus being widely perceived as an initiative too far. Yet, an equality of voices is central not only to co-production and the 3 Keys, but also to recovery practice as a whole. It is to recovery practice and the challenges it faces that we turn next.

GLOSSARY OF KEY TERMS

Assessment in mental health – any process (medical diagnosis, needs based assessment, risk assessment, etc) through which a mental health issue may come to be better understood - assessment should always be a holistic and on-going process of mutual understanding rather than a one-off event

Values-based assessment – any assessment process (including medical diagnosis) that makes central the values of the person concerned (ie what matters to them) in the way the mental issue in question is understood

The 3 Keys – a particular take on values-based assessment based on three aspects of assessment (the 3 Keys) that in a wide ranging consultation all stakeholders agreed were important

> *Key 1: – person-centred assessment*: there should be active participation of the service user concerned in an assessment process aimed at mutual understanding with his or her service providers and where appropriate with their carers

> *Key 2: – multidisciplinary assessment*: wherever possible assessment should include input from different provider perspectives within a multidisciplinary approach

> *Key 3: strengths based assessment*: assessment should focus on the strengths, aspirations and resiliencies of the individual service user concerned as well as identifying his or her needs and challenges

StAR values – an acronym for Strengths, Aspirations and Resources, the positive values high-lighted in values-based practice ('resources' includes but is wider than the 'resiliencies' of the original Key 3)

Aspirations – Personal aspirations, the A in StAR values, and often the key of keys to recovery

FURTHER READING

For further reading on the theory underpinning values-based practice, see Chapter 3. A recent review of philosophical and empirical work on values in assessment and diagnosis is included in Fulford and van Staden (2013); the issues are also explored in Part IV of *The Oxford Textbook of Philosophy and Psychiatry* (Fulford et al., 2006). For a detailed study of the values in the *Diagnostic and Statistical Manual*, see Sadler, 2005).

The 3 Keys report is available as a free download from the VBP website, available at: http://www.go.warwick.ac.uk/values-basedpractice, or simply search on "values-based practice". Chapter 10 of this book explores strengths-based approaches further, including resources for strengths-based assessment as a key component of recovery practice.

A fuller version of Sally Coombs' story is given in Fulford et al. (2012): ch. 4, "Recovery in Schizophrenia: A Values Wake-up Call".

REFERENCES

Atwell, R. and Fulford, K.W.M. (2006) "The Christian tradition of spiritual direction as a sketch for a strong theology of diversity" in Cox, J., Campbell, A.V. and Fulford, K.W.M. (eds) *Medicine of the Person: Faith, Science and Values in Health Care Provision.* London: Jessica Kingsley Publishers.

Department of Health (2004) *The Ten Essential Shared Capabilities: A Framework for the Whole of the Mental Health Workforce.* London: The Sainsbury Centre for Mental Health, the National Health Service University (NHSU), and the National Institute for Mental Health England (NIMHE).

Fulford, K.W.M. and van Staden, W. (2013) "Values-based practice: Topsy-turvy take home messages from ordinary language philosophy (and a few next steps)" in Fulford, K.W.M., Davies, M., Gipps, R. Graham, G., Sadler, J., Stanghellini, G. and Thornton, T. (eds), *The Oxford Handbook of Philosophy and Psychiatry.* Oxford: Oxford University Press.

Fulford, K.W.M., Duhig, L., Hankin, J., Hicks, J. and Keeble, J. (2015) "Values-based assessment in mental health: The 3 keys to a shared approach between service users and service providers" in Sadler, J.Z. van Staden, W. and Fulford, K.W.M. (eds), *The Oxford Handbook of Psychiatric Ethics.* Oxford: Oxford University Press.

Fulford, K.W.M., Peile, E. and Carroll, H. (2012) *Essential Values-based Practice: Clinical Stories Linking Science with People.* Cambridge: Cambridge University Press.

Fulford, K.W.M., Thornton, T. and Graham, G. (2006) *The Oxford Textbook of Philosophy and Psychiatry.* Oxford: Oxford University Press.

Hicks, J., Keeble, J. and Fulford, K.W.M., (forthcoming, 2015) "Mental health co-production in Bristol Seeking to address the challenges", *Mental Health Today.*

National Institute for Mental Health in England (NIMHE) and the Care Services Improvement Partnership (2008) *3 Keys to a Shared Approach in Mental Health Assessment.* London: Department of Health.

Sadler, J.Z. (2005) *Values and Psychiatric Diagnosis.* Oxford: Oxford University Press.

Skills for Health (2013) *Revised National Occupational Standards for Mental Health.* Bristol: Skills for Health.

Worthington, A. and Hannan, R. (2013) *The Triangle of Care – Carers Included: A Guide to Best Practice in Mental Health Care in England* (2nd edn). London: Carers Trust (www.carers.org).

10 | Values, ethics and recovery

Chapter Summary

This chapter will:

- Explore recovery and the different ways that this term has been used in mental health services.

- Describe how therapeutic approaches such as the strengths model, therapeutic risk taking and shared decision making can facilitate a person's recovery journey.

- Consider the personal recovery journey of mental health staff, exploring peer support roles alongside the benefits and challenges of mental health staff disclosing their own experiences of being wounded.

The concept of recovery is one which grew from the people who have experienced mental distress themselves, from people who identified that services had given up hope that their lives could change. Recovery has emerged as an important philosophy within contemporary mental health services. The need for mental health professionals to support people towards recovery is clearly outlined within professional governing frameworks (Department of Health 2004, 2006; College of Occupational Therapists, 2006) and underpinned by policy (Department of Health 2001, 2011). It is apparent that recovery is recognised by the key stakeholders within mental health care, creating potential that service users, professionals and policy share the same goal for mental health practice.

Recovery, however, is a concept that is open to multiple interpretations (Allott et al., 2002; Davidson and Roe, 2007; Stickley and Wright, 2011). The diverse meanings of recovery can create difficulties for collaborative working between mental health professionals and people who use services (Aston and Coffey, 2012). This section examines two frameworks commonly used to interpret recovery and explores their implications for mental health practice.

Recovery

The literal meaning of recovery is to return to a normal state of health, or to regain a position (Thompson, 1996). This interpretation of recovery within the context of mental health has been described as "recovery from mental illness" (Davidson and Roe, 2007), or clinical recovery (Shepard et al., 2008) and, until recently, dominated professional understandings of the term.

Getting back to normal

Recovery from mental illness shares many elements with the notion of cure. There is an expectation that symptoms will lessen and even disappear; that the illness will no longer interfere with daily life, enabling the individual to return to the activities and relationships that they held before. Recovery in this framework clearly has its origins within a biomedical approach. Adopting this perspective has implications for the way in which the experience of mental health problems is defined. A biomedical approach will also imply certain roles for professionals to promote such recovery. Emphasis is placed on the importance of treatment to enable the reduction of symptoms which, in itself, provides the opportunity to return to normal functioning. A mental health professional's expertise lies in understanding the person's illness, offering treatment and support to regain activities.

Over many years, psychiatry has sought to find such a cure for mental health problems, yet it has struggled with maintaining therapeutic optimism in the light of treatments with limited effects and, sometimes, major unwanted side effects. Some mental health problems have been perceived as chronic conditions from which there is restricted opportunity for clinical recovery. Kraepelin, a key theorist in developing the diagnosis of schizophrenia (see Chapter 8), defined it as a progressive condition with inevitable significant deterioration. Such a perspective on the opportunity for cure, effective treatment and, therefore, recovery for people diagnosed with mental health problems creates a pessimistic outlook. People with lived experience of mental distress highlight the devastating impact that such perceptions can have. Deegan (2009) describes her experiences: as a young person, hoping to train as a gym teacher, she was informed that after developing mental health problems she would be sick for the rest of her life, that her best hope was treatments to help her cope on a daily basis.

Research has shown that between one quarter and two thirds of people diagnosed with serious mental health problems will experience recovery from their problems to such an extent that it does not interfere with their daily lives (Harding et al.,1987; Harding, 1988). This offers a more positive view of the potential for recovery *from* mental illness yet, using this framework leaves up to half of those given a diagnosis of serious mental health problems with limited hope for a fulfilled life. Consequently, the value of such an interpretation of recovery within mental health care has to be questioned.

These challenges came in the form of the service user/survivor movements. The movement itself represented a wide range of perspectives in relation to mental distress but was united in a desire for a greater voice for service users, to challenge power relationships and question the consensus view of mental illness as defined by others (Pilgrim, 2005; Campbell, 2009). The movement helped to create more opportunities for service users to share experiences and, collectively, question accepted ideas regarding mental health problems. Within this context, different frameworks for conceptualising recovery are developed by those with direct experience of mental distress.

Exercise 10.1

- What does recovery mean to you?
- Think of an event or experience in your life from which you have "recovered".
- What were some of the characteristics of this recovery?

Discovery and adaptation

One of the most significant aspects of this interpretation of recovery is that it is an approach that is owned by service users. Gosling (2010:31) suggests this means "we decide what we mean by being well, we do not need someone else to tell us". Recovery is about a personal journey of discovery based on the values of the person concerned and, as such, defies a one-size-fits-all definition. However, there have been critiques of this concept of individualised recovery for remaining too reliant on Western notions of individualism, and downplaying structural inequalities and more collective identities and cultures (Kalathil et al., 2011; Harper and Speed, 2012). Recovery entails accepting the possibility of multiple interpretations of mental distress, influenced by a person's world view, rather than working within an imposed medical framework (Collier, 2010). However, there are common themes which appear in relation to this approach to recovery. This section draws on literature and the work of service users to outline these key themes.

Hope Hope offers a vision that the person can live a meaningful and valued life (Repper and Perkins, 2009) and, therefore, that the prospect of recovery is possible. As highlighted by Anthony (1996), hope relates to a belief in the possibility of regaining a sense of self beyond the limits of a disability. Hope is also an important resource to help survive when times are challenging (Wisdom et al., 2008). Hope can mean a way of resisting the pessimism of others, which can develop when a person is diagnosed with mental health problems and expectations of that person's goals, strengths and achievements decrease (Deegan, 1996).

According to Deegan (1996), anguish and apathy can be a common part of experiencing a mental health problem and the link between hopelessness and suicide is well-documented (Repper and Perkins, 2009). Deegan (1996) argues that the right conditions are needed to pull that person out from their anguish and apathy and, while a person needs to discover hope for themselves, mental health professionals can have an important role in nurturing this hope. Hope can be hard to maintain for professionals who only come into contact with people when they are unwell and most in need. However, having hopeful mental health workers is an important part of supporting recovery. Hope may be facilitated through meaningful therapeutic relationships, valuing the individual and recognising their strengths (see the putting the person at the heart of mental health care section – p. 156), accepting problems as part of the recovery journey and finding ways to learn and grow from difficulties (Basset and Repper, 2005; Roberts, 2008).

Identity The experience of mental health problems can damage a person's own identity, causing them to question their values, beliefs and view of themselves (Higgens and McBennett, 2007; Stickley and Bonney, 2008; Wisdom et al., 2008; Raptopoulos, 2012). Recovery has been associated with the development of a new sense of self which, according to Roberts (2008: 747), involves identifying "who or what they need to become" in order to accept their experience of mental distress.

Once diagnosed with a mental illness, a person's identity can be defined negatively by others. Experiencing stigma, prejudice and discrimination is common; such perceptions can become internalised, further contributing to problems with identity (Wisdom et al. 2008). The role of a mentally ill person can dominate how people are viewed, so their self-perception becomes defined by this. Recovery entails having opportunities to build a valued life to access relationships and build positive identities. This involves being recognised for the many other roles and skills a person may have, and that mental health problems may be only part of their identity. This process is described by Davidson and Roe (2007) as "recovery in", as opposed to from, mental health problems. As with hope, acceptance and building new identities are relational; they are facilitated by relationships and contexts that enable exploration and the accessing of new opportunities.

However, research by Kalathil et al. (2011) highlights that this view of recovery can oversimplify the development of damaged identities. For the African, African-Caribbean and South Asian women who narrated their experiences of distress, racism, prejudice and marginalisation (including at the hands of mental health services) contributed to internalised negative self-image. When cultural and gender identities are devalued by attitudes that may be held at a societal level, developing positive identity is more complex. The women in the study by Kalathil et al. (2011) outline that mental health services need to be able to support people to deal with the impact of discrimination and prejudice. For them "recovery is regaining a positive sense of self, re-negotiating personal and cultural expectations and having a sense of control over who you are" (Kalathil et al., 2011: 38).

Control and self-management Recovery involves accepting different means of understanding mental distress. Making sense of these experiences (and those that may have contributed to developing mental health problems) is an important and underestimated aspect of recovery.

Recovery has also been associated with a person taking on more control (Repper and Perkins, 2003). This may relate to the experiences linked with a mental health problem itself – such as hearing voices, and involves the person using their own techniques and ways of coping to manage that experience. Self-help and sharing with other people with shared identity has been recognised as an important way for people to help manage their distress (Mead and Copeland, 2000). Wellness and Recovery Action Planning (see http://www.mentalhealthrecovery.com/) is one example of how this has been used. Taking back control will involve a recognition of the person's own expertise in understanding themselves and how they may best cope with their distress. This may be challenging not only for service users struggling with gaining a positive self-identify, but also for mental health professionals imbued with responsibilities associated with "professionally"-based knowledge. Repper and Perkins (2003) highlight that this involves mental health workers making transitions in our views of the role of professionals from one of prescription to one where our knowledge and skills are made available to service users.

Control in relation to recovery entails being able to make choices about care, taking back control from services. Using mental health services can involve a loss of control over daily life or handing this over to others. The actions of mental health professionals can lead to further loss of power (Social Perspectives Network, 2007). Having control is an important part of recovery (Kartalova-O'Doherty and Tedstone-Doherty, 2010). This means being involved in making decisions about their own care and daily lives. It may seem difficult at times when people are particularly distressed; Davidson (2005) suggests that self-management can be maximised when people may be struggling to retain control through professionals and service users planning together and recording what may help and hinder that person during those times.

Clearly, making choices and taking charge of their own lives is a key aspect of control and recovery. It is in this aspect that recovery presents its greatest challenge for mental health services, as those labelled as mentally ill are subject to controls and forced treatment in the context of mental health care (Mancini, 2007). This creates tensions for service users being permitted to take back control. The second section of this chapter explores some of the therapeutic approaches that may promote recovery; Chapter 6 has already examined some of the potential dilemmas raised by these approaches.

Within this approach to recovery, it is clear that the term refers to much more than reducing symptoms and getting back to normal. It acknowledges that a mental health crisis is only one aspect of what a person may need to recover from. A person's journey of discovery is taking place in the context of negative views of mental illness from society and services, loss of relationships, loss of identity and potentially damaging effects of treatment. Recovery is therefore conceptualised as related to the person not an illness; as connected to rights, roles, values, relationships and opportunities within society. Such an interpretation has been referred to as personal, social or life recovery (Shepard et al., 2008; Collier, 2010; Stickley and Wright, 2011).

Implications

It is apparent that the term "recovery" has multiple interpretations with the frameworks presented here, offering quite divergent views. Though some argue that these interpretations are actually more similar than they first appear (Mountain and Shah, 2008), a position resisted by many people with experience of mental health problems (Social Perspectives Network, 2007). However, the frameworks discussed represent different value positions through the ways in which they understand the experience of mental distress and, consequently, the role of mental health professionals. Pilgrim (2008) highlights that this has very clear implications for practice; for example, that for one position a lack of insight is the barrier to recovery, whereas for the other it is denied opportunity to exercise rights, and choices which may be removed by mental health services themselves. For him, the false consensus view of recovery presented by its appearance in policy, professional practice and service user narratives leads to the risk that recovery comes to mean whatever the different stakeholders want it to mean to serve their interests (Pilgrim, 2008). This is clearly problematic whereas, we saw in Chapters 5 and 6, certain stakeholders hold more power to define recovery than others.

Recovery is recognised as having a number of limitations, some of which have been identified by people with experience of mental health problems (Social Perspectives Network, 2007, Imonioro, 2009). The focus of recovery on individual factors fails to recognise the context in which people develop distress. Damaging and oppressive social environments are not accounted for in these elements of recovery. People from marginalised and minority groups have had a limited voice within the recovery movement (Social Perspectives Network, 2007). The foregrounding of individualistic notions of identity within recovery is seen as a reflection of this (Imonioro, 2009). Research by Kalathil et al. (2011) suggested that, for the African-Caribbean and South Asian women in their study, recovery was perceived as a professionalised term that failed to address the circumstances in which they developed distress. For recovery to be meaningful to people from racialised groups, there should be much greater focus on relationships with others, spirituality, role of family members, tackling oppression and racism, and recognising the social experiences that contribute to mental distress (Social Perspectives Network, 2007; Imonioro, 2009; Kalathil et al., 2011).

The widespread acceptance of recovery in policy may be a reflection of the fact that an emphasis on choice and autonomy suits current political ideologies. Employment has increasingly been presented by some as an important part of enabling recovery. This suits political agendas to reduce the costs of benefits for the unemployed. Yet, full-paid employment may not be a goal for everyone (Coutts, 2007), instead representing socially and culturally defined aspirations. Recent changes to the health care system make a commitment to increase choice for health care "consumers" (Department of Health, 2010). Choice is a key element of recovery values; however, this emphasis at a political level masks increased privatisation and funding cuts. The convergence of political and recovery values are evident within personalisation. This system provides the structure for individuals to purchase and manage their own support services (Mind, 2009). From a recovery perspective, it enables choice, self-determination and power sharing. A person is able to arrange support that suits their individual needs. However, concerns have been raised that this detracts funding from services that provide spaces for social and community engagement. This could result in further isolation for people with mental health problems (Mind, 2009). It also reflects Western political and economic ideologies, risking further stigmatisation of users of the welfare state while failing to tackle social inequality (Ferguson, 2007; Mind, 2009)

The professionalisation of the term "recovery" is problematic. The adoption of recovery approaches by mental health services has been seen to lead to reinterpretations that more closely reflect models of rehabilitation than a genuine shift towards empowerment (Social

Perspectives Network, 2007). In finding the way forward for mental health practice, it is important to underline that personal recovery is a conceptualisation that has been defined and driven by those with direct experience of mental distress. In this respect, arguably, it has the most potential for a positive influence on mental health practice, a person's experience of services and journey to moving on from mental health problems (Collier, 2010). Collier (2010) and Aston and Coffey (2012) agree that this is facilitated by professionals reflecting on their values and engaging in conversations with service users with whom they are working about their own personal meanings of recovery. This is why the skills for values-based practice described in Chapter 4 are important for putting the person concerned at the heart of recovery practice.

Recovery emphasises people's rights to self-determination, increasing their opportunities to take back control (Repper and Perkins, 2003). However, doubts have been raised regarding the reality of recovery facilitating increased control. Recovery, particularly self-management, suggests individuals learn about and adopt strategies that enable them to cope with daily life alongside their distressing experiences (Davidson, 2005). This process may itself act as a system of control. Scott and Wilson (2011) highlight that the Wellness and Recovery Action Planning (WRAP) approach to self-management perpetuates the view that people with mental health problems are in constant danger of losing control. Through its emphasis on monitoring, triggers and early warning signs, it acts as a system of self-surveillance focussed on maintaining wellbeing. In addition, WRAP specifically advocates the need for others to take control when a crisis occurs (Scott and Wilson, 2011). Adams and Drake (2006) also confirm frameworks such as advanced statements promoted within recovery and shared decision making approaches still hand decision making power back to the institution.

According to Scott and Wilson (2011), an individual's constant review of health and wellbeing results in this surveillance being absorbed into the accepted subjectivity of the person. As such, recovery forms part of a neo-liberalist system of governmentality (Scott and Wilson, 2011 Braslow, 2013). Neo-liberal values emphasise individual autonomy while presenting the good citizen as one who is able to govern themselves (Rose, 1999). Conduct is regulated through informed individual decision making based on goals of self-development and risk aversion (Rose, 1999; Larner, 2000; Braslow, 2013). Self, rather than state, regulation is achieved as a technique of control (Rose,1999). Genuine choice becomes a myth, as behaviour that does not conform to these expected values and norms risks ostracism (O'Byrne and Holmes, 2007). Recovery – and, in particular, self-management – offers a framework to encourage individuals to regulate their own conduct in line with the expected behaviours of an autonomous, rational, good citizen. This is underpinned by the individualistic focus of recovery at the cost of considering social environments that may cause and perpetuate distress. Despite these critiques, some authors have offered perspectives on how recovery-orientated practice can better account for social contexts (Yates et al., 2012; Tew, 2013).

Recovery provides a complimentary philosophy to that underpinning neo-liberal welfare reform, according to Braslow (2013). Recent changes to the health care system have been underpinned by commitments to increase choice for health care "consumers" (Department of Health, 2010). The neo-liberal emphasis on choice, free market principles and a reduced role for the state are reflected in these reforms (Larner, 2000). Repper and Perkins (2009) highlight how such amendments to increase choice and control embody principles of recovery. As Rose (1999) claims, such welfare changes form part of the redefinition of citizens as autonomous individuals exercising choices. Those who fail in this self-government will be defined as "'failed citizens'". Recovery potentially perpetuates this viewpoint as responsibility for recovery, and maintenance of wellbeing essentially rests with the individual while social inequality is ignored (Braslow, 2013).

The focus on "getting people back to work" in recent policies, and in the context of welfare reforms and the increasing professionalisation of the recovery agenda, has created a backlash. Within the service user/survivor movement, there is an increasing disaffection with the recovery agenda, including Recovery Colleges, use of recovery models within services and so on, which is reflected in the emergence of an "anti-recovery" movement. The survivor group Recovery in the Bin has produced a document of 18 key principles that challenge and critique the "colonisation" of recovery by market forces and by professional agendas (See Recovery in the Bin (2015)). A key principle is the proposal of the term "UnRecovered" as a valid and legitimate self-definition. "UnRecovered" does not mean that people want to remain unwell, but that they choose to reject the use of outcome measures based on recovery models (for example, the Recovery Star), and the individualised notions of success and progress. Instead, they assert that autonomy and self-determination can only be achieved through collective action against "the effects of social and economic circumstances such as poor housing, poverty, stigma, racism, sexism, unreasonable work expectations, and countless other barriers".

Putting the person at the heart of mental health care

There are a number of therapeutic approaches that may be used to promote recovery-oriented mental health practice. This section explores four key areas to examine how these may be adopted to promote recovery.

Strengths model

In Chapter 9, when outlining the 3 Keys approach, we saw the important focus on strengths-based approaches and including the aspirations of the service user at the heart of mental health care. The strengths model offers both a values base and practical tools for mental health care (Fukui et al., 2012). It is grounded within a critical view of existing frameworks for providing mental health support. Currently, these are defined by identifying and treating a problem or deficit. Rapp and Goscha (2012) suggest that this is unhelpful, as problems become conceptualised in a way that is defined by professionals and professional systems (for example, through diagnosis). This serves to oversimplify people's experiences and provides an individualistic interpretation, divorcing people from their social-cultural context. Such an emphasis on defining and treating a problem creates the expectation that the problem has a resolution, which may not always be the case (Rapp and Goscha, 2012).

Instead, a strengths model assumes all people have skills, abilities and goals, and that all environments can offer resources (Rapp and Goscha, 2012). A strength approach focuses on an individual's goals; problems are only considered as they may arise in relation to a person working towards their goals. Six key principles of the strengths model have been outlined:

- *People with mental health problems can develop, grow and change*
  The values of a recovery approach clearly identify with this principle. It rests on values upheld by the beliefs of mental health professionals and services that change is possible

- *The focus is on individual strengths and abilities*
  Recognising what a person can do is held to be more powerful than focusing on what they cannot. This links with recovery themes of building positive identities and acknowledging people's expertise.

- *The community offers a wealth of resources and people: it is not an obstacle*
  People can be supported to be active members of the community. The sources of support to help this happen are not necessarily to be found in statutory services.

- *The therapeutic relationship between service user and mental health worker is essential*
  The strengths approach is also a model of "case management"; this means it is an approach that can help structure care when working with a number of service users. It emphasises the need for one-to-one working with a person, rather than them being visited by a number of different people. The relationship is viewed as an important tool to support people to work towards their goals.

- *Support is based on individual self-determination*
  Individuals have the right to make choices about their lives and workers should support individuals in these choices. This principle clearly reflects recovery values of taking back control. However, Chopra et al. (2009) highlight that this is still governed by professional, ethical and legal frameworks which might influence negotiation of short-, medium- and long-term goals in relation to, for example, going back to work.

- *The main place of contact should be in the community*
  It suggests that, wherever possible, meetings should take place in the community, rather than professional settings in order to help the person feel comfortable (if this is their own environment) and create more opportunity for exploring interests and abilities.
  (Barry et al., 2003; Chopra et al., 2009; Rapp and Goscha, 2012)

Using the strengths approach in practice can start with a strengths assessment, which not only provides a detailed insight into individuals' current strengths and resources, but also their past achievements. This is followed by a recovery or goals plan that details short-, medium- and long-term goals, including the steps involved in reaching these (Chopra et al., 2009).

The strengths approach offers an alternative to focussing on weaknesses and problems which, all too often, is the concern of mental health services. As a model of providing mental health care, it has been empirically demonstrated that adopting a strengths approach can impact positively on people's life satisfaction, hospital use, symptoms, employment, leisure activities, social support and family stress (Barry et al., 2003; Fukui et al., 2012).

Therapeutic risk taking

Enabling service users to take risks is an important part of promoting recovery. Therapeutic or positive risk taking involves individuals having the opportunity to make choices, decide and follow different options (Morgan, 2000). Positive risk taking is characterised by a process of enabling the person to make decisions about the level of risk they are prepared to take with their health and safety (Department of Health, 2004).

Factors identified by service users as being important for their recovery included the ability to have hope and trusting in their own thoughts. Being supported to take positive risks can help to achieve this, as it allows the person to experiment and identify their own limitations and abilities. This should be guided by the person, rather than defined and decided by a mental health professional on their behalf, and, as such, involves a shift in the balance of power. Deegan's (2001) exploration of the process of recovery acknowledges that taking risks and recovery are synonymous, and that taking risks facilitates the acceptance stage of recovery.

The concept of risk is one that has come to dominate the mental health literature, policy and practice (Godin, 2004; Holloway, 2004). Risk is predominantly understood within a negative framework. Focus is maintained on the losses, rather than the gains that may be associated with risk. In mental health practice, this is reflected in the preoccupation with the assessment of risk of violence to others, suicide and self-harm (Muir-Cochrane, 2006). Such an emphasis overlooks not only the losses to which a person may be exposed as a result of their mental health problems and service use (such as side effects of medication, employment), but also the benefits that may be gained by taking a risk. Focussing on the dangers believed to be posed by service users can serve to justify control being maintained by mental health services, which can be at odds with a person's recovery. The dominance of risk assessment and management in mental health can also perpetuate a focus on the difficulties of the past, rather than the person's hopes and goals for the future.

Promoting positive risk taking therefore involves recognising people with mental health problems as individuals with rights and responsibilities who have an entitlement to live a life that is not unduly restricted (Stalker, 2003).Taking a chance and learning from experience is something that we can all grow from.

There are many decisions and processes that may constitute a positive risk and what these are will obviously depend on individual circumstances. However, examples of positive risk taking could include coming off medication, moving accommodation and applying for jobs.

Shared decision making

Shared decision making is defined as a "process by which clinicians and patients work together to clarify treatment, management or self-management, support goals ... with the aim of reaching mutual agreement on the best course of action" (Coulter and Collins, 2011: 2). Emphasis is placed on a process of understanding the person's own values and attitudes, identifying their own goals. Achieving shared decision making entails recognising the person's expertise developed through the experience of health problems. Shared decision making, therefore, reflects the values underpinning a recovery approach.

Adopting such an approach to making decisions represents a departure from traditional models of health care. Within such paternalistic styles of decision making, the role of a health care professional is to inform the person of the options and persuade them to accept the option that the professional perceives is best for that person; shared decision making involves sharing information, identifying the person's preferences, and jointly agreeing an option (Schauer et al., 2007; Hamann et al., 2011).

Shared decision making applies to a wide variety of scenarios which may include a decision;

- To undertake a particular intervention such as counselling or an education programme.
- Whether to take medication.
- To introduce a change in lifestyle.
- Arrangements regarding follow up appointments.

(Coulter and Collins 2011; Matthias et al., 2012)

Shared decision making is supported by certain skills and approaches: the values, skills and competence of the professional; communication and sharing information; social and cultural context; shared decision making; and peer support.

Values, skills and competence of the professional

In order to make negotiated decisions with service users, a health care professional has to recognise this as the desired goal within decision making (Dy and Purnell, 2012). Incorporated in this is understanding that the person's views values and beliefs are important. Historically being defined as "mad" and, more recently, "mentally ill" has carried with it the assumption that that person is irrational and incompetent, and therefore cannot be trusted. These suppositions at the very heart of our definitions of mental illness may present a challenge for health care professionals to have the conviction to follow a person's preferences, particularly if these options are perceived as risky or a "bad choice".

Communication and sharing information

Shared decision making is dependent on enabling people to be involved. Developing a trusting therapeutic relationship provides the conditions in which a person can be open and share their goals and concerns, and acknowledge their wishes and preferences. To support shared decisions this needs to be supported by ensuring that the person has the opportunity to share these preferences when a decision is being made.

Social and cultural context

Being able to recognise the influence of a person's culture on their experience of mental distress, lifestyle, choices and beliefs about their health facilitates shared decision making with diverse populations. This includes understanding the impact of cultural oppression and racism on the development of and maintenance of distress. Responding to an individual's cultural context while also enabling their participation through awareness of factors such as language, values, community and family relationships is important to negotiating decisions and reflects a "culturally competent" approach to care (Dy and Purnell, 2012). Mental health services themselves can be a source of discrimination. Shared decision making with people from diverse groups should recognise that previous experiences of prejudice or discrimination can cause people to be cautious about developing relationships with professionals, further emphasising the need for empathy and trust to enable decision making.

Shared decision making: Potential problems

Yet, mental health services are perceived to be lagging behind other health and social care arenas when it comes to promoting shared decision making. Health care professionals question the abilities of service users to be involved in decision making, highlighting issues such as cognitive abilities, insight and paranoia as barriers to service users being able to communicate their views to providers (Chong et al., 2013). Studies have shown, however, that people with serious mental health problems want to, and feel able, to be involved in decision making (Matthias et al., 2012). Such a position is emphasised by service user/survivor movements themselves.

The context in which health professionals have expressed these views is one in which discourses surrounding mental illness emphasise a lack of rationality and competence associated with the person with that illness (Adams and Drake, 2006). These perceptions of mental illness would clearly undermine a shared approach to decision making, as a person is presented as unable to make clear decisions when diagnosed.

The power of mental health services, and therefore mental health professionals, to contain and control service users endorsed by legislation questions the values on which shared decision making is based. Negotiated decisions emphasise respect for the individuals' autonomy. According to Beauchamp and Childress (2001), key components of autonomy are liberty, freedom from coercive influences and agency, and the capacity for meaningful action. Capacity is often used as an argument for why autonomy is applied differently in mental health compared with other health care settings (Schauer et al., 2007). However, it is apparent that an individual's liberty is frequently affected by using mental health services, not only in the sense of being held in hospital and potentially treated against their will, but also in the experience of coercion (discussed in more depth in Chapter 7). Service users have consistently described how, for example, being admitted to hospital is not perceived as a voluntary decision even when, legally, it is (Vassilev and Pilgrim, 2007). This means that professionals have the power to override a person's preferences and that people with mental health problems are using services with this awareness. It would be naive to assume that such a gulf in power would not impact on the dynamic of negotiation and mutual agreement at the heart of shared decisions. Much of the literature discussing shared decision making and mental health lacks an analysis of this influence.

Shared decision making is an approach within mental health practice that can promote recovery. It involves valuing and responding to an individual's values, social context and preferences and recognising their expertise, which promotes person centred care. Caution needs to be exercised in adopting an uncritical acceptance of shared decision making. However, an awareness of the complexities in implementing it within mental health settings is an important step in enabling more equal power relationships to share decisions.

Exercise 10.2

Below are links to two people's narratives of recovery, shared with the Scottish Recovery Network as part of their project on stories of recovery.
Read Michelle's Story.

http://www.scottishrecovery.net/Submitted-thoughts-and-stories/keeping-my-glass-half-full-the-story-of-my-recovery.html

Read Jean's story.

http://www.scottishrecovery.net/Submitted-thoughts-and-stories/hindsight-is-a-wonderful-thing.html

When they discuss the input of professionals and mental health services, consider:

- How could the strengths model be used to support recovery?
- What opportunities were there to enable Michelle and Jean to take a risk?
- What strategies could be used to facilitate a shared decision making approach within the care Michelle and Jean received?

You could also reflect on what they identify as the key influences on their recovery.

Peer support

Peer support is an approach that has been used and valued by people with experience of mental distress for many years. A peer support approach may include self-help groups, survivor or peer-led services, activism and collective mutual support (Faulkner and Kalathil, 2012). More recently, peer support has received greater attention in statutory services. Peer support workers are becoming an important part of health and social care delivery. Here, peer support is characterised by a helping relationship between a person who has experienced mental distress and someone who has progressed less in their recovery journey, and is likely to involve the provision of support (Davidson et al., 2006). Peer support provides the opportunity for the sharing of experiences, and the offering of acceptance, understanding and empathy alongside the offering of practical and emotional support. This is housed within a relationship with someone who has a shared identity in terms of their experience of mental distress.

While the definition and application of peer support approaches is varied, the literature consistently highlights the positive impact that working with a peer can have on a person's recovery journey. Working with a peer support worker can help people feel more in control, experience a sense of empowerment, and improve confidence and self-esteem (Repper and Carter, 2011). Social contacts and friends have been found to be higher in those who have experienced peer support, perhaps underpinned by findings that suggest social functioning may also be improved (Repper and Carter, 2011).

Explanations have been offered as to how peer support exerts this positive influence on recovery, particularly as some of the features (such as acceptance, understanding, support) should also define relationships with non-peer professionals. A peer support worker may act as a role model; this helps provide hope that recovery and growth is possible. According to Dennis (2003), this is linked to Bandura's social cognitive theory (1986), where learning is explained through observation. Peer support work provides the opportunity for people to observe the positive ways that others use to cope; it can help to normalise some feelings and reactions. Encouragement also acts as an important influence to improve self-efficacy and, therefore, peer support can positively influence people's interpretations. This can be even more powerful when a role model is someone similar to that individual. Dennis (2003) also suggests that peer support may have a positive influence through impacting on how a person views their coping abilities and stressors (the buffering effect model). Information provided by peers could influence the way in which a stressor, such as a diagnosis or stressful event, is seen and discourage self-blame. Through the sharing of problem solving techniques or suggested ways of managing distress that are based on insights gained by experience, perceptions of coping resources may also be changed. Dennis (2003) therefore argues that this can act to "buffer" the impact of stress.

Benefits of peer support are not confined to those who may be receiving help from a peer. Peer support workers themselves have highlighted that their recovery has benefited from being in the role, with significant impact on identity and confidence, enabling people to feel they are making a positive contribution (Mental Health Foundation, 2012).

Challenges of the peer support worker role are evident, too. In increasingly stretched health and social care services, there is a danger that peer support worker posts become cheap alternatives to professional roles. Consequently, the unique peer aspects of the role become overshadowed with a potential expectation that workers are involved in the "controlling" aspects of health care (such as restraint). Some argue that power differences have already been exacerbated by the introduction of peer roles through training, role structures and their paid employment in statutory organisations, therefore making it diffi-cult to protect the uniqueness of a peer support worker. Professionalisation of peer support is also seen as a threat to the range and diversity of peer support approaches that exist. It risks masking the diversity of experiences and values that peer support can encompass. A need to protect these is essential as peer support is expanded in mainstream services (Faulkner and Kalathil, 2012).

Tensions may arise where peer support workers have a role linked to a team that may have previously treated them, contributing to them being perceived as a "patient" with lower status. Repper and Carter (2011) argue this is a form of discrimination, which the peer support worker role itself has proved a powerful advocate in challenging, as it can have a positive impact on staff attitudes.

Peer support work has been recognised as helping to facilitate recovery. One of the main characteristics of peer support is that it is a relationship in which parties share common experiences of mental distress. As we have seen, tensions may arise as boundaries between helper and helped are blurred. The following section explores mental health workers' experi-ence of mental health issues, questioning whether these boundaries may have been falsely created.

Recovery journey of mental health staff

Many people within the mental health and social care professions experience mental health problems. Lived experience of mental distress or trauma may be a motivator for being drawn to roles that provide support to others. As the discussion of peer support has highlighted, having a shared experience can be of benefit within a helping profes-sion. Being wounded yourself may aid in promoting healing in others. This notion has its origins in ancient Greek, Hebrew, Chinese and Norse legends where the ability to heal comes from experiencing suffering or illness (Benziman et al., 2012). Carl Jung drew on

Greek mythology to relate the experience of wounded healer to psychotherapy, expressing that therapists' own emotional distress is an important part of promoting healing in the therapeutic process.

Central to the constructs of a wounded healer is the perception that both healer and wounded are closely bound, not different or separate from one another. "The wounded healer ... tells us that the patient has a healer within as much as the healer has a patient within" (Benziman et al., 2012: 3). Within some cultures practicing shamanism, part of the journey to becoming a shaman involves inducing illness or emotional distress. This provides a demonstration that the person's role as shamen has been validated by the spirits and is a crucial part of their training to heal others (Benziman et al., 2012).

The erosion of the boundary between helper and helped in the concept of wounded healers provides a key indication of the formidable impact that wounded healers can have within mental health care. It provides the opportunity for more equal power relationships, as experiences of vulnerability are shared and the paternalism of professionalism is challenged. Recognising that, as helpers, we have our own emotional trauma can challenge assumptions that the mentally ill are in some way separate or different from us; as Brandon (1999) highlights, people move in and out of mental health problems throughout life. Sharing personal experiences can demonstrate greater empathy for the person and their struggles, as well as the challenges of working towards recovery. Being open about our own mental distress can also help mental health workers demonstrate that recovery is possible, understand this process and inspire hope in others.

Being open about experiencing mental health problems as a mental health worker can clearly bring its own risks. Many have expressed concerns at experiencing prejudice at the hands of colleagues. Zerubavel and Wright (2012) suggest that this may be related to fears regarding humiliation and shame, particularly in relation to certain diagnosis or experiences (such as violence or abuse) that may carry additional stigma. This may be exacerbated by an awareness of negative perceptions of mental health problems in wider society, which may reinforce a desire for mental health workers to keep this part of their identity hidden. Unfortunately, there is some evidence that professionals have struggled with the reactions of colleagues. A study by Joyce et al. (2007) suggests that some nurses adopted a negative attitude to colleagues who were open about their mental illness and engaged in behaviours to try and manage their conduct; for example, giving them a heavier workload. It was suggested this aims to reinforce what was perceived an appropriate role of a nurse. Those who had experienced mental health problems in the study also reflected on the challenges of their identity changing from nurse to patient. Brandon (1999) similarly noted how he felt rejected by other service users due to his professional qualification. However, this perhaps highlights the dualism within the notion of the wounded healer and the potential of this identity to challenge the false separation between those defined as mentally ill and those who are not.

There is a fear that sharing experiences of mental health problems as a professional may bring into question that person's competence successfully to satisfy the requirements of their position. Beliefs regarding mental illness being associated with a lack of rationality and dangerousness risk perpetuating the perception that having experienced a mental health problem a person's capabilities as a professional are undermined. Such concerns may deter people from being open.

The opportunities and challenges presented by being open, as a mental health professional, about experiencing psychological distress can lead to a dilemma about whether to disclose this or not. Making this decision is clearly a complex process. It is influenced by recognising the reasons why disclosure may be beneficial, such as the development of a relationship or self-expression, and is reinforced by positive responses and outcomes to the disclosure (Chaudoir and Fisher, 2010). Disclosure may be a one off or ongoing event, and may include sharing with other professionals and service users. Revealing experiences of mental health problems may enhance levels of support. This can be particularly important within the mental health field, where the nature of the work may be emotionally challenging. Effective support from managers and mechanisms such as clinical supervision can be valuable for enabling people to disclose. Fostering a working environment that acknowledges that we are all susceptible to stress and, sometimes, difficulties at work and creating supportive spaces can also engender a culture of openness (Zerubavel and Wright, 2012).

Exercise 10.3

Think about a time where you have "disclosed" something about yourself.

- Was there anything that you were worried about before you shared this information about yourself?
- What was the other person's reaction?
- How did you feel after you had been open?
- How could this help you offer support to others?

Sharing experiences as wounded healers may be transformative, not only for the individual and those that they are supporting, but also for services, as it facilitates the tackling of prejudice and challenges the segregation between "them" and "us". Whether wounded or not, this is a responsibility that all mental health workers have: to be aware of our own values and beliefs, to guard against blame and fear, providing support and compassion to enable healing.

CONCLUSION

Recovery is an important concept within contemporary mental health services. However, the very nature of recovery as a personal journey means that the term is open to multiple interpretations. This can create problems with certain stakeholders maintaining the power to impose unhelpful and restrictive interventions in the name of recovery.

Part of the move to recovery-orientated mental health services is accepting that we have our own wounds and being open about this can have a powerful impact. The strengths model, therapeutic risk taking and shared decision making are approaches that can be utilised to support recovery *in* mental health. All these frameworks are united in their value base, which recognises people's potential, values their expertise and encourages their right to make choices. These values support mental health workers to facilitate people's journeys of recovery.

GLOSSARY OF KEY TERMS

Peer support - a helping relationship between a person who has experienced mental distress and someone who has progressed less in their recovery journey

Wounded healer – A healer (or professional) who has experienced mental health problems

Strengths model – Therapeutic approach that focuses on strengths, skills and abilities rather than problems.

Therapeutic risk taking – Process that recognises the benefits that can be gained from taking a risk and involves working with service users to support them to make decisions about their safety.

Disclosure – Sharing an experience of mental distress, trauma or crisis with another or more than one person.

Shared decision making – Mutual agreement of a course of action between professional and a service user based on negotiation and sharing of information

Recovery from – Definition of recovery that relates to returning back to a 'normal' state with reduction in symptoms and improvement in ability to function.

Recovery in – Definition of recovery based on recognising recovery as an individual journey which may be linked to regaining hope, identity and control.

FURTHER READING

Web Resources

Deegan P.E (1996) *Recovery and The conspiracy of hope: There's a Person In Here*: The Sixth Annual Mental Health Services Conference of Australia and New Zealand. Brisbane, Australia (Available at: https://www.patdeegan.com/pat-deegan/lectures/conspiracy-of-hope).

Scottish Recovery network: resources, narratives and recovery work http://www.scottishrecovery.net/

Resources for recovery and recovery planning: http://www.mentalhealthrecovery.com/

Kalathil, J., Collier, B., Bhakta, R., Daniel, O., Joseph, D. and Trivedi, P. (2011) *Recovery and Resilience: African, African-Caribbean and South Asian Women's Narratives of Recovering from Mental Distress.* London: Mental Health Foundation (Available from the Mental Health Foundation at www.mentalhealth.org.uk

For a discussion of links between values and recovery and the role of web-based learning, see Allott et al. (2005).

Books and Documents

Rapp, C. and Goscha, R. (2012) *The Strengths Model: A Recovery Orientated Approach to Mental Health Services,* 3rd edn. New York: Oxford University Press.

Shepard, J., Boardman, G. and Slade, M. (2008) Making Recovery a Reality. London: Centre for Mental Health.

Watkins, P. (2007) Recovery: *A Guide for Mental Health Practitioners*. Edinburgh: Churchill Livingstone. Elsevier.

Articles

Stickley, T. and Wright, N. (2011) "The British research evidence for recovery. Papers published between 2006 and 2009 (inclusive). Part I: A review of the peer-reviewed literature using a systematic approach", *Journal of Psychiatric and Mental Health Nursing*, 18: 247–56.

Mead, S. and Copeland, M. (2000) "What recovery means to us: Consumer perspectives", *Community Mental Health Journey*, 36(3), 315–28.

REFERENCES

Adams, J. and Drake, R. (2006) "Shared decision making and evidence based practice", *Community Mental Health Journal*, 42(1): 87–105.

Allott, P., Fulford, K.W.M., Fleming, B., Williamson, T. and Woodbridge, K. (2005) "Recovery, values and e-learning", *Mental Health Review*, 10(4): 34–8.

Allott, P., Loganathan, L. and Fulford, K.W.M. (2002) "Discovering hope for recovery" in *Innovation in Community Mental Health: International Perspectives*, Special issue of the *Canadian Journal of Community Mental Health*, 21(2): 13–33.

Anthony, W.A. (1996) "Recovery from mental illness: The guiding vision of the mental health system in the 1990s", *Innovation and Research*, 2(3): 17–23.

Aston, V. and Coffey, M. (2012) "Recovery: What mental health nurses and service users say about the concept of recovery", *Journal of Psychiatric and Mental Health Nursing*, 19: 257–63.

Bandura, A. (1986) *Social Foundation of Thought and Action: A Social Cognitive Theory*. Englewood Cliffs: Prentice Hall.

Barry, K., Zeber, J., Blow, F. and Valenstein, M. (2003) "Effect of strengths model versus assertive community treatment model on participant outcomes and utilisation: Two year follow up", *Psychiatric Rehabilitation Journal*, 26(3): 268–77.

Basset, T. and Repper, J. (2005) "Travelling hopefully", *Mental Health Today*, 16–18 November

Beauchamp, T. and Childress, J. (2001) *Principles of Biomedical Ethics* (5th edn). Oxford: Oxford University Press.

Benziman, G., Kannai, R. and Ahmad, A. (2012) "The wounded healer as cultural archetype", *Comparative Literature and Culture*, 14: 1.

Brandon, D. (1999) "Melting straitjackets", *Journal of Psychiatric and Mental Health Nursing*, 6: 321–6.

Braslow, J.T. (2013) "The manufacture of recovery", *Annual Review of Clinical Psychology*, 9: 781–809.

Campbell, P. (2009) "The service user/survivor movement" in Reynolds, J., Muston, R., Heller, T., Leach, J., McCormick, M., Wallcraft, J. and Walsh, M. (eds) *Mental Health Still Matters*. Basingstoke: Palgrave

Chaudoir, S. and Fisher, J. (2010) "The disclosure process model: Understanding disclosure decision making and postdisclosure outcomes among people living with a concealable stigmatized identity", *Psychological Bulletin*, 136(2): 236–56.

Chong, W., Asiani, P. and Chen, T. (2013) "Shared decision-making and interprofessional collaboration in mental healthcare: A qualitative study exploring perceptions of barriers and facilitators", *Journal of Interprofessional Care*, 27(5): 373–9.

Chopra, P., Hamilton, B., Castle, D., Smith, J., Mileshkin, C., Deans, M., Wynne, B., Prigg, G., Toomey, N. and Wilson, M. (2009) "Implementation of the strengths model at an area mental health service", *Australian Psychiatry*, 17(30): 203–6.

College of Occupational Therapists (2006) *Recovering Ordinary Lives: The Strategy for Occupational Therapy in Mental Health Services 2007-2017: A Vision for the Next Ten Years.* London: College of Occupational Therapists.

Collier, E. (2010) "Confusion of recovery: One solution", *International Journal of Mental Health Nursing*, 19: 16-21.

Coulter, A. and Collins, A. (2011) *Making Shared Decision Making a Reality. No Decision About Me, Without Me.* London: Kings Fund.

Coutts, P. (2007) *Mental Health, Recovery and Employment. SRN Discussion Paper Series,* Report No. 5. Glasgow: Scottish Recovery Network.

Davidson, L. (2005) "Recovery, self-management and the expert patient – Changing the culture of mental health from a UK perspective", *Journal of Mental Health*, 14(1): 25-35.

Davidson, L. and Roe, D. (2007) "Recovery from versus recovery in serious mental illness: One strategy for lessening confusion plaguing recovery", *Journal of Mental Health*, 16(4): 459-70.

Davidson, L., Chinman, M., Sells, D. and Rowe, M. (2006) "Peer support among adults with serious mental illness: A report from the field", *Schizophrenia Bulletin*, 32(3): 443-50.

Deegan, P.E. (2009) "Recovery: The lived experience of rehabilitation" in Reynolds, J., Muston, R., Heller, T., Leach, J., McCormick, M., Wallcraft, J. and Walsh, M. (eds) *Mental Health Still Matters.* Basingstoke: Palgrave Macmillan.

Deegan, P.E. (1996) *Recovery and the Conspiracy of Hope: There's a Person In Here,* The Sixth Annual Mental Health Services Conference of Australia and New Zealand. Brisbane, Australia.

Deegan, P.E. (2001) "Recovery as a self-directed process of healing and transformation", *Occupational Therapy in Mental Health*, 17(3/4): 5-21.

Dennis, C.L. (2003) "Peer support within a health care context: A concept analysis", *International Journal of Nursing Studies*, 40: 321-32.

Department of Health (2001) *The Journey to Recovery: The Government's Vision for Mental Health Care.* London: TSO.

Department of Health (2004) *Essential Shared Capabilities: A Framework for the Whole of the Mental Health Workforce.* London: TSO.

Department of Health (2006) *From Values to Action: The Chief Nursing Officer's Review of Mental Health Nursing.* London: Crown Copyright.

Department of Health (2010) *Equity and Excellence: Liberating the NHS.* London: Crown Copyright.

Department of Health (2011) *No Health without Mental Health: A Cross Governmental Mental Health Outcomes Strategy.* London: TSO.

Department of Health (2012) *No Decision About Me Without Me: Liberating the NHS.* London: TSO.

Dy, S. and Purnell, T. (2012) "Key concepts relevant to quality of complex and shared decision making in healthcare: A literature review", *Social Science and Medicine*, 74: 582-7.

Faulkner, A. and Kalathil, J. (2012) *The Freedom to Be, the Chance to Dream: Preserving User-led Peer Support in Mental Health,* commissioned by Together at: http://www.survivor-research.com/publications/99-the-freedom-to-be-the-chance-to-dream (accessed 29 May 2015).

Ferguson, I. (2007) "Increasing user choice or privatising risk? The Antinomies of Personalisation", *British Journal of Social Work*, 37: 387-403.

Fukui, S., Goscha, R., Rapp, C., Mabry, A., Liddy, P. and Marty, D. (2012) "Strengths model case management fidelity scores and client outcomes", *Psychiatric Services*, 163(7): 708-10.

Godin, P. (2004) "'You don't tick boxes on a form': A study of how community mental health nurses assess and manage risk", *Health, Risk & Society*, 6: 347-60.

Gosling, J. (2010) "The ethos of involvement as the route to recovery" in Weinstein, J. (ed.) *Mental Health Service User Involvement and Recovery.* London: Jessica Kingsley.

Hamann, J., Mendel, R., Buhner, M., Kissling, W., Cohen, R., Knipfer, E. and Eckstein, H.H. (2011) "How should patients behave to facilitate shared decision making: The doctors' view", *Health Expectations*, 15: 360–6.

Harding, C. (1988) "Course types in schizophrenia: An analysis of European and America studies", *Schizophrenia Bulletin*, 14: 633–43.

Harding, C., Brooks, G., Ashikaga, T., Strauss, J.S. and Breier, A. (1987) "The Vermont longitudinal study of persons with severe illness II: Long-term outcome of subjects who retrospectively met DSM-III criteria for schizophrenia", *American Journal of Psychiatry*, 144(6): 727–35.

Harper, D. and Speed, E. (2012) "Uncovering recovery: The resistible rise of recovery and resilience", *Studies in Social Justice*, 6(1): 9–25.

Higgens, A. and McBennett, P. (2007) "The petals of recovery in a mental health context", *British Journal of Nursing*, 16(4): 852–6.

Holloway, F. (2004) "Risk: More questions than answers", *Advances in Psychiatric Treatment*, 10: 273–4.

Imonioro, O. (2009) *The Recovery Star Model and Cultural Competency: Report of the Recovery Star*, BAME Pilot Study. London: Mental Health Providers Forum.

Joyce, T., Hazelton, M., McMillan, M. (2007) "Nurses with mental illness: Their workplace experiences", *International Journal of Mental Health Nursing*, 16: 373–80.

Kalathil, J., Collier, B., Bhakta, R., Daniel, O., Joseph, D. and Trivedi, P. (2011) *Recovery and Resilience: African, African-Caribbean and South Asian Women's Narratives of Recovering from Mental Distress*. London: Mental Health Foundation.

Kartalova-O'Doherty, Y. and Tedstone-Doherty, D. (2010) "Recovering from recurrent mental health problems: Giving up and fighting to get better", *International Journal of Mental Health Nursing*, 19: 3–15.

Larner, W. (2000) "Neo-liberalism; Policy, ideology, governmentality", *Studies in Political Economy*, 63: 5–25.

Mancini, M. (2007) "A qualitative analysis of turning points in the recovery process", *American Journal of Psychiatric Rehabilitation*, 10: 223–44.

Matthias, M., Salyers, M., Rollins, A. and Frankel, R. (2012) "Decision making in recovery orientated mental health care", *Psychiatric Rehabilitation Journal*, 35(4): 305–14.

Mead, S. and Copeland, M. (2000) "What recovery means to us: Consumer perspectives", *Community Mental Health Journey*, 36(3): 315–28.

Mental Health Foundation (2012) "Peer support". Available at: http://www.mentalhealth.org.uk/help-information/mental-health-a-z/P/peer-support/ (accessed October 2013).

Mind (2009) *Personalisation in Mental Health: Our View of the Evidence*. London: Mind.

Morgan, S. (2000) *Clinical Risk Management: A Clinical Tool and Practitioner Manual*. London: Sainsbury Centre for Mental Health.

Mountain, D. and Shah, P. (2008) "Recovery and the medical model", *Advances in Psychiatric Treatment*, 14: 241–4.

Muir-Cochrane, E. (2006) "Medical co-morbidity risk factors and barriers to care for people with schizophrenia", *Journal of Psychiatric and Mental Health Nursing*, 13: 447–52.

O'Byrne, P. and Holmes, D. (2007) "The micro-fascism of Plato's good citizen: Producing dis(order) through the construction of risk", *Nursing Philosophy*, 8(2): 92–101.

Pilgrim, D. (2005) "Protest and co-option: The voice of mental health service users" in Bell, A. and Lindley, P. (eds) *Beyond the Water Towers: The Unfinished Revolution in Mental Health Services 1985–2005*. London: Sainsbury Centre for Mental Health.

Pilgrim, D. (2008) "Recovery and mental health policy", *Chronic Illness*, 4: 295–304.

Rapp, C. and Goscha, R. (2012) *The Strengths Model: A Recovery Orientated Approach to Mental Health Services* (3rd edn). New York: Oxford University Press.

Raptopoulos, A. (2012) "Becoming an expert by experience" in Weinstein, J. (ed.) *Mental Health Service User Involvement and Recovery*. London: Jessica Kingsley.

Recovery in the Bin (2015) "18 key principles". Available at: http://studymore.org.uk/binrec.htm (accessed 29 May 2015).

Repper, J. and Carter, T. (2011) "A review of the literature on peer support in mental health services", *Journal of Mental Health*, 20(4): 392–411.

Repper, J. and Perkins, R. (2003) *Social Inclusion and Recovery: A Model for Mental Health Practice*. Edinburgh: Balliere Tindall.

Repper, J. and Perkins, R. (2009) "Recovery and social inclusion: Changing the mental health agenda" in Brooker, C. and Repper, J. (eds) *Mental Health From Policy to Practice*. Edinburgh: Churchill Livingstone.

Roberts, M. (2008) "Facilitating recovery by making sense of suffering: A Nietzschean perspective", *Journal of Psychiatric and Mental Health Nursing*, 15: 743–8.

Rose, N. (1999) *Powers of Freedom*. Cambridge: Cambridge University Press.

Schauer, C., Everett, A,. del Vecchio, P. and Anderson, L. (2007) "Promoting the value and practice of shared decision-making in mental health care", *Psychiatric Rehabilitation Journal*, 31(1): 54–61.

Scott, A. and Wilson, L. (2011) "Valued identities and deficit identities: Wellness recovery action planning and self-management in mental health", *Nursing Inquiry*, 18(1): 40–9.

Shepard, J., Boardman, G. and Slade, M. (2008) *Making Recovery a Reality*. London: Centre for Mental Health.

Social Perspectives Network (2007) *Whose Recovery Is It Anyway?* London: SPN.

Stalker, K. (2003) "Managing risk and uncertainty in social work: A literature review", *Journal of Social Work*, 3(2): 211–33.

Stickley, T. and Bonney, S. (2008) "Recovery and mental health: A review of the British literature", *Journal of Psychiatric and Mental Health Nursing*, 15(2): 140–53.

Stickley, T. and Wright, N. (2011) "The British research evidence for recovery. Papers published between 2006 and 2009 (inclusive). Part One: A review of the peer-reviewed literature using a systematic approach", *Journal of Psychiatric and Mental Health Nursing*, 18: 247–56.

Tew, J. (2013) "Recovery capital: What enables a sustainable recovery from mental health difficulties?", *European Journal of Social Work*, 16(3): 360–74.

Thompson, D. (ed.) (1996) *Oxford English Dictionary*. Oxford: Oxford University Press.

Vassilev, I. and Pilgrim, D. (2007) "Risk, trust and the myth of mental health services", *Journal of Mental Health*, 16(3): 347–57.

Walsh, J., Stevenson, C., Cutcliffe, J. and Zinck, K. (2008) "Creating a space for recovery focused psychiatric nursing care", *Nursing Inquiry*, 15(3): 251–9.

Wisdom, J., Bruce, K., Saedi, G., Weis, T. and Green, A. (2008) "'Stealing me from myself': Identity and recovery in personal accounts of mental illness", *Australian and New Zealand Journal of Psychiatry*, 42(6): 489–95.

Yates, I., Holmes, G. and Priest, H. (2012) "Recovery, place and community mental health services", *Journal of Mental Health*, 21(2): 104–13.

Zerubavel, N. and Wright, M. (2012) "The dilemma of the wounded healer" *Psychotherapy*, 49(4): 482–91.

11 | Valuing persons

Chapter Summary

This chapter will:

- Build on the ideas of recovery and autonomy introduced in previous chapters and apply them to the notion of "personhood".

- Identify the role of narrative in exploring the person within their experience of dementia.

- Identify how these principles and approaches could apply to working with people with other mental health problems.

- Consider the ethical implications of these approaches to care and how they may influence the practitioner's ability to demonstrate compassion and empathy within their practice.

- Offer case examples and exercises which will encourage you to apply the theoretical ideas introduced here to practice scenarios and reflect on the potential challenges which may present when implementing these approaches.

The concept of personhood

McCormack (2004) suggests the term "personhood" refers to the attributes of a person which represent humanness. For example, Cassel (1982) describes the different facets of a person as having a past, having cultural background, roles, relationships with "others", being political, doing things including action and creation, engaging in regular behaviours, having a body, a secret life, a perceived future and a transcendent or spiritual dimension. Cassel stresses that people do not exist without "others" and it is through relationship with "others" that the experience of a full sense of being a person evolves.

Cognitive perspectives of personhood

There are, however, problems with describing personhood as a status, or even where attributes are used as criteria for inclusion as a person. This is because it inevitably leads to exclusion for some. Post (1995) argues Western cultures are "hypercognitive" because cognition is prized to the point where other equally valuable aspects of being human are no longer considered important. Conventional Western philosophy tends to offer rigidly defined criteria for personhood and the status of being a person. Westernised values about the criteria or attributes for personhood highly prize cognitive attributes that enable functions such as rationality, informed choice, decision making and responsible action, with attributes such as expressiveness or the ability to feel and express emotion and spirituality having less value. This is exemplified by Quinton (1973), who offers five criteria for assigning the status of person to a human being: consciousness and self-consciousness; morality, in particular living by principles and accounting for one's own actions; rationality; agency; and the capacity to form and hold social relationships coming last.

Traditional Western ideas, according to Engelhardt (1986), portray persons as either a rational cognitive actor or a driven creature; the former from Kantian philosophy and the latter from Freudian psychology. Traditional explanations can be said to sit within a Cartesian duality framework, with mind and body and mind and brain essentially viewed as separate or dual. In many ways, traditional explanations based on Kantian ideals as exemplified by the Cartesian position are still dominating the personhood and person-centred literature, although the focus is moving more towards the brain than the mind and on one particular set of attributes of the brain; cognition (Dewing, 2008). Thus, a flaw with theories of personhood is that they either positively or inadvertently promote certain attributes (Post, 2006). Consequently, McCurdy (1998) and Post (1995), among others, have been highly critical of traditional personhood theories and describe that, as constructed so narrowly, they bestow a higher moral status on human beings who are regarded as self-legislating moral agents.

Additionally, John Locke famously identified the self with memory. Whereas Descartes had found the self in the immediate conscious experience of thinking ("I think, therefore I am"), Locke found identity in the extension of consciousness backward in time. In Locke's view, a person's identity extends to whatever of his or her past he or she can remember. Consequently, past experiences, thoughts, or actions that the person does not remember are not part of his identity. For Locke, identity and selfhood have nothing to do with continuity of the body, or even continuity of mind. Selfhood consists entirely in continuity of memory. A person who remembers nothing of his or her past literally has no identity (Leary and Tangney, 2002). Consequently, this implies a person who has suffered significant memory loss through trauma or disease has no identity.

Relational perspectives of personhood

Kitwood (1997) informs us that the term "personhood" can be found in three main types of literature: theology and spiritual, ethics, and social psychology. Each body of literature ascribes different weighting to certain attributes of personhood. For example, Tournier (1978), writing from a theological tradition, stresses the value of (Christian) faith-based subjective or inner experience, and considers personhood is arrived at through self-discovery carried along by a force coming from God. He argues that personhood is a potential, rather than a status; a current of energy that continually surges up. This would suggest personhood is more spiritual than cognitive or intellectual.

Several psychological perspectives have common elements. Harré (1998) describes personhood as a threefold phenomenon: a sense of personal distinctiveness, a sense of personal continuity and a sense of personal autonomy. Heron (1992) and Kitwood (1997) refer to transcendence (a state of going beyond the material or usual existence) as a necessary feature in descriptions of personhood. Rogers (1980) and Maslow (1970), as does Heron (1992), focus on the future and achievement of full potential through continuing cycles or states of personal development as a result of entering into, being affected by and reflecting on life experiences. Thus suggesting personhood is dynamic, both a state in the here and now, but also with future potential to evolve.

Social psychology descriptions draw on other perspectives such as spirituality, or social constructionism. Some – for example, Heron (1992) – integrate Eastern perspectives into Western thinking on personhood. Heron sets outs a series of evolutionary levels to becoming a more complete person. The person is progressively actualised through a series of eight states of personhood (primal person, spontaneous person, compulsive person, conventional person, creative person, self-creating person, self-transfiguring person and charismatic person), some of which run concurrently; thus, personhood is always present and always has potential.

Ideas such as these challenge the notion that personhood is a fixed status and one that can be switched on or off. They contradict traditional approaches focusing on seeing a person as a status or position and the preoccupation with exploring when status starts and ends and under what conditions it can be withdrawn. Further, such ideas suggest, personhood evolves and comes into an ever-increasing presence over time.

Exercise 11.1

- Reflect on the factors and influences which you feel make you who you are.
- Compare these to the criteria or definitions discussed above.
- Consider your position in relation to these arguments.
- Consider how you would explain the concept of personhood to a friend or colleague.

Personhood and its relationship with dementia

Dementia is associated with a progressive decline in cognitive functions. Therefore, the disease has historically been assumed to strip the individual of their personhood status – leading, for example, to a loss of self (Bartlett and O'Connor 2010). Within this perspective, the person with dementia is considered mindless; with the mind either somewhere else or no longer existing. Another consequence is the body and embodied experience is ignored, hence the "empty shell" scenario in dementia described by Gubrium (1986). In the late 1980s, the notion of "personhood" was reconceptualised and introduced into the dementia literature as a critical component of the dementia experience. For example, Tom Kitwood, perhaps one of the most recognised pioneers of this approach, defined personhood as "a standing or status that is bestowed upon one human being by others in the context of particular social relationships and institutional arrangements" (Kitwood, 1997: 7). Kitwood, soon followed by others, began to stress the influence of interpersonal relations as an essential aspect for understanding the dementia experience, theorising that at least some of the deterioration seen in persons with dementia was caused not by the disease process itself but, rather, by how the person was treated, which resulted in his or her subsequent loss of personhood (Kitwood and Bredin, 1991 Sabat and Harré, 1997).

Kitwood (1997: 14) describes a set of interpersonal processes occurring between people when a person with dementia enters a social arena, which results in the erosion of person-hood and consequent invisibility for the person with dementia, while simultaneously making very visible the effects of dementia. Similarly, Sabat (2001) contends that the way people with dementia are socially positioned affects how they are related to, considered and conceptual-ised; this, in turn, affects how they are as people, their personhood, behaviours and interac-tions with another. Thus, rather than a person with dementia, what emerges is a "demented" human being in need of "micro-management". Additionally, Kitwood controversially intro-duces the concept of rementia or rementing. By this, Kitwood (1997) means there remains the possibility of a return, however, temporary, to some previous level of ability and function. Thus, dementia is seen not as an irreversible process of decline but, rather, as a dialectical process mediated by a number of factors, such as interpersonal relationships, positioning by 'others', and by the quality or culture of care. Accepting the possibility of rementia means persons with dementia have capacity for increased communication, feeling and learning, which it has generally been thought is not possible (Mozley et al., 1999; Dewing, 2002).

Kitwood (1997) further argues the psycho-social processes are underpinned by a social psychology that is malignant in its effects (even where the intention might be positive). Sabat (2001) builds on Kitwood's work, describing this process as malignant positioning, whereby the person with dementia is stripped of their primary social persona and rights, becomes a "patient" and is seen by "others" as being inferior and having less ability and status in relationship with "others". Kitwood (1997) describes two sets of deep-rooted anxi-eties on which malignant social psychology is founded; a fear of becoming frail and highly dependent through memory loss, and a fear of long drawn out dying in old age. Dementia can be said to be the paradigm case for such anxieties. Given Westernised culture's value on normative brain function, particularly memory (Post, 2006), when dementia "shatters" brain and mind function, what is left – an empty shell – is not seen as having much value. More than this, what is left is even considered as dangerous, and to be controlled and avoided.

Kitwood and Post, argue that, despite many losses in function and capacity, persons with dementia do not lose their essential non-cognitive attributes of humanity. However, there is little doubt persons with dementia become different in some ways to who they were before the onset of dementia. That others around the person with dementia consequently see them as a lesser or non-person does not mean, in an absolute moral sense, they are lesser. Kitwood (1997) forcefully concludes that historical patterns in care of older people with dementia in Western cultures meant care practices had residues of bestialisation, attributes of moral deficit, warehousing and unnecessary use of the medical model. It is this position he uses as a basis for developing a number of specific categories and levels of malignant social psychology. These are being widely taken up as indicators of non-person-centred care and also feature in the observation method, Dementia Care Mapping (Innes and Surr, 2001).

Application of personhood to mental health practice

The concept of "person" is one of the foundations of nursing theories and models yet, in nursing, the focus is on the person as a patient and, most recently, on patient-centred care. Moving from patient-centred to person-centred care is not simply about adopting new terminology but, rather, is an opportunity to break away from any historic association of care with depersonalised and institutionalised care (Nolan et al, 2001:13) and revisit the values on which practice is based. Person-centred practice requires health care professionals to put the person first and the evidence base for technical or clinical interventions second (McCormack and Reed, 2006).

Kitwood (1997) identified a number of psychological and social factors which people need to have met in order to maintain wellbeing. To practice person-centred care it is necessary to focus on these needs by using responses and approaches that help to:

Uphold the person's identity
For example:

- Respecting the person by addressing them by the name they wish to be called.
- Seeking out opportunities to explore the life history of the person through talking to friends and family members.

Engage the person in occupation
For example:

- Supporting and encouraging the person to engage in meaningful tasks at whatever level the person is able and comfortable to do.

Provide comfort
For example:

- Demonstrating warmth and acceptance of the person when talking with them.

Enable attachment
For example:

- Recognising the important feelings a person may have for past or present relationships.
- Being sensitive to recognise the person's sense of reality.

Include the person in what is happening
For example:

- Enabling a person to be involved both physically and psychologically.

Upholding these needs will have an effect on the person's wellbeing. Not having these needs met will potentially lead to ill-being – that is, feelings of distress and discomfort.

Promotion of personhood has meant that the way people are spoken about has improved dramatically since the turn of the millennium. For example, until relatively recently, older people with dementia were often described as though they were living "the death that leaves the body behind" or a "social death" (Sweeting and Gilhooly, 1997). Care providers were therefore urged to "look after the carer" since the person with dementia had, to all appearances, died and gone (Bartlett and O'Connor, 2010). In addition, people with dementia were generally regarded as a "sufferer" lacking insight into, and ability to articulate, their situation. This discourse silenced people with dementia. However, since attention was drawn to personhood and the exclusion of the perspectives of persons with dementia in understanding and influencing the dementia experience, the focus has shifted to incorporating the voices and understandings of persons with dementia into both research and practice.

A result of this shift is that, gradually, research has begun to emerge aimed at capturing the perspectives of persons with dementia. This body of research now clearly documents that persons with dementia are often quite aware of their situation, and can contribute important and unique insights about their experiences and needs. The net result is that, since the introduction of personhood into the dementia literature, research and practice has shifted from failing even to consider whether persons with dementia have anything to say, to acknowledging that, indeed, they do and recognising the importance of hearing their perspectives. Emphasis is now being placed on seeking creative and innovative methods to overcome communication deficits associated with the condition. The use of a personhood lens has effectively and explicitly brought the person with dementia into the picture (Bartlett and O'Connor, 2010).

A second way that the shift to personhood has contributed to transformations in the culture of dementia care is by offering hope that positive change can occur. Kitwood (1997) and others clearly accorded primacy to the interpersonal environment for helping to shape the dementia experience; the linear link between personal experience of deterioration and organic changes is challenged and one's interactions with one's worlds are recognised as having the potential to foster or erode one's sense of personal competence, uniqueness and, hence, personhood. This understanding promotes a shift from the disease process itself to the interpersonal environment as the focus of efforts for change. Countering the pessimism and hopelessness historically attached to working with "the demented", the new vision offers exciting possibilities for positively influencing the dementia experience; neurological factors might not be readily modified but there is growing evidence that psychosocial interventions, environmental changes and assistive technologies can mitigate the extent of the disability and improve quality of life (Bartlett and O'Connor 2010). A focus on personhood, then, offers hope and validates the importance of developing person-centred approaches to practice and research.

Although there is developmental work being performed to offer alternative framings or understandings of dementia and to promote better care for older people with dementia, for most health care professionals person-centred care continues to remain either an ideal, to be elusive, or as McCarthy (2006) found, professionals themselves are sceptical about the theory of person-centredness actually working in practice. As a consequence, people with dementia, both as individuals and collectively, are still continually subjected to debate over the legitimacy of personhood in regard to health care. In practice settings, it is still common to encounter situations where people with dementia are positioned as "other" and related to as "it" in varying degrees. This has, as Kitwood and Bredin (1991) say, created a misplaced licence for a different type of approach to relationships and care. Whereas, Kitwood (1997) proposes all persons have fundamental needs for love, inclusion, attachment, comfort, identity and occupation which, it could be argued, become more critical with dementia.

❏ **Case Example 11.1**

You walk onto a health care of the older adult ward and take a moment to observe your surroundings. The ward is stark, rather cold and impersonal. You observe six older men in a bay. Two are sitting by their beds asleep in a chair, one is shouting out for his wife, two are laid in their beds appearing unaware and the last is attempting to climb out of his bed without support. You notice a nurse and a health care assistant run to the chap who is climbing out of his bed and hear one speak sternly to him and the other reprimand him for attempting to move. They return him to his bed and leave the bay without interacting with the remaining patients.

- In light of the theoretical discussion presented above, list 10 ways in which your observations are in conflict with promoting a person-centred approach to practice.
- Suggest ways in which the environment and approach of the health care staff could be changed in order to improve this situation.

The role of biographical narrative in dementia care

In light of these arguments, it is relevant to consider the role of narrative in relation to both improving dementia care and its wider role in understanding the person's experience of mental distress, thus promoting empathy and compassion. This is due to the claim that narrative approaches can be effective in enhancing the relationship between the patient and the practitioner, and address issues associated with detached and impersonal care environments (Kirkpatrick, 2008). They provide the person with opportunities, if they so desire to talk about their life experiences – family, friends, work history, hobbies – often using photographs and personal belongings as triggers to discussion. Exploring a person's past and present lives with them, particularly the circumstances which have shaped their experiences potentially provides greater insights into their needs and aspirations (IRISS 2010)

Listening to a person's life story is a powerful way of showing that they are valued as an individual and may also have a cathartic affect. The person's stories may subsequently be recorded formally in a life story book – either by the patient themselves, their family carers, or members of the ward team – thereby assisting practitioners to focus their efforts on the individual's needs in a manner consistent with their life perspectives (Patton 2012). A biographical approach thus enables practitioners to gain a better understanding of the person by providing knowledge which may directly influence decisions made about appropriate care. A biographical approach is valued by older people themselves. The older participants in the study by Nolan et al. (2001) indicated that they wanted to have their personal biographies recognised and valued as a basis for individualised care. Similarly, the evaluation by McKee et al. (2002: 13) of the impact of reminiscence on the quality of life of older people concluded that most older people in long-term care enjoyed talking about their lives, and that being listened to accorded personhood, identity and significance to the older person. Relatives also appreciate staff taking an interest in the older person's life and focusing on more than their physical needs (Nagai-Jacobson and Burkhardt, 1996).

Exercise 11.2

- How might listening to the story of a person with a diagnosis of dementia impact on person-centred approaches to care?
- What might be the difficulties of gaining the story of a person who has a diagnosis of dementia?
- How might you overcome these difficulties?
- How might the principles and approaches identified so far in this chapter be applied to working with people with other mental health problems?
- What would be the similarities and differences?

Compassion and empathy

The descriptions of both person-centred care and narrative approaches have recognised the importance of empathy, which is a core component of compassion. Buddhism defines compassion as a nonjudgemental open heartedness to the suffering of self and others with a strong desire to alleviate suffering in all living things (Dalai Lama, 1995; 2001). Developing compassion for self and others is central to the processes of reducing suffering. Buddhist concepts of compassion are based on the idea that we suffer because we are ignorant of how our minds really are. Western philosophers have also given much thought to the issue and value of compassion. Aristotle suggested compassion "is a painful emotion directed at the other's misfortune or suffering" (Nussbaum, 2003: 306). Nussbaum (2003) suggested three key cognitive elements to Aristotle's view, summarised as: The first cognitive element of compassion is a belief or appraisal that the suffering is serious, rather than trivial. The second is the belief that the person does not deserve the suffering. The third is the belief that the possibilities of the person who experiences the emotions are similar to those of the sufferer.

Compassion also links to a Buddhist notion of common humanity – that we all find ourselves on this planet constituted by a set of genes and shaped by our social conditions, none of which we choose. Also, that we are all seeking to avoid suffering and to prosper guided only by our evolved minds and social conditioning. We can also grasp that, in each human being, is a struggling consciousness and had we been born with the same genes and life circumstances as someone else then "I" would be "him or her".

Gilbert (2005) identifies the following facets which constitute a compassionate mind and maintains that the desire to care for another activates these processes: care for wellbeing, distress and the need for sensitivity, sympathy, distress tolerance, empathy, non-judgement and warmth. Alternatively, threat-focused emotions act to turn off these components and result in ones which are focused on self-preservation and protection.

Care for wellbeing: This involves a motivation to be caring of others' distress and also to promote their wellbeing. We can direct these desires to all living things and the environment. When directed at the self, the self becomes focused on genuine desires to nurture the self. Caring for the self is about looking after and is different to the more competitive goal of promoting the self for competitive advantage.

Distress and the need for sensitivity: This involves a capacity to be sensitive to the nature and complexity of distress; to be able to read emotion cues and have an awareness of distress. It also involves the emotional ability to be sensitive to other people's needs and requirements that will help them prosper. When directed at the self, it involves the ability to be sensitive to one's own distress and needs, rather than condemning, ignoring or avoiding them.

Sympathy: Sympathy is the ability to be emotionally moved by both the distress and the joys of other people. We can lose feelings of sympathy for others, or for the harm we do them, if we see them as threats to ourselves. Sympathy for the pain of our friends is easier than for our enemies and, indeed, seeing our enemies suffer may be felt positively. One reason for this is because too much sympathy (when we need to defend ourselves or only focus on our own self-interests) could stop us taking protective actions. So, we can see that, when threatened, our brains may actual turn off the "sympathy module".

Distress tolerance: Research has shown that we can, at times, feel overwhelmed by the distress of others, become distressed ourselves and feel that there is nothing we can do to help. These are unpleasant feelings that we might try to avoid. The ability to stay with, tolerate and think about the distress of others is an important element of compassion. Health care professionals may struggle to tolerate painful feelings in their patients and engage in rescuing behaviours. It is possible for people to be emotionally sensitive and sympathetic but to feel overwhelmed by distress and, thus, avoidant or try to be over-controlling.

For some people, inner feelings, thoughts, memories, fantasies or situations can be frightening; they engage in a range of safety strategies to try to avoid or rid themselves of them. Learning how to accept, tolerate and "bear" painful emotions and to reduce emotional intolerance and avoidance can be of key importance to change. Distress tolerance related to oneself involves abilities to tolerate aversive emotions, alter negative thoughts about emotions, and reduce avoidance.

Empathy: Empathy involves emotional resonance with the other, trying to put oneself in their shoes, feeling and thinking in a similar way, but also with cognitive awareness about the reasons for others people's behaviour, intentions, feelings and motivations.

Nonjudgement: Nonjudgement is the ability to engage with the complexities of people's (and our own) emotions and lives without judging them in a condemning fashion. This is not, then, to deny responsibility but, rather, to understand these processes, and what we need to do to help ourselves become mindfully and compassionately responsible for our actions. It is through becoming compassionate (rather than condemning) and harnessing compassionate qualities of the mind that opens the door for understanding the passions of our evolved minds and taking responsibility for them.

Warmth: This is an emotional quality of gentleness and kindness that operates through all the facets we have just discussed. Warmth is a difficult quality to define accurately but it involves being nonthreatening while having a genuine caring orientation. Commonly, experiences of warmth are noted by non-verbal communications and interpersonal manner. People who are viewed as warm as usually seen as safe and nonthreatening, but not dull or passive – they have a calming impact on the minds of others.

Compassion in health care services is currently the source of a great deal of media controversy as a result of significant failures within the health care system which have been partly attributed to a lack of compassion amongst the health care workforce (Francis, 2010). The discussion above identifies the facets of a compassionate mind. You might believe that you possess these qualities and can identify how they are influential in the way you approach and communicate with patients. However, it is evident factors which impinge on an individual's ability to express compassion within the health care environment are present. Gilbert (2005) suggests that the lack of compassion expressed in health care is as a result of the health care professionals' constant defensive reaction to the threat culture of the health service. In a way, compassion begins by recognising that many of our mental mechanisms are survival-oriented, trying as best they can to enact strategies that maximise our survival and protect us from harm. If some of our basic emotions and fears are triggered, these can then drive thinking and behaviour. "Thinking" is then recruited to serve our desires for vengeance or self-protection, not subdue them.

Exercise 11.3

Refer back to the Case Example 11.1. This time, consider the situation from the perspective of the nurse and the health care assistant. Identify the factors which might have contributed to her lack of compassion towards the man getting out of his bed and the other patients in the bay.

CONCLUSION

This chapter has discussed the related concepts of personhood, narrative, compassion and empathy. It has applied them to a health care context to identify how nursing practice can benefit from approaches which attempt to encompass these ideas. It is proposed that current criticisms of the lack of compassion and person-centred care observed in health care services could be explained by an individual's self-protective response to the threat culture. This exists as a result of poor resources and negative media representations which influence public perception. In this environment, it is likely that the practitioner will feel unable to invest the time or emotion in approaches which promote person-centred care. It is pertinent, therefore, to consider ways of harnessing the compassion mind of health care professionals. The role of narrative as a precursor for change could be considered as part of this agenda.

KEY TERMS

Personhood the way in which the factors which make us who we are are related to by others and regarded by society

Empathy the ability to view a situation from another perspective and understand their response to it

Compassion a bio-psycho-social response initiated by a desire to care for another

FURTHER READING

Mental Heath Foundation: http://www.mentalhealth.org.uk/help-information/mental-health -a-z/R/recovery/

> Aims to promote recovery, survival or prevention of mental health problems through research, campaigning and raising awareness.

Compassionate Mind Foundation: http://www.compassionatemind.co.uk

> Aims to promote wellbeing through the scientific understanding and application of compassion founded by Paul Gilbert.

Dementia Partnership: http://www.dementiapartnerships.org.uk

> A resource for people, partnerships and networks working to improve outcomes for people living with dementia.

There is an extensive philosophical literature linking values, personhood and mental distress. Early examples from the journal *Philosophy, Psychiatry and Psychology* include Moore et al. (1994) and Sabat and Harré (1997). The edited collection by Hughes et al. (2006) includes a range of more recent work by key authors. Stephen Sabat has drawn together his work on personhood and dementia in his book *The Experience of Alzheimer's Disease: Life through a Tangled Veil* (2001). This includes good practice examples of the communication skills that crucially support compassionate and empowering care. An account of the relationship between values-based practice, personhood and spiriitual aspects of healing inspired by Paul Tournier's work is developed with a detailed case example in Atwell and Fulford (2006). An explicitly values-based approach to supporting good practice in dementia care is Julian Hughes' and Toby Williamson's (forthcoming) *The Dementia Manifesto: Values-Based Practice (VBP) and Dementia Care.*

> Bartlett, R. and O'Connor, D. (2010) *Broadening the Dementia Debate: Towards Social Citizenship.* The Policy Press: University of Bristol

> IRISS (2010) "Supporting those with dementia: Reminiscence therapy and life story work" *Insights No. 4.* The Institute for Research and Innovation in Social Services

> Pattoni, L. (2012) "Strengths-based approaches for working with individuals". *Insights No 16.* The Institute for Research and Innovation in Social Services

> Sweeting, H. and Gilhooly, M. (1997), "Dementia and the phenomenon of social death", *Sociology of Health and Illness* 19:1, 93-117.

REFERENCES

Adams, T. (2005) "Communication and interaction within dementia care triads: Developing a theory for relationship-centred care", *Dementia International Journal of Social Research and Practice,* 4: 185–205

Atwell, R. and Fulford, K.W.M. (2006) "The Christian tradition of spiritual direction as a sketch for a strong theology of diversity" in Cox, J., Campbell, A.V. and Fulford, K.W.M. (eds) *Medicine of the Person: Faith, Science and Values in Health Care Provision*. London: Jessica Kingsley.

Bartlett, R. and O'Connor, D. (2010) *Broadening the Dementia Debate: Towards Social Citizenship*. Bristol: Policy Press.

Bowlby, J. (1969) *Attachment: Attachment and Loss*, Volume 1., inc., London: Hogarth Press.

Bowlby, J. (1973) *Separation, Anxiety and Anger. Attachment and Loss*, Volume 1., inc., London: Hogarth Press.

Cassel, E.J. (1982) "The nature of suffering", *New England Journal of Medicine*, 306: 639–45.

Dalai Lama (1995) *The Power of Compassion*. India: HarperCollins.

Dalai Lama (2001) *An Open Heart: Practising Compassion in Everyday Life*, edited by N. Vreeland. London: Hodder & Stoughton.

Dewing, J. (2002) "From ritual to relationship: A person centred approach to consent in qualitative research with older people who have a dementia", *Dementia: The International Journal of Social Research & Practice*, 1: 156–71.

Dewing, J. (2008) "Personhood and dementia: Revisiting Tom Kitwood's ideas", *International Journal of Older People Nursing*, 3(1): 3–13.

Downs, M., Clare, L. and Mackenzie, J. (2006) "Understandings of dementia: Explanatory models and their implications for the person with dementia and therapeutic effort" in *Dementia: Mind, Meaning and the Person*, (Hughes, J.C., Louw. S.J. and Sabat, S.R. (eds). Oxford: Oxford University Press.

Engelhardt, H.T. (1986) *The Foundations of Bioethics*. New York, NY: Oxford University Press.

Francis, R. (2010) *Final Report of The Independent Inquiry Into Care Provided By Mid Staffordshire NHS Foundation Trust*. London: TSO.

Frank, A.W. (2000) "The standpoint of storyteller", *Qualitative Health Research*, 10: 354–65.

Geary, D.C. (2000) "Evolution and proximate expression of human parental investment", *Psychological Bulletin*, 126: 55–77.

Gerhardt, S. (2004) *Why Love Matters. How Affection Shapes a Baby's Brain*. London: Brunner-Routledge.

Gilbert, P. (2005) *Compassion: Conceptualisations, Research and Use in Psychotherapy*. London: Routledge.

Gubrium, J. (1986) *Old Timers and Alzheimer's: The Descriptive Organisation of Senility*. London, UK: Jai Press.

Harding, N. and Palfrey, C. (1997) *The Social Construction of Dementia. Confused Professionals?* London: Jessica Kingsley.

Harré, R. (1998) *The Singular Self: An Introduction to the Psychology of Personhood*. London: Sage.

Heron, J. (1992) *Feeling and Personhood*. London: Sage.

Hughes, J.C., Louw, S.J. and Sabat, S.R. (eds) (2006) *Dementia: Mind Meaning and the Person*. Oxford: Oxford University Press.

Hughes, J.C. and Williamson, T. (forthcoming, 2015) *The Dementia Manifesto: Values-Based Practice (VBP) and Dementia Care*. Cambridge: Cambridge University Press.

Innes, A. and Surr, C. (2001) "Measuring the well-being of people with dementia living in formal care settings: The use of dementia care mapping", *Aging & Mental Health*, 5: 258–68.

RISS (2010) "Supporting those with dementia: Reminiscence therapy and life story work", *Insights No 4*. London: Institute for Research and Innovation in Social Services.

Jacobson, N. (2001) "Experiencing recovery: A dimensional analysis of recovery narratives", *Psychiatric Rehabilitation Journal*, 24: 248–56.

Kirkpatrick, H. (2008) "A narrative framework for understanding experience of people with severe mental illness", *Archives of Psychiatric Nursing*, 22(2): 61–8.

Kitwood, T. (1993) "Person and process in dementia", *International Journal of Psychiatry*, 8: 541–5.

Kitwood, T. (1997) *Dementia Reconsidered: The Person Comes First.* Buckingham, UK: Open University Press.

Kitwood, T. and Bredin, K. (1991) *Person to Person: A Guide to the Care of Those with Failing Mental Powers* (2nd edn). Loughton, UK: Gale Centre.

Leary, M.R. and Tangney, J. (eds) (2002) *Handbook of Self and Identity.* New York: Guilford Press.

Maslow, A. (1970) *Motivation and Personality* (2nd edn). New York: Harper & Rowe.

McCarthy, B. (2006) "Translating person-centred care: A case study of preceptor nurses and their teaching practices in acute care areas", *Journal of Clinical Nursing*, 15: 629–38.

McCormack, B. (2003) "A conceptual framework for person-centred practice with older people", *International Journal of Nursing Practice*, 9: 202–9.

McCormack, B. (2004) "Person-centredness in gerontological nursing: An overview of the literature", *Journal of Clinical Nursing*, 13: 31–8.

McCormack, B. and Reed, J. (2006) "Editorial: Evidence-based health-care – A lot of bull?", *International Journal of Older Peoples Nursing*, 1: 129–30.

McCurdy, D.B. (1998) "Personhood, spirituality, and hope in the care of human beings with dementia", *Journal of Clinical Ethics*, 9: 81–91.

McKee, K., Wilson, F., Elford, H., Goudie, F., Chung, M.C., Bolton, G. and Hinchliff, S. (2002) *Evaluating the Impact of Reminiscence on the Quality of Life of Older People.* Sheffield: Sheffield Institute of Studies on Ageing, University of Sheffield.

Moore, A., Hope, T. and Fulford, K.W.M. (1994) "Mild mania and well-being", *Philosophy, Psychiatry, & Psychology*, 1(3): 165–78.

Mozley, C.G., Huxley, P., Sutcliffe, C., Bagley, H., Burns, A., Challis, D. and Cordingley, L. (1999) "'Not knowing where I am doesn't mean I don't know what I like': Cognitive impairment and quality of life responses in elderly people", *International Journal of Geriatric Psychiatry*, 14: 776–83.

Nagai-Jacobson, M.G. and Burkhardt, M.A. (1996) "Viewing persons as stories: A perspective for holistic care", *Alternative Therapies*, 2, 54–8.

Nolan, M., Davies, S. and Grant, G. (2001) "Integrating Perspectives" in *Working with Older People and Their Families: Key Issues in Policy and Practice*, Nolan, M., Davies, S. and Grant, G. (eds). Buckingham: Open University Press.

Nolan, M.R., Davis, S. and Grant, G. (eds) (2003) *Working with Older People and Their Families: Key Issues in Policy and Practice.* Buckingham: Open University Press.

Nussbaum, M. (2003) "Capabilities as fundamental entitlements: Sen and social justice", *Feminist Economics*, 9 (2–3): 33–59.

Pattoni, L. (2012) "Strengths-based approaches for working with individuals", *Insights No. 16.* London Institute for Research and Innovation in Social Services.

Post, S.G. (1995) *The Moral Challenge of Alzheimer's Disease.* Baltimore, MD: John Hopkins University Press.

Post, S.G. (2006) "Respectare: Moral respect for the lives of the deeply forgetful" in *Dementia: Mind Meaning and the Person*, Hughes, J.C., Louw, S.J. and Sabat, S.R. (eds). Oxford: Oxford University Press.

Quintin, A. (1973) *The Nature of Things.* London: Routledge.

Rappaport, J. (2000) "1999 Seymour B. Sarason Award. Community narratives: Tales of terror and joy" *American Journal of Community Psychology*, 28: 1–24.

Redman, R. (2005) "The power of narratives", *Research and Theory for Nursing Practice: An International Journal*, 19: 5–7.

Reed, J. and Ground, I. (1997) *Philosophy for Nursing.* London: Arnold.

Rogers, C. (1980) *A Way of Being.* New York: Houghton Mifflin.

Sabat, S.R. (2001) *The Experience of Alzheimer's Disease - Life Through a Tangled Veil*. Oxford: Blackwell.

Sabat, S.R. and Harré, R. (1997) "The Alzheimer's disease sufferer as semiotic subject", *Philosophy, Psychiatry, & Psychology*, 4(2): 145–60.

Sweeting, H. and Gilhooly, M. (1997) "Dementia and the social phenomenon of social death", *Sociology of Health and Illness*, 19(1): 93–117.

Tournier, P. (1978) *Meaning of Persons*. London: SCM Press.

Woods, R.T. (2001) "Discovering the person with Alzheimer's disease: Cognitive, emotional and behavioural aspects", *Ageing and Mental Health*, 5(Suppl. 1): S7–S16.

12 | Daring to care: Maintaining our values in practice

Chapter Summary

This chapter will:

- Summarise and emphasise the key themes of the book.
- Explore of the challenge of maintaining our values in practice.
- Look at the particular difficulties this raises in the transition from student to professional and review some of the resources that can support us in this.

Key themes of the book

Our book began with the familiar consideration of ethical theories for mental health practice, and the importance of understanding four such theories: deontology, consequentialism, virtue ethics and an ethics of care. We then considered how these theories might be embedded in a practical approach for health care, which is commonly known as "principlism" (Beauchamp and Childress, 2012). We outlined the four principles of biomedical ethics: beneficence, non-maleficence, autonomy and justice, and considered how they might help us in ethical reasoning when we face dilemmas in practice.

However, we quickly realised that even a detailed understanding and application of ethical theories and principles does not give us straightforward answers to ethical issues in health care practice. We considered the complex case of giving a person medication against their will in the reflective example in Chapter 1, and we came to the conclusion that there was no straightforward manner in which to apply a principle to the case which would give us an obvious answer to balancing the relative demands of autonomy versus beneficence. Ethical reasoning needed to be supplemented with a richer context of understanding the situation in which a decision takes place. A consideration of narrative ethics led us to the recognition of the importance of a context wider than ethical principles alone (while not forgetting the importance of ethical theories and principles).

The diversity of values

We found that wider context embedded in what we called the "tool kit" for working with values and we explored, in particular, the skills-based approach of values-based practice. Throughout the book, we have emphasised and explored three key points about values and values-based practice. First, values are diverse and plural. We have discussed how the plurality of different values and interpretations of mental distress impact on a range of scenarios and key processes in mental health care. We have discussed decisions about risk in Chapter 7, values in diagnosis and assessment in Chapters 8 and 9, and what it might mean to value identity and personhood in Chapter 11. We have seen how even the process of naming disorders in mental health care brings in a diversity of values and perspectives. In Chapter 6, we considered the diversity of survivor voices in mental health care and how these voices have, too often, been silenced in the history of psychiatry, to the extent that the understanding of madness became what Foucault famously termed a "monologue of reason about madness" (Foucault, 1993). This central chapter of our book demonstrated that any values-based practice that is truly inclusive needs to work with the perspective and values of the service user at the heart of any care. Indeed, the story of Sally Coombs, to which we returned throughout the book, demonstrated the difficulties that arise if we presume that we know and understand the values of the person at the centre of care, without truly attempting to listen and understand them.

Diversity and dissensus

The diversity and plurality of values with the service user's perspective as the key narrative is central to values-based practice. Nevertheless, conflicts still arise. Therefore, the second key point we have emphasised is that working with conflicts in values is the norm, rather than the exception, in mental health care. Throughout the book, our reflective examples have drawn your attention to the multiple difficulties, dilemmas and demands of mental health practice. The key task of the mental health practitioner is neither to dissolve nor resolve these conflicts but, rather, to work with them creatively and respectfully – the aim being to balance conflicting demands according to the particular circumstances presented by a given situation. In Chapters 3 and 4, we considered how an appreciation of values in health care enables us to work in this balanced way with a plurality of perspectives that are in conflict without completely rejecting any one perspective. The important concept of "dissensus" seeks to capture the idea of keeping different values in play with one or another perspective coming to the fore according to the balance required in any particular context. When thinking through participation in shared decision making and recovery, which we discussed extensively in Chapters 5, 6 and 10, it is important to work through conflict, while integrating the highest level of involvement for the service user and the least amount of restriction.

Power inequalities

This emphasis on plurality and diversity appears highly democratic and unproblematic. Indeed, the NHS constitution emphasises the right of service users to make choices, to be involved in decisions and to be given appropriate treatment (Department of Health, 2009). This is why values-based practice starts from the principle of mutual respect.

However, the reality is that service users often do not feel involved in their care (Karnieli-Miller and Eiskovits, 2009). An emphasis on diversity of values and perspectives needs to be supplemented with an understanding and awareness of power inequalities and discrimination that continues in mental health care. We introduced the concept of power in Chapter 5 and we have considered the impact of inequalities in power throughout this book. We have emphasised the discrimination that many people face based on race, gender and sexuality. This discrimination is compounded when it encounters notions of madness and mental illness. In Chapter 8, we explored the important problem of how diagnostic categories such as schizophrenia can lead to added discrimination for members of minority ethnic groups facing the pressures of cultural misunderstanding, racism and migration. In Chapter 6, we considered the manner in which service user voices are silenced and represented in psychiatric care and mental health literature. As Kirmayer (2012) has pointed out, skills-based approaches to increasing work with a diversity of values are of only limited use without acknowledging power imbalances. He writes that we need to be open to different understandings, and to try and make the clinical encounter safer by "acknowledging and addressing structural inequality" (Kirmayer, 2012: 251). This leads us to the third key point about values-based practice, which is concerned with awareness of values.

Awareness of values

By now, the reader of this book should be attuned to an awareness of values in situations, and an awareness of power differentials and potential inequalities that exist in mental health care. Throughout the book, we have provided reflective examples and exercises for the reader to engage with their values, and to stimulate reflection and awareness. Awareness of values not only brings conflicts to the fore, but also shared goals that might lie beneath those conflicts. In Sally Coombs' story, we emphasised conflicts between practitioners over care that expressed diverse values, but that were both based on a genuine desire to work for the benefit of Sally. However, as we saw also, it was Sally's perspective that was sadly missing, and it took work to bring that key perspective into play.

We return now to the importance of raising awareness of values as a key resource, among others, for maintaining our values of care. We look first at the challenges of maintaining our values particularly as these arise in the transition from student to professional status.

The challenge of maintaining our values in practice

Mead (1934) noted that internalisation of values is integral to the development of a socially active individual because considering oneself as a "moral being" is fundamental to becoming a professional. Mackintosh (2006) however, identified a juxtaposition between different and opposing sets of values within health care. She maintains that the emotional caring ethos of the profession is discouraged in order for the practitioner to prioritise tasks. This is at the expense of providing emotional support and developing a personal relationship with the service user, which is assumed to be an essential element of the health care professional's role. This was found to result in personal disillusionment among health care students and the development of cynical attitudes about the caring aspect of their role. These findings are reinforced by Curtis et al. (2012) who conducted a grounded theory analysis of interviews with student nurses. The data indicates that students aspire to the professional ideal of compassionate practice, although they have concerns about how compassionate practice might fit within the nursing role because of constraints in practice. Students felt vulnerable to dissonance between professional ideals and practice reality, and managed their uncertainty by attempting to balance the intention to uphold professional ideals and challenge constraints, while accepting the realisation that they might need to adapt their ideals and conform to constraints.

Barnard et al (2008) has written about issues of a values base and professionalisation in social work practice, and how social work students have increasingly come to adopt more managerial and risk averse values due to changes in the nature of the role of social workers. Barnard et al (2008) writes of the need to reinvigorate a values base for social work practice.

From training to practice

Maben et al. (2006) attempted to consider the specific aspects of health care practice that may be contributing to the dissonance. She indicates that, although health care practitioners emerge from their educational programme with a strong set of professional values, a number of organisational factors sabotage their implementation. The factors at play include a lack of support, poor role models, time pressure, role constraints, staff shortages and work overload. Kelly (1998: 1134) identified the importance of "preserving moral integrity" as the basic psychosocial process when newly qualified health care professionals adapt to the "real world" of work. She suggests moral distress results from a health care professional believing that they are not living up to their moral convictions, and highlights the prevalence of self-criticism and self-blame in this process. Here, the person becomes intensely aware of the discrepancy between their perception of good practice and what they observe, and cope with this by redefining their perceptions of their role.

Mackintosh (2006) supports the view that health care students are coping with this moral distress and identified that a minority recognised the practice of poor role models but rejected this influence. However, others rationalised these practices as a consequence of the working organisation or the type of service users with whom they were working. Some felt that the ability to "switch off" from the emotional aspects of practice was essential in order to cope with the emotional demands of the role and, therefore, a skill which they hoped to acquire. A further factor, which is viewed as significant within the professional socialisation process, is the established workforce. Evidence suggests poor role models who devalue personal care have been shown to cause personal disillusionment and significantly influence the maintenance of humanistic values (Greenwood, 1993; Mackintosh, 2006). It has been suggested that this can lead to a willingness amongst students to shift their self-identity in order to justify the loss of ideals and become proficient in their new role. Therefore, the disposition to resist may coexist with a desire to appear to conform, as professionals who initiate challenges about issues of concern are quickly discouraged when not supported by senior colleagues. Jowett et al. (1991) suggest that this process will have a negative effect on newly qualified practitioners who may lose their skills as "knowledgeable doers" and "confident analytical thinkers" as they become socialised into a culture where routine and task-based work approaches are valued. More seriously, Brookfield (Brookfield, 1993: 200) referred to the term "cultural suicide" in suggesting that practitioners who choose to take "a critical stance towards conventional assumptions and accepted procedures face the prospect of finding themselves excluded from the culture that has defined and sustained them up to that point".

Conflict, compliance and conformity

This view of professional socialisation suggests that the health care profession exists as a powerful structural reality and that newcomers are little more than passive recipients of knowledge, who are being moulded into a type of professional (Clouder, 2003). Initially, this determinist view was questioned by Becker et al. (1961: 436), who suggested students were developing "a way of acting" that enabled them to avoid conflict with established and experienced colleagues. This action was termed reactive and challenged previous assumptions by suggesting that individual students may only be *appearing* to conform. The influence of interaction and context on the student was recognised by Bucher and Strauss (1961), who identified continually changing subcultures within medicine and, therefore, further challenged the earlier assumptions of the uniformity and stability of a profession that is purely maintained by structure. This body of research has been reinforced by evidence from professional groups in non-health care settings including teachers, who were found to employ similar strategies that were termed compliance as opposed to conformity. This involved bowing to the power of the professional structures without changing personal beliefs, attitudes or intentions (Abrams, 1992).

Clouder (2003) explains this apparent conformity in two ways: "learning to play the game" and "presentation of self". Playing the game involves becoming aware of rules, both written and unwritten, and learning to comply with the systems in place. This process requires recognition of the power differentials inherent in being a newcomer seeking to join the profession. Clouder (2003) recognised that students perceive a need to present themselves or act in accordance with expectations throughout the identification process and draws on Goffman (1959), who argues that impression management, which is a fundamental component of all social interaction, is "a rhetoric of training" (Goffman 1961: 189).

Therefore, rather than being solely reactive, as has been previously assumed, these strategies illustrate the ways in which students respond to expectations that appear to be aimed at evoking confirmatory feedback and may lead to the verification of self-conceptions. This is consistent with a social constructivist perspective, as individuals are simultaneously working together to create shared meanings and learning continuously about how to become a part of the shared culture that is generated. This encourages a more sceptical view of the ways in which students and newly qualified practitioners identify with professional norms and discourses, within the context of health and social care, due to the recognition of the role of performance management.

Constructing a professional identity

The application of social constructionist principles suggests that individuals enter the social world of a profession and, predominantly through face-to face interaction with others, establish what it is to be a professional. Structural determinants are also moderated because, although structures constrain members and therefore regulate professional conduct, they also enable members by providing opportunities to debate and change aspects of practice over time. Therefore, if it is agreed that the individual feels a need to seek validation from others, it is feasible to see how professional socialisation proceeds. Positive feedback reinforces a particular sense of self as a professional person that incorporates desirable behaviour, fitting in with social practices identified by the profession (Goffman, 1959) and it is vital that newcomers begin to position themselves in relation to expectations. However, some established "fronts" within the health and social care professions can be more difficult for students to handle (Clouder, 2003) and may contribute to the experience of conflict during the transition from student to qualified mental health worker (Stacey et al., 2011).

Ricoeur (1992) offers an explanation for the route of this conflict in light of his theory concerning the construction of self-identity. He promotes the idea that a healthy self-identity happens when a self is constructed based on a foundation that does not change so much that all former identity is lost, while being aware that self does change so that experiences can be incorporated into a coherent self-narrative. This implies that situations which require the newly qualified practitioner to act against their beliefs will lead to conflict, as it will challenge their self-identity. In order to contend with this they must be able to justify their actions in a way that they are not forced to change their perception of themselves, which is a challenging task. Research findings show nurses may contend with this conflict by pursuing an alternative career path and choosing to leave the profession due to their rejection of the structures within which they are working (Robinson et al, 2005; Forsyth and McKenzie, 2006; Lu et al, 2012). However, some recognise the constraints of the system and work within it to orchestrate change despite the potential to be ostracised and excluded (Stacey et al., 2011)

Resources for maintaining our values in practice

So, with all these difficulties to face, how can we maintain our values in practice? The challenges are there at every stage in our careers. As students, although we are relatively free to entertain new ideas, there is simply a great deal to learn. As fully-fledged professionals, we have the pressures of targets and other systemic constraints. But it is, as we have seen in the transition from student to professional, that the challenges are most acute. So, if our very education as professionals puts us at risk of losing our values of care, what resources are available to us for maintaining those same values as we move towards becoming a skilled practitioner?

First, there are resources aplenty for countering plain bad practice. Ethics and law provide increasingly powerful resources for countering bad practice in areas such as human rights and anti-discrimination. But the continuing (some would say, deepening) crisis of care shows that these are not enough. Besides resources for countering bad practice, we also need resources for the positive process of building up good practice.

There is also a danger in this discourse around maintaining values of discussing issues of practice as though there is a "we" who care and a "they" who are cared for. As we have seen throughout the book when discussing issues of co-production and emphasising shared decision making, there is a need to think about values as something produced in an encounter between workers and service users. It can be dispiriting and demoralising to feel as though you are constantly being "cared for", rather than being an active participant in constructing your own recovery from mental distress.

It is with building good practice that this book has been concerned. We hope you will have found the ideas we discussed helpful. But the challenge now is to turn these ideas into effective practice in the real world of everyday care. In the remainder of this section, we draw together the themes of the book around the growing resources available for meeting the challenge of maintaining positive values of care in practice.

Recognising the challenge

Perhaps the first step towards maintaining our values is to recognise that this really *is* a challenge. Lists of good values are just so easy to come up with that we fail to see just how difficult it can be to translate values into practice. Every organisation nowadays has their "values". Our professional bodies provide us with lengthy codes of practice. These are, indeed, helpful and important – up to a point. But the danger is that just in "talking the talk" so readily we fail to recognise how little we are "walking the walk".

This was one of the main findings in the 3 Keys project on assessment in mental health described in Chapter 9. Everyone involved, you will recall, agreed readily enough on the 3 Keys. There was a clear consensus that assessment in mental health should be person-centred, multidisciplinary and strengths-based. Simple! But examples of the 3 Keys actually being implemented in practice were very much the exception, rather than the rule. Of the whole programme, there was only one group in which all three of the 3 Keys were being used: the Bradford-based non-governmental organisation Sharing Voices. It probably is no coincidence that this group has a community orientation and an understanding of the importance of inequalities and discrimination at the heart of the issues that it strives to address.

Raising awareness of values

So, a first step towards maintaining our values is to recognise and embrace the challenge. Hand-in-hand with this goes the importance of raising awareness of the particular values actually in play. All too often, there is a gap between the values to which we subscribe and the values that drive the way we actually behave in a given context. We had an example of this in Chapter 3 with the mental health team who asked Kim Woodbridge for training in values-based practice to support their work as what they believed to be person-centred practice. Much was their surprise, therefore, to find in their first session with Kim that their decision making as a team reflected not the values of the service users with whom they were working, but their *own values* as service providers.

This was not a criticism of the team in question. It was a graphic illustration of how easily our true values become hidden in what, in Chapter 3, we called the "background". And raising awareness of values, with this team as elsewhere, proved to be the first step towards more effective values-based practice.

There are many resources for raising awareness of values. We have covered a number of them in this book. They include exercises such as "the three words that mean values to you" (in Chapter 3). Many other awareness raising exercises are included in resources such as the training manual *Whose Values?* (Woodbridge and Fulford, 2004). This manual, which can be used for self-training, includes exercises also on the other skills areas for values-based practice, knowledge of values, and reasoning about values and communication skills. Developing your skills in each of these areas is a powerful way of building positive practice. There are, for example, specific communication skills concerned with eliciting and understanding values, and also with conflict resolution. Chapter 7 of *Essentials Values-based Practice* (Fulford et al., 2012), which is about diabetic control in a teenager, provides an example of these skills in action.

There are further resources targeted at specific contexts. The 3 Keys document offers a whole series of good practice exemplars for values-based assessment in mental health (as illustrated in Chapter 9). These examples should not be read prescriptively as somehow being the gold standard. However, they provide a rich resource of ideas on which we can build in the context of our own practice. There is also a whole manual of training materials concerned with coercive treatment (Care Services Improvement Partnership (CSIP) and the National Institute for Mental Health in England (NIMHE), 2008) – available at http://www.go.warwick.ac.uk/values-basedpractice). As we saw in Chapter 7, this is a particularly contentious area of practice and there are arguments against the use of coercion at all. But, as a reality of practice, we should at least be using the Mental Health Act as far as possible in a balanced way that minimises compulsion and maximises service user participation (these are two of the Guiding Principles for the use of the Act, see Department of Health, 2008; Fulford et al. (forthcoming, 2015), for an account of how the Act, the Code of Practice and the values-based training materials fit together). As with *Whose Values?*, these resources are all available as free downloads on the VBP website (http://www.go.warwick.ac.uk/values-basedpractice) and can be used either for group work, or for individual study.

Another powerful way of raising awareness is through narrative. Here, though, as we saw in Chapters 3 and 4 and in the discussion of personal narratives in Chapter 6, we need to be careful. The danger is that service users' stories become framed and positioned in terms that reflect not their perspectives but, rather, the perspectives of workers and researchers. Sally Coombs' story, running through Chapters 3, 4 and 6, brought out a range both of our own and of others' values. But the key message from Sally's story was just how easily the values of the service user concerned in a given situation (Sally, in this instance) get lost or ignored. As workers, we have a fatal tendency to assume we know what matters to those with whom we are working, rather than actually finding out. This was reflected in our own reading of Sally's story. In the early stages of this, in Chapter 3, we remained unaware that we had heard almost nothing about what mattered to Sally. It was not until towards the end of Chapter 9 that we eventually found out!

But read carefully, with an awareness of how readily they are shaped and reframed by our own values, personal narratives are a powerful source of understanding. A review of narrative sources in mental health collected by one of us (Kalathil) was published in a companion website to the *Oxford Handbook of Philosophy and Psychiatry* (Fulford et al., 2013). This is available at: http://fdslive.oup.com/www.oup.com/booksites/uk/booksites/content/9780199579563/narratives/fulford_narratives.pdf. Among other narrative sources, the Oxford DiPEX programme has a whole collection of patient narratives illustrating important value dimensions of the experiences of patients and their families in various areas of bodily medicine (http://www.self-help.org.uk/directory/general-health-advice/?entryid54=94762&tp=2). *Essentials of Values-based Practice* (Fulford et al., 2012) is based on a series of clinical stories illustrating the roles of different elements of values-based practice in a number of clinical contexts ranging from psychiatry through primary care to vascular surgery.

Team work

A further important resource for working with values is team work. Team work is nowadays the norm in most areas of practice, and brings a vital resource of diverse knowledge and skills to the complexities of contemporary practice. The *extended* multidisciplinary team of values-based practice, as we saw in Chapter 4, adds to these a resource of *diverse values*.

Again, this was illustrated by Sally Coombs' story. The "wait and watch" decision adopted on admission represented a balance between Nurse Matthews' concern for establishing a trusting therapeutic relationship and Dr Brown's priorities around excluding undiagnosed and potentially serious medical conditions, such as diabetes. Values-based team work also emerged as the key to establishing Sally's own values. It was Jenny Khan, the STR worker, who recognised that, contrary to what everyone else had assumed, Sally actually did *not* want to become an artist. This was vital to recovery practice. As we saw in Chapters 10 and 11, understanding and responding to a person's aspirations is often the turning point in an individual's journey towards recovery.

Power and a role for dissensus

None of this could have happened had the team concerned in Sally Coombs' story been more hierarchical. Teams need leadership; but, where one or other team member automatically has the last say, there can be no balance of values in decision making. This is why values-based practice starts from mutual respect. It is also why it works through dissensual processes that leave different values in play, rather than allowing one or another value to become dominant.

The reality, of course, is all too often not leadership and mutual respect but, rather, the dominance of this or that individual or professional voice. We explored the power inequalities between service user/survivor and service provider "voices" in Chapter 6 and in the particular contexts, respectively, of coercive treatment and assessment in Chapters 7 and 8. There is no magic bullet for countering these inequalities. The tool kit, though, as we called it (Chapter 3) for working with values offers a range of relevant resources. Ethics and law, as noted earlier, in principle, provide a back-stop to bad practice: no one, for instance, whether service user or service provider, should be subject to discrimination or bullying.

On the positive side, furthermore, values-based practice simply by opening up space for the diversity of values validates the minority voice. In the early days of developing training resources for values-based practice, trainees used expressions such as "giving us oxygen" or "space to breathe" to describe their experience (Fulford et al., 2013). What they meant is illustrated by the following story. One social worker trainee reported how, on a home visit, instead of doing a formal needs assessment with her client she had spent their time together helping him find his dog (which had strayed). Her values of care made this the priority in the particular situation in which she found her client but she had been reprimanded by her line manager. Although she had expected this, and understood the requirements of the system, she had felt nonetheless diminished in "getting it wrong". The idea of dissensus by creating space for her values as well as those of the system allowed her to see her decision quite differently. It was not that the system was now wrong and she was right. The difference was that she was no longer wrong and the system right.

Policy "headroom"

You will recognise parallels between that story from the early days of values-based practice and the themes explored throughout this book. Important as systems are, it is people and their individual values that are the key to recovery. Again, the realities of practice remain all too often "system first" not "persons first". But there are growing policy resources for countering this. As we have seen throughout the book, the concept of recovery in mental health has embedded notions of service user involvement at the heart of modern mental health care. Allied to this, there are also specific personalisation initiatives such as "personal budgets" . Co-production, too, has a growing influence: a recent announcement from the Department of Health on personalisation has co-production right at its heart (http://www.england.nhs.uk/2014/08/29/personalised-resource/). There have been helpful initiatives, too, in areas such as Values-based Commissioning of services (Heginbotham, 2012; see also a review of recent initiatives by the National Service User Network (NSUN), Perry et al., 2013) and value-based pricing (www.2020selection.co.uk/images/pdfs/**value-based-pricing**.pdf). For carers also, co-production is a priority (Worthington and Hannan, 2013). The recently revised (National Occupational Standards for Mental Health (NOS) reflect these shifts in policy and practice by making co-production and values-based practice the twin training resources for recovery practice (Skills for Health, 2013).

Such initiatives are readily subverted to the needs of the system. Recovery itself, as we saw in Chapter 10, has been widely high-jacked to serve the needs of the system (Harper and Speed, 2012). And recall here from Chapter 4 how the originally rich concept of evidence-based medicine – as integrating best research evidence, experience and values – has become thinned down to a narrow conception not just of research evidence, but also of a particular restricted range of research evidence (paradigmatically, RCTs). The values-based approach to balanced decision making under the Mental Health Act 2007 noted, although actually required by the Act itself (through its Guiding Principles), has been replaced in practice with decision making dominated largely by the single value of risk averse practice (Fulford et al., forthcoming, 2015).

So, there is no room for complacency here. "Values monism" not "values pluralism" seems to be our "default position". As service providers, we remain under pressure to value the system. As service users, we still have to struggle too hard for our voices to be heard. But there is increasing policy headroom for what we called, in Chapter 11, "valuing persons".

Valuing persons

The different resources for maintaining our values in practice all come together in valuing persons. Call it what you will – "human rights" in ethics and law, or "mutual respect" in values-based practice, or "equality of voices" in political philosophy, or "co-production" in recovery practice – it is in supporting each other that we find the mainspring of care. Certainly, this has been our experience in working on this book together. We hope that, in sharing our experience, you will have found resources for building and sustaining your own positive values of care.

REFERENCES

Abrams, D. (1992) "Processes of social identification", in Breakwell, G. (ed.) *Social Psychology of Identity and the Self Concept.* London: London Academic Press and Surrey University.

Barnard, A., Horner, N. and Wild, J. (eds) (2008) *The Value Base of Social Work and Social Care: An Active Learning Handbook.* Maidenhead: Open University Press.

Beauchamp, T. and Childress, J. (2012) *Principles of Biomedical Ethics.* Oxford: Oxford University Press.

Becker, H.S., Geer, B., Hughes, E.C. and Strauss, A.L. (1961) *Boys in White.* Chicago: University of Chicago.

Brookfield, S. (1993) "On impostership, cultural suicide, and other dangers: How nurses learn critical thinking", *Journal of Continuing Education in Nursing*, 24(5): 197–205.

Bucher, R. and Strauss, A. (1961) "Professions in process", *American Journal of Sociology*, 66: 325–34.

Care Services Improvement Partnership (CSIP) and the National Institute for Mental Health in England (NIMHE) (2008) *Workbook to Support Implementation of the Mental Health Act 1983 as Amended by the Mental Health Act 2007.* London: Department of Health.

Clouder, L. (2003) "Becoming professional: Exploring the complexities of professional socialization in health and social care", *Learning in Health and Social Care*, 2(4): 213–22.

Curtis, K., Horton, K. and Smith, P. (2012) "Student nurse socialization in compassionate practice: A grounded theory study", *Nurse Education Today*, 32(7): 790–5.

Department of Health (2008) *Mental Health Act 1983 Code of Practice – 2008 Revision.* London: TSO.

Department of Health (2009) *The NHS Constitution.* London: TSO.

Forsyth, S. and McKenzie, H. (2006) "A comparative analysis of contemporary nurses' discontents", *Journal of Advanced Nursing*, 56(2): 209–16.

Foucault, M. (1993) *Madness and Civilisation. A History of Insanity in the Age of Reason.* Cambridge: Routledge.

Fulford, K.W.M., Davies, M., Gipps, R., Graham, G., Sadler, J., Stanghellini, G. and Thornton, T. (2013) *The Oxford Handbook of Philosophy and Psychiatry.* Oxford: Oxford University Press.

Fulford, K.W.M., Dewey, S. and King, M. (2015) "Values-based involuntary seclusion and treatment: Value pluralism and the UK's Mental Health Act 2007" in Sadler, J.Z., van Staden, W. and Fulford, K.W.M. (eds), *The Oxford Handbook of Psychiatric Ethics.* Oxford: Oxford University Press.

Fulford, K.W.M., Peile, E. and Carroll, H. (2012) "Diabetic control and controllers: Nothing without communication" in Fulford, K.W.M., Peile, E. and Carroll, H. *Essential Values-based Practice: Clinical stories linking science with people.* Cambridge: Cambridge University Press.

Fulford, K.W.M., Williamson, T. and Woodbridge, K. (2002) "Values-added practice (a values-awareness workshop)", *Mental Health Today*, October: 25–7.

Goffman, E. (1959) *The Presentation of Self in Everyday Life*. London: Penguin.

Goffman, E. (1967) *Interaction Ritual*. Penguin: London.

Greenwood, J. (1993) "The apparent desensitization of nursing students during their professional sociali-sation: A cognitive perspective", *Journal of Advanced Nursing*, 18: 1471–9.

Harper, D. and Speed, E. (2012) "Uncovering recovery: The resistible rise of recovery and resilience", *Studies in Social Justice*, 6(1): 9–25.

Heginbotham, C. (2012) *Values-Based Commissioning of Health and Social Care*. Cambridge: Cambridge University Press.

Jowett, S., Walton, I. and Payne, S. (1991) *The NFER Project 2000 Research: An Introduction and Some Interim Issues. Interim Paper 2*, Slough, UK: NFER.

Karnieli-Miller, O. and Eiskovits, Z. (2009) "Physician as partner or salesman? Shared decision making in real-time encounters", *Social Science and Medicine*, July, 69(1): 1–8.

Kelly, B. (1998) "Preserving moral integrity: A follow-up study with new graduate nurses", *Journal of Advanced Nursing*, 28(5): 1134–45.

Kirmayer, L. (2012) "Cultural competence and evidence-based practice in mental health: Epistemic communities and the politics of pluralism", *Social Science and Medicine*, 75: 249–56.

Lu, H., Barriball, K.L., Zhang, X. and While, A.E. (2012) "Job satisfaction among hospital nurses revisited: A systematic review", *International Journal of Nursing*, 49(8): 1017–38.

Maben, J., Latter, S. and Macleod Clark, J. (2006) "The theory-practice gap: Impact of professional-bureaucratic work conflict on newly-qualified nurses", *Journal of Advanced Nursing*, 55(4): 465–77.

Mackintosh, C. (2006) "Caring: The socialisation of pre-registration student nurses: A longitudinal qualita-tive descriptive study", *International Journal of Nursing Studies*, 43: 953–62.

Mead, G.H. (1934) *Mind, Self and Society from the Standpoint of a Social Behaviourist*. Chicago: University of Chicago Press.

Perry, E., Barber, J., and England, E. (2013) *A Review of Values-based Commissioning in Mental Health. London and Birmingham*. National Service User Network (NSUN) and NHS East Midlands.

Ricoeur, P. (1992) *Oneself as Another*, translated by Kathleen Blamey. Chicago: University of Chicago Press.

Robinson, S., Murrells, T., Hickey G., Clinton, M. and Tingle, A. (2005) *A Tale of Two Courses: Comparing Careers and Competencies of Nurses Prepared via Three-year Degree and Three-year Diploma Courses*. Kings College London Nursing Research Unit, Careers and Working Lives Research. Available at: http://www.kcl.ac.uk/nursing/nru/nru_res_rep.html (accessed 20 September 2005).

Skills for Health (2013) *Revised National Occupational Standards for Mental Health*. Bristol: Skills for Health. Also available at: https://tools.skillsforhealth.org.uk/competence_search/

Stacey, G., Johnson, K., Stickley, T. and Diamond, B. (2011) "How do nurses cope when values and practice conflict?", *Nursing Times*, 107(5): 20–4.

Woodbridge, K., and Fulford, K.W.M. (2004) *"Whose Values?" A Workbook for Values-based Practice in Mental Health Care*. London: Sainsbury Centre for Mental Health.

Worthington, A., and Hannan, R. (2013) *The Triangle of Care – Carers Included: A Guide to Best Practice in Mental Health Care in England* (2nd edn). London: Carers Trust.

Bibliography

Abhay, S. et al. (2012) "Critical perspectives on the NIMH initiative 'grand challenges to global mental health'", *Indian Journal of Medical Ethics*, 4.

Abrams, D. (1992) "Processes of social identification", in Breakwell, G. (ed.) *Social Psychology of Identity and the Self Concept*. London: London Academic Press and Surrey University.

Achebe, C. (1994) "The art of fiction". Interview by J. Brooks, *Paris Review*, 133, Winter. Available at http://www.theparisreview.org/interviews/1720/the-art-of-fiction-no-139-chinua-achebe (accessed 2 April 2014).

Adams, J. and Drake, R. (2006) "Shared decision making and evidence based practice", *Community Mental Health Journal*, 42(1): 87–105.

Adams, T. (2005) "Communication and interaction within dementia care triads: Developing a theory for relationship-centred care", *Dementia International Journal of Social Research and Practice*, 4: 185–205.

Adorno, T.W. (1990) *Negative Dialectics*, translated by E.B. Ashton. London and New York: Routledge.

Adorno, T.W. (2000) *Problems of Moral Philosophy*, translated by Rodney Livingstone. Cambridge, UK: Polity Press.

Agamben, G. (2005) *State of Exception*. Chicago and London: University of Chicago Press.

Allmark, P. (1995) "Can there be an ethics of care?", *Journal of Medical Ethics*, 21(1): 19–24.

Allmark, P. (2013) "Virtue and austerity", *Nursing Philosophy*, 14(1): 45–52.

Allott, P. (2004) "What is mental health, illness and recovery", in Ryan, T. and Pritchard, J. (eds) *Adult Mental Health, Good Practice Series 10*. London: Jessica Kingsley.

Allott, P., Fulford, K.W.M., Fleming, B., Williamson, T. and Woodbridge, K. (2005) "Recovery, values and e-learning", *Mental Health Review*, 10(4): 34–8.

Allott, P., Loganathan, L. and Fulford, K.W.M. (2002) "Discovering hope for recovery" in *Innovation in Community Mental Health: International Perspectives*, Special issue of the *Canadian Journal of Community Mental Health*, 21(2): 13–33.

Amery, J. (1980) *At the Mind's Limits: Contemplations of a Survivor on Auschwitz and its Realities*, translated by Sidney Rosenfeld and Stella Rosenfeld. Bloomington and Indianapolis: Indiana University Press.

Anand, S. and Hanson, K. (1998) "DALYs: Efficiency versus equity", *World Development*, 26: 30710.

Anderson, S., "Coercion", *The Stanford Encyclopaedia of Philosophy* (2014) (spring edn), Edward N. Zalta (ed.). Available at: http://plato.stanford.edu/archives/spr2014/entries/coercion/ (accessed 10 April 2014).

Anonymous (1620) *The Petition of the Poor Distracted People in the House of Bedlam*. London.

Anonymous (1855) "Autobiography of the insane", *Journal of Psychological Medicine and Mental Pathology*, 11, July: 338–53.

Anthony, W.A. (1996) "Recovery from mental illness: The guiding vision of the mental health system in the 1990s", *Innovation and Research*, 2(3): 17–23.

APA (American Psychiatric Association) (2013) "Major depressive disorder and the bereavement exclusion". Available at: http://www.dsm5.org/Documents/Bereavement%20Exclusion%20Fact%20Sheet. pdf (accessed 10 April 2014).

APA (American Psychiatric Association) (2013) DSM-5 – Diagnostic and Statistical Manual of Mental Disorders (5th edn). Washington, DC: American Psychiatric Association.

Appleby, L., Kapur, N., Shaw, J., Hunt, I., While, D., Flynn, S., Windfuhr, K. and Williams, A. (2013) *The National Confidential Inquiry into Suicide and Homicide by People with Mental Illness.* Manchester: University of Manchester.

Arendt, H. (1970) *On Violence.* San Diego, New York, London: Harcourt Publishers.

Arendt, H. (1986) "Communicative power" in Lukes, S. (ed.) *Power.* Cambridge: Blackwell.

Aristotle (2009) *Nicomachean Ethics*, translated by David Ross. Oxford: Oxford University Press.

Armstrong, A. (1999) "Enforced medication and virtue ethics", *Journal of Psychiatric and Mental Health Nursing*, 6(4): 329–34.

Arnold, D. (2001) "Coercion and moral responsibility", *American Philosophical Quarterly*, 38(1): 53–67.

Ash, T.G. (1999) *We the People: The Revolution of '89 Witnessed in Warsaw, Budapest, Berlin and Prague.* London: Penguin Books.

Aston, V. and Coffey, M. (2012) "Recovery: What mental health nurses and service users say about the concept of recovery", *Journal of Psychiatric and Mental Health Nursing*, 19: 257–63.

Atkinson, A., Douglas, C., Francis, D., Laville, M., Millin, S., Pamfield, J., Smith, P. and Smith, R. (2008) *Lifting Barriers: African and Caribbean People Tell Stories of Struggle, Strength and Achieving Mental Health.* London: Mellow, SAFH, THACMHO, East London NHS Trust.

Atwell, R. and Fulford, K.W.M. (2006) "The Christian tradition of spiritual direction as a sketch for a strong theology of diversity" in Cox, J., Campbell, A.V. and Fulford, K.W.M. (eds) *Medicine of the Person: Faith, Science and Values in Health Care Provision.* London: Jessica Kingsley.

Badcock, J.C. and Hugdahl, K. (2014) "A synthesis of evidence on inhibitory control and auditory hallucinations based on the Research Domain Criteria (RDoC) framework", *Frontiers in Human Neuroscience*, 8(180). doi: 10.3389/fnhum.2014.00180

Bandura, A. (1986) *Social Foundation of Thought and Action: A Social Cognitive Theory.* Englewood Cliffs: Prentice Hall.

Banks, S. and Gallagher, A. (2009) *Ethics in Professional Life: Virtues for Health.* Basingstoke: Palgrave Macmillan.

Barker, P. (ed.) (2011) *Mental Health Ethics: The Human Context.* Oxon: Routledge.

Barnard, A., Horner, N. and Wild, J. (eds) (2008) *The Value Base of Social Work and Social Care: An Active Learning Handbook.* Maidenhead: Open University Press.

Barry, K., Zeber, J., Blow, F. and Valenstein, M. (2003) "Effect of strengths model versus assertive community treatment model on participant outcomes and utilisation: Two year follow up", *Psychiatric Rehabilitation Journal*, 26(3): 268–77.

Bartlett, R. and O'Connor, D. (2010) *Broadening the Dementia Debate: Towards Social Citizenship.* Bristol: Policy Press.

Basaglia, F. (2004) "Breaking the circuit of control", in Ingleby, D. (ed.) *Critical Psychiatry. The Politics of Mental Health.* London: Free Association Books.

Basset, T. and Repper, J. (2005) "Travelling hopefully", *Mental Health Today*, November 16–18.

Basset, T. and Stickley, T. (eds) (2010) *Voices of Experience: Narratives of Mental Health Survivors.* Chichester, UK: Wiley.

Beach, M.C. and Inui, T. (2006) "Relationship-centered care. A constructive reframing", *Journal of General Internal Medicine*, 21(1 Suppl): S3–8.

Beauchamp, T. (1999) "The philosophical basis of psychiatric ethics", in Bloch, S., Chodoff, P. and Green, S. (eds) *Psychiatric Ethics*. Oxford: Oxford University Press.

Beauchamp, T. and Childress, J. (2012) *Principles of Biomedical Ethics*. Oxford: Oxford University Press.

Becker, H.S., Geer, B., Hughes, E.C. and Strauss, A.L. (1961) *Boys in White*. Chicago: University of Chicago.

Bentall, R. (2009) *Doctoring the Mind. Is Our Current Treatment of Mental Illness Really Any Good?* New York: New York University Press.

Bentall, R. (2004) *Madness Explained: Psychosis and Human Nature*. London: Penguin.

Bentall, R. (2006) "Madness explained: Why we must reject the Kraepelinian Paradigm and replace it with a 'complaint-orientated' approach to understanding mental illness", *Medical Hypotheses*, 66: 220–33.

Bentall, R. (2013) "Too much coercion in mental health services", *The Guardian*, 1 February. Available at: http://www.theguardian.com/commentisfree/2013/feb/01/mental-health-services-coercion (accessed 29 June 2014).

Bentham, J. (2007) *An Introduction to the Principles of Morals and Legislation*. New York: Dover Publications.

Ben-Zeev, D., Young, M. and Corrigan, P. (2010) "DSM-5 and the stigma of mental illness", *Journal of Mental Health*, 19(4): 318–327.

Benziman, G., Kannai, R. and Ahmad, A. (2012) "The wounded healer as cultural archetype", *Comparative Literature and Culture*, 14: 1.

Bhabha, H. (1994) *The Location of Culture*. New York: Routledge.

Bhui, K. (2003) "Cultural identity and mental health", *International Journal of Social Psychiatry*, 49(4) 243–6.

Bindman, J., Reid, Y., Szmukler, G., Tiller, J., Thornicroft, G. and Leese, M. (2005) "Perceived coercion at admission to psychiatric hospital and engagement to follow-up", *Social Psychiatry Psychiatric Epidemiology*, 40: 160–6.

Bird, V., Leamy, M., Le Boutillier, C., Williams, J. and Slade, M. (2011) *REFOCUS: Promoting Recovery in Community Mental Health Services*. London: Rethink.

Bleuler, E. (1950) *Dementia Praecox or the Group of Schizophrenias*, translated by J. Zinkin. New York International Universities Press.

Bloch, S. and Green, S.A. (eds) (2009) *Psychiatric Ethics* (4th edn). Oxford: Oxford University Press.

Blum, L.A. (1988) "Gilligan and Kohlberg – implications for moral theory", Ethics, 98(3): 472–91.

Bowlby, J. (1969) *Attachment: Attachment and Loss, Volume 1*. London: Hogarth Press.

Bowlby, J. (1973) *Separation, Anxiety and Anger. Attachment and Loss, Volume 2*. London: Hogarth Press.

Boyle, M. (2002) *Schizophrenia: A Scientific Delusion?* London and New York: Routledge.

Bracken, P. and Thomas, P. (2005) *Postpsychiatry. Mental Health in a Postmodern World*. Oxford: Oxford University Press.

Bracken, P. and Thomas, P. (2010) "From Szasz to Foucault: On the role of critical psychiatry", *Philosophy Psychiatry, & Psychology*, 17(3): 219–28.

Bracken, P. and Thomas, P. (2013) "Challenges to the modernist identity of psychiatry: User empowerment and recovery", in Fulford, K.W.M, Davies, M, Gipps, R.G.T., Graham, G., Sadler, J., Stanghellini, G and Thornton, T. (eds) *The Oxford Handbook of Philosophy and Psychiatry*. Oxford: Oxford University Press.

Brandon, D. (1999) "Melting straitjackets", *Journal of Psychiatric and Mental Health Nursing*, 6: 321–6.

Braslow, J.T. (2013) "The manufacture of recovery", *Annual Review of Clinical Psychology*, 9: 781809.

Brecher, B. (2011) "Which values? And whose? A reply to Fulford", *Journal of Evaluation in Clinical Practice* 17: 996–8.

Brecher, B. (2014) "VBP: But which values? And whose?" in Loughlin, M. (ed.) *Debates in Values-Based Practice*. Cambridge: Cambridge University Press.

Breeze, J. (1998) "Can paternalism be justified in mental health care"?, *Journal of Advanced Nursing*, 28(2): 260–5.

Brookfield, S. (1993) "On impostership, cultural suicide, and other dangers: How nurses learn critical thinking", *Journal of Continuing Education in Nursing*, 24(5): 197–205.

Bruckner, P. (2010) *Perpetual Euphoria. On the Duty to be Happy.* Princeton: Princeton University Press.

Bruckshaw, S. (1774) *The Case, Petition, and Address of Samuel Bruckshaw, who Suffered a Most Severe Imprisonment, for Very Near the Whole Year, Loaded with Irons, without Being Heard in his Defense, Nay Even without Being Accused, and at Last Denied an Appeal to a Jury. Humbly Offered to the Perusal and Consideration of the Public.* London: The Author.

Buchanan, A. (1999) "Risk and dangerousness", *Psychological Medicine*, 29: 465–3.

Buchanan-Barker, P. and Barker, P. (2009) "The convenient myth of Thomas Szasz", *Journal of Psychiatric and Mental Health Nursing*, 16: 87–95.

Bucher, R. and Strauss, A. (1961) "Professions in process", *American Journal of Sociology*, 66: 325–34.

Bullmore, E., Fletcher, P. and Jones, P. (2009) "Why psychiatry can't afford to be neurophobic?", *British Journal of Psychiatry*, 194: 293–5.

Burgess, P., Bindma, J., Leese, M., Henderson, C. and Szmukler, G. (2006) "Do community treatment orders for mental illness reduce admission to hospital", *Social Psychiatry and Psychiatric Epidemiology*, 41: 574–9.

Burns, T., Rugaska, J., Molodynski, A., Dawson, J., Yeeles, K., Vazquez-Montes, M., Voysey, M., Sinclair, J. and Priebe, S. (2013) "Compulsory treatment orders for patients with psychosis (OCTET): A randomised control trial", *Lancet*, 381(9878): 1627–33.

Burstow, B. and Weitz, D. (eds) (1998) *Shrink Resistant.* Vancouver: New Start Books.

Butler, J. (2005) *Giving an Account of Oneself.* New York: Fordham University Press.

Callard, F. (2014) "Psychiatric diagnosis: The indispensability of ambivalence", *Journal of Medical Ethics*, 40(8): 526–30.

Campbell, P. (2009) "The service user/survivor movement", in Reynolds, J., Muston, R., Heller, T., Leach, J., McCormick, M., Wallcraft, J. and Walsh, M. (eds) *Mental Health Still Matters.* Palgrave: Milton Keynes.

Campbell, R.J. (1989) *Psychiatric Dictionary* (6th edn). Oxford: Oxford University Press.

Cantor-Graee, E. and Selten, J. (2005) "Schizophrenia and migration: A meta-analysis and review", *American Journal of Psychiatry*, 162(1): 12–24.

Caplan, A.L., Engelhardt, H.T. and McCartney, J.J. (eds) (1981) *Concepts of Health and Disease.* Reading: Addison-Wesley.

Care Quality Commission (2014) "Monitoring the Mental Health Act in 2012/2013". Available at: http://www.cqc.org.uk/sites/default/files/media/documents/cqc_mentalhealth_2012_13_07_update.pdf (accessed 14 April 2014).

Care Services Improvement Partnership (CSIP) and the National Institute for Mental Health in England (NIMHE) (2008) *Workbook to Support Implementation of the Mental Health Act 1983 as Amended by the Mental Health Act 2007.* London: Department of Health.

Cassel, E.J. (1982) "The nature of suffering", *New England Journal of Medicine*, 306: 639–45.

Chan, P. (2002) "In whose best interests? An examination of the ethics of the UK government's White Paper 'Reforming the Mental Health Act'", *Journal of Psychiatric and Mental Health Nursing*, 9: 399–404.

Chaudoir, S. and Fisher, J. (2010) "The disclosure process model: Understanding disclosure decision making and postdisclosure outcomes among people living with a concealable stigmatized identity", *Psychological Bulletin*, 136(2): 236–56.

Chong, W., Asiani, P. and Chen, T. (2013) "Shared decision-making and interprofessional collaboration in mental healthcare: A qualitative study exploring perceptions of barriers and facilitators", *Journal of Interprofessional Care*, 27(5): 373–9.

Chopra, P., Hamilton, B., Castle, D., Smith, J., Mileshkin, C., Deans, M., Wynne, B., Prigg, G., Toomey, N. and Wilson, M. (2009) "Implementation of the strengths model at an area mental health service", *Australian Psychiatry*, 17(30): 203–6.

Churchill, R., Owen, G., Singh, S. and Hotopf, M. (2007) *International Experiences of Using Community Treatment Orders.* Institute of Psychiatry: London.

Clouder, L. (2003) "Becoming professional: Exploring the complexities of professional socialization in health and social care", *Learning in Health and Social Care*, 2(4): 213–22.

Coid, J. (1996) "Dangerous patients with mental illness; increased risks warrant new policies, adequate resources and appropriate legislation", *BMJ*, 312: 965–6.

College of Occupational Therapists (2006) *Recovering Ordinary Lives: The Strategy for Occupational Therapy in Mental Health Services 2007–2017: A Vision for the Next Ten Years.* London: College of Occupational Therapists.

Collier, E. (2010) "Confusion of recovery: One solution", *International Journal of Mental Health Nursing*, 19: 16–21.

Collins, P.Y., Patel, V., Joestl, S.S., March, D., Insel, T.R. and Daar, A.S. (2011) "Grand Challenges to Global Mental Health", *Nature*, 475: 27–30.

Colombo, A., Bendelow, G., Fulford, K.W.M. and Williams, S. (2003) "Evaluating the influence of implicit models of mental disorder on processes of shared decision making within community-based multi-disciplinary teams", *Social Science & Medicine*, 56: 1557–70.

Costa, L., Voronka, J., Landry, D., Reid, J., McFarlane, B., Reville, D. and Church, K. (2012) "Recovering our stories: A small act of resistance", *Studies in Social Justice*, 6(1): 85–101.

Coulter, A. and Collins, A. (2011) *Making Shared Decision Making a Reality. No Decision About Me, Without Me.* London: Kings Fund.

Coutts, P. (2007) *Mental Health, Recovery and Employment.* SRN Discussion Paper Series, Report No. 5 Glasgow: Scottish Recovery Network.

Crepaz-Keay, D. and Kalathil, J. (2013) "Introduction", *Personal Narratives of Madness* (annotated bibliography). Available at: http://global.oup.com/booksites/content/9780199579563/narratives/ (accessed 29 May 2015)

Crisp, R. (1994) "Quality of life and health care" in Fulford, K.W.M., Gillett, G. and Soskice, J. (eds) *Medicine and Moral Reasoning.* Cambridge: Cambridge University Press.

Crisp, R. (2013) "Commentary: Values-based practice by a different route", in Fulford, K.W.M. and van Staden, W. (2013) "Values-based practice: Topsy-turvy take home messages from ordinary language philosophy (and a few next steps)" in Fulford, K.W.M., Davies, M., Gipps, R., Graham, G., Sadler J., Stanghellini, G. and Thornton, T. (eds) *The Oxford Handbook of Philosophy and Psychiatry.* Oxford Oxford University Press.

Croft, S., Bewley, C., Beresford, P., Branfield, F., Fleming, J., Glynn, M. and Postle, K. (2011) *Person-centred Support: A Guide to Person-Centred Working for Practitioners.* York: Shaping Our Lives and Joseph Rowntree Foundation.

Cromby, J. (2011) "The greatest gift: Happiness, governance and psychology", *Social and Psychology Personality Compass*, 5(11): 840–52.

Crossley, N. (1998) "R.D. Laing and the British anti-psychiatry movement: A socio-historical analysis" *Social Science and Medicine*, 47(7): 877–89.

Cruden, A. (1739) *The London-Citizen Exceedingly Injured; or, a British Inquisition Display'd, in an Account of the Unparallel'd Case of a Citizen of London, Bookseller to the Late Queen, Who Was in a Most*

Unjust and Arbitrary Manner Sent on the 23rd of March Last, 1738, by One Robert Wightman, a Mere Stranger, to a Private Madhouse. London: T. Cooper.

Curtis, K., Horton, K. and Smith, P. (2012) "Student nurse socialisation in compassionate practice: A grounded theory study", *Nurse Education Today*, 32(7): 790–5.

Curtis, T., Dellar, R., Lestie, E. and Watson, B. (eds) (2000) *Mad Pride: A Celebration of Mad Culture.* London: Spare Change Books.

Cutliffe, J. and Hannigan, B. (2001) "Mass media, monsters and mental health clients: The need to increased lobbying", *Journal of Psychiatric Mental Health Nursing*, 8(4): 315–21.

Dalai Lama (1995) *The Power of Compassion.* India: HarperCollins.

Dalai Lama (2001) *An Open Heart: Practising Compassion in Everyday Life*, edited by N. Vreeland. London: Hodder & Stoughton.

Danquah, M.N.-A. (1998) *Willow Weep for Me: A Black Woman's Journey through Depression.* New York: Ballentine.

Davidson, L. (2005) "Recovery, self-management and the expert patient-changing the culture of mental health from a UK perspective", *Journal of Mental Health*, 14(1): 25–35.

Davidson, L. and Roe, D. (2007) "Recovery from versus recovery in serious mental illness: One strategy for lessening confusion plaguing recovery", *Journal of Mental Health*, 16(4): 459–70.

Davidson, L., Chinman, M., Sells, D. and Rowe, M. (2006) "Peer support among adults with serious mental illness: A report from the field", *Schizophrenia Bulletin*, 3293: 443–50.

Davies, J. (2013) *Cracked – Why Psychiatry is doing More Harm than Good.* London: Icon Books.

Davis, S. (2002) "Autonomy versus coercion: Reconciling competing perspectives in community mental health", *Community Mental Health Journal*, 38(3): 239–51.

Daykin, N., Orme, J., Evans, D., Salmon, D., McEachran, M. and Brain, S. (2008) "The impact of participation in performing arts on adolescent health and behaviour: A systematic review of the literature", *Journal of Health Psychology*, 13 (2): 251–64.

Deegan, P. (1995) "Principles of a recovery model including medication", Available at: http://www.power2u.org/downloads/MedicationMeetingPacket.pdf (accessed January 2014).

Deegan, P. and Drake, R. (2006) "Shared decision making and medication management in the recovery process", *Psychiatric Services*, 57(11): 1636–9.

Deegan, P.E. (1996) *Recovery and the Conspiracy of Hope: There's a Person In Here*, The Sixth Annual Mental Health Services Conference of Australia and New Zealand. Brisbane, Australia.

Deegan, P.E. (2001) "Recovery as a self-directed process of healing and transformation", *Occupational Therapy in Mental Health*, 17(3/4): 5–21.

Deegan, P.E. (2009) "Recovery: The lived experience of rehabilitation" in Reynolds, J., Muston, R., Heller, T., Leach, J., McCormick, M., Wallcraft, J. and Walsh, M. (eds) *Mental Health Still Matters.* Basingstoke: Palgrave Macmillan.

Denbrough, D. (2014) *Retelling the Stories of Our Lives: Everyday Narrative Therapy to Draw Inspiration and Transform Experience.* New York and London: Norton.

Dennis, C.L. (2003) "Peer support within a health care context: A concept analysis", *International Journal of Nursing Studies*, 40: 321–32.

Department for Constitutional Affairs (2006) *Mental Capacity Act Code of Practice.* Code Number CP 05/06. London: TSO.

Department of Health (1998) *Mental Health Services Safe, Sound and Supportive.* London: TSO.

Department of Health (1999) *National Service Framework for Mental Health, Modern Standards and Service Models.* London: TSO.

Department of Health (2001) *The Journey to Recovery: The Government's Vision for Mental Health Care.* London: TSO.

Department of Health (2004) *Essential Shared Capabilities: A Framework for the Whole of the Mental Health Workforce.* London: TSO.

Department of Health (2004) *The Ten Essential Shared Capabilities: A Framework for the Whole of the Mental Health Workforce.* London: The Sainsbury Centre for Mental Health, the National Health Service University (NHSU), and the National Institute for Mental Health England (NIMHE).

Department of Health (2006) *From Values to Action: The Chief Nursing Officer's Review of Mental Health Nursing.* London: Crown Copyright.

Department of Health (2008) *Code of Practice, Mental Health Act 1983.* Norwich: TSO.

Department of Health (2008) *Mental Health Act 1983 Code of Practice – 2008 Revision.* London: TSO.

Department of Health (2009) *The NHS Constitution.* London: TSO.

Department of Health (2010) *Equity and Excellence: Liberating the NHS.* London: Crown Copyright.

Department of Health (2011) *No Health without Mental Health: A Cross Government Mental Health Outcomes Strategy for People of All Ages.* Available at: https://www.gov.uk/government/uploads/system/uploads/attachment_data/fi le/213761/dh_124058.pdf (accessed 11 December 2013).

Department of Health (2011) *No Health without Mental Health: A Cross Governmental Mental Health Outcomes Strategy.* London: TSO.

Department of Health (2012) *Compassion in Practice. Nursing, Midwifery and Care Staff: Our Vision and Strategy.* Available at: http://www.england.nhs.uk/wp-content/uploads/2012/12/compassion-inpractice.pdf (accessed 11 December 2013).

Department of Health (2012) *No Decision About Me Without Me: Liberating the NHS.* London: TSO.

Dewing, J. (2002) "From ritual to relationship: A person centred approach to consent in qualitative research with older people who have a dementia", *Dementia: The International Journal of Social Research & Practice*, 1: 156–71.

Dewing, J. (2008) "Personhood and dementia: Revisiting Tom Kitwood's ideas", *International Journal of Older People Nursing*, 3(1): 3–13.

Dickenson, D. and Fulford, K.W.M. (2000) *In Two Minds: A Casebook of Psychiatric Ethics.* Oxford: Oxford University Press.

Donnelly, M. (1992) *The Politics of Mental Health in Italy.* London and New York: Routledge.

Dowie, J. (2004) "Research implications of science-informed, value-based decision making", *International Journal of Occupational Medicine and Environmental Health*, 17(1): 83–90.

Downs, M., Clare, L. and Mackenzie, J. (2006) "Understandings of dementia: Explanatory models and their implications for the person with dementia and therapeutic effort" in *Dementia: Mind, Meaning and the Person*, Hughes, J.C., Louw. S.J. and Sabat, S.R. (eds). Oxford: Oxford University Press.

Drew, N., Funk, M., Tang, S., Lamichane, J., Chavez, E., Katontoka, S., Pathare, S., Lewis, O., Gostin, L. and Saraceno, B. (2011) "Human rights violations of people with mental and psychosocial disabilities: An unresolved global crisis", *Lancet*, 378: 1664–75.

Dy, S. and Purnell, T. (2012) "Key concepts relevant to quality of complex and shared decision making in healthcare: A literature review", *Social Science and Medicine*, 74: 582–7.

Eagleton, T. (2007) *Ideology. An Introduction.* London: Verso.

Engelhardt, H.T. (1986) *The Foundations of Bioethics.* New York, NY: Oxford University Press.

Escobar, J. (2012) "Diagnostic bias: Racial and cultural issues", *Psychiatric Services*, September, 63(9): 847.

Faulkner, A. and Kalathil, J. (2012) *The Freedom to Be, the Chance to Dream: Preserving User-led Peer Support in Mental Health*, commissioned by Together at: http://www.survivor-research.com/publications/99-the-freedom-to-be-the-chance-to-dream (accessed 29 May 2015).

Fazel, S., Singh, J., Doll, H. and Grann, M. (2012) "Use of risk assessment instruments to predict violence and antisocial behaviour in 72 samples involving 24,827 people: A systematic review and meta analysis", *BMJ*, 345: 1–12.

Ferguson, I. (2007) "Increasing user choice or privatising risk? The Antinomies of Personalisation", *British Journal of Social Work*, 37: 387–403.

Fernando, S. (2010) *Mental Health, Race and Culture*. Basingstoke: Palgrave Macmillan.

Flanagan, O. (1992) *Consciousness Reconsidered*. Cambridge, MA: MIT Press.

Flood, C., Byford, S., Henderson, C., Leese, M., Thornicroft, G., Sutherby, K. and Szmukler, G. (2006) "Joint crisis plans for people with psychosis: Economic evaluation of a randomised controlled trial", *BMJ*, doi:10.1136/bmj.38929.653704.55 (16 August 2006).

Foley, P. (n.d.) "'Black dog' as a metaphor for depression: A brief history". Available at: http://www.blackdoginstitute.org.au/docs/foley.pdf (accessed on 5 April 2013).

Forsyth, S. and McKenzie, H. (2006) "A comparative analysis of contemporary nurses' discontents", *Journal of Advanced Nursing*, 56(2): 209–16.

Foucault, M. (1986) *The History of Sexuality, Volume 1*, London: Penguin.

Foucault, M. (1991) *Discipline and Punish. The Birth of the Prison*. London: Penguin.

Foucault, M. (1993) *Madness and Civilization. A History of Insanity in the Age of Reason*, translated by R. Howard. London: Routledge.

Foucault, M. (2002) "Truth and power" in Faubion, J. (ed.) *Power – Essential Works of Foucault – 1954–1984, Voume.3*. London: Penguin.

Frances, A. (2013) *Saving Normal*. New York: William Morrow.

Francis, R. (2010) *Final Report of The Independent Inquiry Into Care Provided By Mid Staffordshire NHS Foundation Trust*. London: TSO.

Francis, R. (2013) *Report of the Mid Staffordshire NHS Foundation Trust: Public Inquiry – Executive Summary*. London: TSO.

Frank, A.W. (2000) "The standpoint of storyteller", *Qualitative Health Research*, 10: 354–65.

Frank, A.W. (2010) *Letting Stories Breathe: A Socio-Narratology*. Chicago: University of Chicago Press.

Freshwater, D. and Westwood, T. (2006) "Risk, detention and evidence: Humanizing mental health reform", Editorial, *Journal of Psychiatric and Mental Health Nursing*, 13: 257–9.

Fukui, S., Goscha, R., Rapp, C., Mabry, A., Liddy, P. and Marty, D. (2012) "Strengths model case management fidelity scores and client outcomes", *Psychiatric Services*, 163(7): 708–10.

Fulford, K.W.M. (1999 [1989, 1995]) *Moral Theory and Medical Practice*. Cambridge: Cambridge University Press.

Fulford, K.W.M. and Colombo, A. (2004) "Six models of mental disorder: A study combining linguistic-analytic and empirical methods", *Philosophy, Psychiatry, & Psychology*, 11(2): 129–44.

Fulford, K.W.M. and van Staden, W. (2013) "Values-based practice: topsy-turvy take home messages from ordinary language philosophy (and a few next steps)" in Fulford, K.W.M., Davies, M., Gipps, R., Graham, G., Sadler, J., Stanghellini, G., and Thornton, T. (eds), *The Oxford Handbook of Philosophy and Psychiatry*. Oxford: Oxford University Press.

Fulford, K.W.M. and Woodbridge, K. (2008) "Practising ethically: Values-based practice and ethics – Working together to support person-centred and multidisciplinary mental health care" in Stickley, T. and Basset, T. (eds) *Learning About Mental Health Practice*. Chichester: Wiley.

Fulford, K.W.M., Bortolotti, L. and Broome, M. (2014) "Taking the long view: An emerging framework for translational psychiatric science", Special Article for *World Psychiatry*, 13/2: 10817. Also available on the World Psychiatric Association website (www.wpanet.org) and on the Wiley Online Library (http://onlinelibrary.wiley.com/journal/10.1002/%28ISSN%292051-5545).

Fulford, K.W.M., Davies, M., Gipps, R., Graham, G., Sadler, J., Stanghellini, G. and Thornton, T. (2013) *The Oxford Handbook of Philosophy and Psychiatry*. Oxford: Oxford University Press.

Fulford, K.W.M., Dewey, S. and King, M. (2015) "Values-based involuntary seclusion and treatment: Value pluralism and the UK's Mental Health Act 2007" in Sadler, J.Z., van Staden, W. and Fulford, K.W.M. (eds) *The Oxford Handbook of Psychiatric Ethics*. Oxford: Oxford University Press.

Fulford, K.W.M., Duhig, L., Hankin, J., Hicks, J. and Keeble, J. (2015) "Values-based assessment in mental health: The 3 keys to a shared approach between service users and service providers" in Sadler, J.Z., van Staden, W. and Fulford, K.W.M., (eds) (2015) *The Oxford Handbook of Psychiatric Ethics*. Oxford: Oxford University Press.

Fulford, K.W.M., Peile, E. and Carroll, H. (2012) "'Recovery in schizophrenia: A values wake-up call' Values-based practice element 1: Awareness of values" in Fulford, K.W.M., Peile, E. and Carroll, H., *Essential Values-based Practice: Clinical Stories Linking Science with People*. Cambridge: Cambridge University Press.

Fulford, K.W.M., Peile, E. and Carroll, H. (2012) *Essential Values-based Practice: Clinical Stories Linking Science with People*. Cambridge: Cambridge University Press.

Fulford, K.W.M., Peile, E. and Carroll, H. (2012) "Diabetic control and controllers: Nothing without communication" in Fulford, K.W.M., Peile, E. and Carroll, H., *Essential Values-based Practice: Clinical Stories Linking Science with People*. Cambridge: Cambridge University Press.

Fulford, K.W.M., Smirnov, A.Y.U. and Snow, E. (1993) "Concepts of disease and the abuse of psychiatry in the USSR", *British Journal of Psychiatry*, 162: 801–10.

Fulford, K.W.M., Thornton, T. and Graham, G. (2006) *The Oxford Textbook of Philosophy and Psychiatry*. Oxford: Oxford University Press.

Fulford, K.W.M., Williamson, T. and Woodbridge, K. (2002) "Values-added practice (a values-awareness workshop)", *Mental Health Today*, October: 25–7.

Geary, D.C. (2000) "Evolution and proximate expression of human parental investment", *Psychological Bulletin*, 126: 55–77.

Gerhardt, S. (2004) *Why Love Matters. How Affection Shapes a Baby's Brain*. London: Bruner Routledge.

Gert, B., Culver, C. and Clouser, K. (2006) *Bioethics: A Systematic Approach*. Oxford: Oxford University Press.

Gilbert, P. (2005) *Compassion: Conceptualisations, Research and Use in Psychotherapy*. London: Routledge.

Gilligan, C. (1986) "Reply by Carol Gilligan", *Signs*, 11(2): 324–33.

Gilligan, C. (2003) *In a Different Voice: Psychological Theory and Women's Development*. Cambridge, MA: Harvard University Press.

Gilman, C.P. (1935) *The Living of Charlotte Perkins Gilman: An Autobiography*. New York and London: Appleton-Century.

Gilman, C.P. (1973 [1892]) *The Yellow Wallpaper*. New York: Feminist Press.

Gleeson, J., Cotton, S., Alvarez-Jimenez, M., Wade, D., Gee, D., Crisp, K. Pearce, T., Spiliotacopoulos, D., Newman, B. and McGorry, P. (2013) "A randomized controlled trial of relapse prevention therapy for first-episode psychosis patients: Outcome at 30-month follow-up", *Schizophrenia Bulletin*, 39(2): 436–48.

Glynn, M. and Beresford, P. with Bewley, C., Branfield, F., Jabeer Butt, Croft, S., Dattani Pitt, K., Fleming, J., Flynn, R., Patmore, C., Postle, K. and Turner, M. (2008) *Person-centred Support: What Service Users and Practitioners Say*. York: Joseph Rowntree Foundation.

Godin, P. (2004) "'You don't tick boxes on a form': A study of how community mental health nurses assess and manage risk", *Health, Risk & Society*, 6: 34760.

Goffman, E. (1959) *The Presentation of Self in Everyday Life*. London: Penguin.

Goffman, E. (1967) *Interaction Ritual*. Penguin: London.

Goffman, E. (1990) *Stigma: Notes on the Management of Spoiled Identity.* London: Penguin.

Goldacre, B. (2006) "It's not easy to predict murder – Do the maths". Available at: www.guardian.co.uk/science/2006/dec/09/badscience.uknews (accessed 29 May 2015).

Gosling, J. (2010) "The ethos of involvement as the route to recovery" in Weinstein, J. (ed.) *Mental Health Service User Involvement and Recovery.* London: Jessica Kingsley.

Gramsci, A. (1999) *The Gramsci Reader,* edited by D. Forgacs. London: Lawrence & Wishart.

Greenberg, G. (2013) *The Book of Woe. The DSM and the Unmaking of Psychiatry.* London and Melbourne: Scribe Press.

Greenberg, J. (1964) *I Never Promised You a Rose Garden.* London: Signet.

Greenwood, J. (1993) "The apparent desensitization of nursing students during their professional socialisation: A cognitive perspective", *Journal of Advanced Nursing,* 18: 1471–9.

Grisso, T. and Appelbaum, P. (1998) *Assessing Competence to Consent to Treatment: A Guide for Physicians and Other Health Care Professionals.* New York: Oxford University Press. ISBN 0195103726, 9780195103724.

Gubrium, J. (1986) *Old Timers and Alzheimer's: The Descriptive Organisation of Senility.* London, UK: Jai Press.

Habermas, J. (1986) "Hannah Arendt's communications concept of power" in Lukes, S. (ed.) *Power.* Cambridge: Blackwell.

Hall, S. (1990) "Cultural identity and diaspora", in Rutherford, J. (ed.) *Identity: Community, Culture, Difference.* London: Lawrence & Wishart.

Hamann, J., Mendel, R., Buhner, M., Kissling, W., Cohen, R., Knipfer, E. and Eckstein, H.H. (2011) "How should patients behave to facilitate shared decision making: The doctors' view", *Health Expectations,* 15: 360–6.

Harding, C. (1988) "Course types in schizophrenia: An analysis of European and American studies", *Schizophrenia Bulletin,* 14: 633–43.

Harding, C., Brooks, G., Ashikaga, T., Strauss, J.S. and Breier, A. (1987) "The Vermont longitudinal study of persons with severe illness II: Long-term outcome of subjects who retrospectively met DSM-III criteria for schizophrenia", *American Journal of Psychiatry,* 144(6): 727–35.

Harding, N. and Palfrey, C. (1997) *The Social Construction of Dementia. Confused Professionals?* London: Jessica Kingsley.

Harper, D. and Speed, E. (2012) "Uncovering recovery: The resistible rise of recovery and resilience", *Studies in Social Justice,* 6(1): 9–25.

Harré, R. (1998) *The Singular Self: An Introduction to the Psychology of Personhood.* London: Sage.

Harris, J. (1991) "Unprincipled QALYs: A response to Cubbon", *Journal of Medical Ethics,* 17: 185–8.

Health and Social Care Information Centre (2012) *Inpatients Formally Detained in Hospitals Under the Mental Health Act 1983 and Patients Subject to Supervised Community Treatment – England, 2011–2012, Annual figures,* 24 October. Available at: http://www.hscic.gov.uk/catalogue/PUB08085 (accessed January 2014).

Heginbotham, C. (2012) *Values-Based Commissioning of Health and Social Care.* Cambridge: Cambridge University Press.

Held, V. (2006) *The Ethics of Care: Personal, Political and Global.* Oxford: Oxford University Press.

Heron, J. (1992) *Feeling and Personhood.* London: Sage.

Hicks, J., Keeble, J. and Fulford, K.W.M., (2015) "Mental health co-production in Bristol: Seeking to address the challenges", *Mental Health Today,* January/February: 18–19.

Higgens, A. and McBennett, P. (2007) "The petals of recovery in a mental health context", *British Journal of Nursing,* 16(4): 852–6.

Ho, B.-C., Andreasen, N., Ziebell, S., Pierson, R. and Magnotta, V. (2011) "Long-term antipsychotic treatment and brain volumes: A longitudinal study of first-episode schizophrenia", *Archives of General Psychiatry*, 68(2): 128–37.

Hobbes, T. (2008) *Leviathan*. Oxford: Oxford University Press.

Holland, S. (2010) "Scepticism about the virtue ethics approach to nursing ethics", *Nursing Philosophy*, 11(3): 151–8.

Holloway, F. (2004) "Risk: More questions than answers", *Advances in Psychiatric Treatment*, 10: 273–4.

Hopper, K. and Wanderling, J. (2000) "Revisiting the developed versus developing country distinction in course and outcome in schizophrenia: Results from ISoS, the WHO collaborative follow-up project", *Schizophrenia Bulletin*, 26(4): 835–46.

Hopton, J. (1996) "Towards a critical theory of mental health nursing", *Journal of Advanced Nursing*, 25: 492–500.

Horkheimer, M. (1973) *Critical Theory – Selected Essays*. London and New York: Continuum.

Hornstein, G. (2009) *Agnes's Jacket: A Psychologist's Search for the Meaning of Madness*. New York: Rodale.

Hughes, J.C. and Beatty, A. (2013) "Understanding the person with dementia: A clinicophilosophical case discussion", *Advances in Psychiatric Treatment*, 19: 337–43 doi: 10.1192/apt.bp.112.011098

Hughes, J.C. and Williamson, T. (forthcoming, 2015) *The Dementia Manifesto: Values-Based Practice (VBP) and Dementia Care*. Cambridge: Cambridge University Press.

Hughes, J.C., Louw, S.J. and Sabat, S.R. (eds) (2006) *Dementia: Mind Meaning and the Person*. Oxford: Oxford University Press.

Hustvedt, A. (2011) *Medical Muses: Hysteria in Nineteenth-Century Paris*. London: Blooomsbury.

Hutchinson, P. and Read, R. (2014) "Reframing health care: Philosophy for medicine and human flourishing" in Loughlin, M. (ed.) *Debates in Values-based Practice*. Cambridge: Cambridge University Press.

Huxley, A. (2007) *Brave New World*. London: Vintage.

Hyman, S. (2010) "The diagnosis of mental disorders: the problem of reification", *Annual Review of Clinical Psychology*, 6: 155–79.

Imonioro, O. (2009) *The Recovery Star Model and Cultural Competency: Report of the Recovery Star, BAME Pilot Study*. London: Mental Health Providers Forum.

Ingleby, D. (2008) *New Perspectives on Migration, Ethnicity and Schizophrenia*. Malmo: Malmo University.

Innes, A. and Surr, C. (2001) "Measuring the well-being of people with dementia living in formal care settings: The use of dementia care mapping", *Aging & Mental Health*, 5: 258–68.

Inquiry into the Schizophrenia Label (2014) "Preliminary findings", International Universities Press. Available at: http://www.schizophreniainquiry.org/news/isl-releases-preliminary-fi ndings (accessed 29 May 2015).

Insel, T.R. (2013) "Transforming diagnosis". Available at: www.nimh.nih,gov (accessed 29 May 2015).

IRISS (2010) "Supporting those with dementia: Reminiscence therapy and life story work", *Insights No. 4*. London: Institute for Research and Innovation in Social Services.

Jackson, V. (2001) *In Our Own Voice: African-American Stories of Oppression, Survival and Recovery in Mental Health Systems*. Massachusetts: National Empowerment Center.

Jacobson, N. (2001) "Experiencing recovery: A dimensional analysis of recovery narratives", *Psychiatric Rehabilitation Journal*, 24: 248–56.

Jamison, K. (2011) *An Unquiet Mind. A Memoir of Moods and Madness*. Surrey: Picador.

Jaspers, K. (1997) *General Psychopathology, Volume 2*, translated by J. Hoeing and M. Hamilton, Baltimore: Johns Hopkins University Press.

Johnston, J. (1985) *Paper Daughter*. New York: Knopf.

Joseph, J. (2003) *The Gene Illusion: Genetic Research in Psychiatry and Psychology under the Microscope*. Ross-On-Wye: PCCS Books.

Jowett, S., Walton, I. and Payne, S. (1991) *The NFER Project 2000 Research: An Introduction and Some Interim Issues*, Interim Paper 2, Slough, UK: NFER.

Joyce, T., Hazelton, M., McMillan, M. (2007) "Nurses with mental illness: Their workplace experiences", *International Journal of Mental Health Nursing*, 16: 373–80.

Kalathil J., Russo, J. and Shulkes, D. (2013) *Personal Narratives of Madness: Annotated Bibliography*. Available at: http://global.oup.com/booksites/content/9780199579563/narratives/ (accessed 29 May 2015).

Kalathil, J. (2011) *Recovery and Resilience: African, African-Caribbean and South Asian Narratives of Recovering from Mental Distress*. London: Mental Health Foundation.

Kalathil, J. and Perry, E. (2014) "Speaking about ourselves", *Mental Health Today*, May–June: 21.

Kalathil, J., Collier, B., Bhakta, R., Daniel, O., Joseph, D. and Trivedi, P. (2011) *Recovery and Resilience: African, African-Caribbean and South Asian Women's Narratives of Recovering from Mental Distress*. London: Mental Health Foundation.

Kant, I. (1985) *Foundations of the Metaphysics of Morals*, translated by Lewis White Beck (2nd edn). New York: Macmillan.

Karnieli-Miller, O. and Eiskovits, Z. (2009) "Physician as partner or salesman? Shared decision making in real-time encounters", *Social Science and Medicine*, July, 69(1): 1–8.

Kartalova-O'Doherty, Y. and Tedstone-Doherty, D. (2010) "Recovering from recurrent mental health problems: Giving up and fighting to get better", *International Journal of Mental Health Nursing*, 19: 3–15.

Kaysen, S. (1995) *Girl, Interrupted*. London: Virago.

Kearney, R. and Williams, J. (1996) "Narrative and ethics", *Proceedings of the Aristotelian Society*, Supplementary Papers, 70: 47–61.

Kelly, B. (1998) "Preserving moral integrity: A follow-up study with new graduate nurses", *Journal of Advanced Nursing*, 28(5): 1134–45.

Kempe, M. (1985 [1436]) *The Book of Marjory Kempe*, translated by B.A. Windeatt. New York: Penguin.

King, C., Bhui, K., Fulford, K.W.M., Vasiliou-Theodore, C. and Williamson, T. (2009) *Model Values? Race, Values and Models in Mental Health*. London: Mental Health Foundation.

Kirkpatrick, H. (2008) "A narrative framework for understanding experience of people with severe mental illness", *Archives of Psychiatric Nursing*, 22(2): 61–8.

Kirmayer, L. (2012) "Cultural competence and evidence-based practice in mental health: Epistemic communities and the politics of pluralism", Social Science and Medicine, 75: 249–56.

Kisely, S., Campbell, L.A. and Preston, N. (2005) "Compulsory community and involuntary outpatient treatment for people with severe mental disorders", *Cochrane Database of Systematic Reviews 2005*, 20.

Kitwood, T. (1993) "Person and process in dementia", *International Journal of Psychiatry*, 8: 541–5.

Kitwood, T. (1997) *Dementia Reconsidered: The Person Comes First*. Buckingham, UK: Open University Press.

Kitwood, T. and Bredin, K. (1991) *Person to Person: A Guide to the Care of Those with Failing Mental Powers* (2nd edn). Loughton, UK: Gale Centre.

Kleinman, A. (1977) "Depression, somatization and the 'new cross-cultural psychiatry'", *Social Science and Medicine*, 11: 3–10.

Klerman, G.L. (1978) "The evolution of a scientific nosology" in Shershow, J.C. (ed.) *Schizophrenia, Science and Practice*. Cambridge, MA: Harvard University Press.

Kramer, P. (1997) *Listening to Prozac*. London: Penguin.

Kupfer, D., First, M. and Regier, D. (eds) (2002) *A Research Agenda for DSM-V*. Washington, DC: American Psychiatric Association.

Kutchins, H. and Kirk, S. (1997) *Making Us Crazy: DSM: The Psychiatric Bible and the Creation of Mental Disorders*. New York: Free Press.

Laing, R.D. (1967) *The Politics of Experience and the Bird of Paradise.* London: Penguin.

Laing, R.D. (1990) *The Divided Self.* London: Penguin.

Larner, W. (2000) "Neo-liberalism; Policy, ideology, governmentality", *Studies in Political Economy,* 63: 5–25.

Laurence, J. (2003) *Pure Madness: How Fear Drives the Mental Health System.* London: Routledge.

Layard, R. (2011) *Happiness: Lessons from a New Science* (2nd edn). London: Penguin.

Lean, M. and Pajonk, F.-G. (2003) "Patients on atypical anti-psychotic drugs. Another high-risk group for type 2 diabetes", *Diabetes Care,* 26(5): 1597–605.

Leary, M.R. and Tangney, J. (eds) (2002) *Handbook of Self and Identity.* New York: Guilford Press.

LeCroy, C. and Holschuh, J. (2012) *First Person Accounts of Mental Illness and Recovery.* Chichester: Wiley.

Lester, H. and Glasby, J. (2006) *Mental Health Policy and Practice.* New York: Palgrave Macmillan.

Littlewood, R. and Lipsedge, M. (1997) *Aliens and Alienists: Ethnic Minorities and Psychiatry.* London: Routledge.

Lombardo, P.A. (1985) "Three generations, no imbeciles: new light on Buck v. Bell", *New York University Law Review,* 60: 30–62.

Lowe, L. (1872) *Gagging in Madhouses as Practised by Government Servants in a Letter to the People, by One of the Gagged.* London: Burns.

Lu, H., Barriball, K.L., Zhang, X. and While, A.E. (2012) "Job satisfaction among hospital nurses revisited: A systematic review", *International Journal of Nursing,* 49(8): 1017–38.

Lukács, G. (1971) *History and Class Consciousness,* translated by R. Livingstone. London: Merlin Press.

Lukes, S. (1986) *Power. A Radical View.* Basingstoke: Palgrave Macmillan.

Lupton, D. (1997) "Foucault and the medicalisation critique" in Petersen, A. and Bunton, R. (eds) (1997) *Foucault, Health and Medicine.* London and New York: Routledge.

Maben, J., Latter, S. and Macleod Clark, J. (2006) "The theory-practice gap: Impact of professional-bureaucratic work conflict on newly-qualified nurses", *Journal of Advanced Nursing,* 55(4): 465–77.

MacIntyre, A. (1982) *After Virtue – A Study in Moral Theory.* London: Duckworth.

Mackintosh, C. (2006) "Caring: The socialisation of pre-registration student nurses: A longitudinal qualitative descriptive study", International Journal of Nursing Studies, 43: 953–62.

Macpherson, W. (1999) The Stephen Lawrence Inquiry. Available at: https://www.gov.uk/government/uploads/system/uploads/attachment_data/file/277111/4262.pdf (accessed 14 July 2015).

Maden, T. (2006) *Review of Homicides by Patients with Serious Mental Illness.* London: Imperial College.

Mancini, M. (2007) "A qualitative analysis of turning points in the recovery process", *American Journal of Psychiatric Rehabilitation,* 10: 223–44.

Marx, K. (1988) *Selected Writings,* edited by D. McLellan. Oxford: Oxford University Press.

Maslow, A. (1970) *Motivation and Personality* (2nd edn). Harper & Rowe, New York, NY: Harper & Rowe.

Matthias, M., Salyers, M., Rollins, A. and Frankel, R. (2012) "Decision making in recovery orientated mental health care", *Psychiatric Rehabilitation Journal,* 35(4): 305–14.

MCA (Mental Capacity Act) (2005) *Code of Practice.* London: TSO.

McCarthy, B. (2006) "Translating person-centred care: A case study of preceptor nurses and their teaching practices in acute care areas", *Journal of Clinical Nursing,* 15: 629–38.

McCormack, B. (2003) "A conceptual framework for person-centred practice with older people", *International Journal of Nursing Practice,* 9: 202–9.

McCormack, B. (2004) "Person-centredness in gerontological nursing: An overview of the literature", *Journal of Clinical Nursing,* 13: 31–8.

McCormack, B. and Reed, J. (2006) "Editorial: Evidence-based health-care – A lot of bull?", *International Journal of Older Peoples Nursing,* 1: 129–30.

McCormick, M., Wallcraft, J. and Walsh, M. (eds) *Mental Health Still Matters*. Palgrave. Milton Keynes.

McCurdy, D.B. (1998) "Personhood, spirituality, and hope in the care of human beings with dementia", *Journal of Clinical Ethics*, 9: 81–91.

McKee, K., Wilson, F., Elford, H., Goudie, F., Chung, M.C., Bolton, G. and Hinchliff, S. (2002) *Evaluating the Impact of Reminiscence on the Quality of Life of Older People*. Sheffield: Sheffield Institute of Studies on Ageing, University of Sheffield.

McMahon, D. (2006) *The Pursuit of Happiness. A History from the Greeks to the Present*. London: Penguin Books.

McNamara, A. and du Brul, S. (eds) (2004) *Navigating the Space between Brilliance and Madness: A Reader and Roadmap of Bipolar Worlds*. New York: Icarus Project.

Mead, G.H. (1934) *Mind, Self and Society from the Standpoint of a Social Behaviourist*. Chicago: University of Chicago Press.

Mead, S. and Copeland, M. (2000) "What recovery means to us: Consumer perspectives", *Community Mental Health Journey*, 36(3): 315–28.

Mental Health Act (1983/2007) *Code of Practice*. London: TSO.

Mental Health Alliance (2005) "Towards a better Mental Health Act: The Mental Health Alliance Policy Agenda", Mental Health Alliance. Available at: http://www.mentalhealthalliance.org.uk/pre2007/documents/AGENDA2.pdf (accessed 29 May 2015)

Mental Health Foundation (2012) "Peer support". Available at: http://www.mentalhealth.org.uk/helpinformation/mental-health-a-z/P/peer-support/ (accessed October 2013).

Metzl, J. (2010) *The Protest Psychosis: How Schizophrenia became a Black Disease*. Boston: Beacon Press.

Mill, J.S. (2004) "Utilitarianism", in Mill, J.S. and Bentham, J. (2004) *Utilitarianism and Other Essays*, edited by Alan Ryan. London: Penguin.

Mill, J.S. (2006) *On Liberty*. London: Penguin Classics.

Miller, P. and Rose, N. (1986) (eds) *The Power of Psychiatry*. Cambridge, UK: Polity Press.

Mills, C. (2014) *Decolonising Global Mental Health: The Psychiatrisation of the Majority World*. London: Routledge.

Mind (2009) *Personalisation in Mental Health: Our View of the Evidence*. London: Mind.

Mind (2011) *Listening to Experience: An Independent Inquiry into Acute and Crisis Mental Health Care*. London: Mind.

Minkowitz, T. and Dhanda, A. (eds) (2006) *First Person Stories on Forced Interventions and Being Deprived of Legal Capacity*. Pune: WNUSP and BAPU Trust.

Mishler, E.G. (1986) *Research Interviewing: Context and Narrative*. Cambridge, MA: Harvard University Press.

Moncrieff, J. (2003) *Is Psychiatry for Sale? An Examination of the Influence of the Pharmaceutical Industry on Academic and Practical Psychiatry*, Maudsley Discussion Paper. London: Institute of Psychiatry.

Moncrieff, J. (2008) *The Myth of the Chemical Cure: A Critique of Psychiatric Drug Treatment*. Basingstoke: Palgrave Macmillan.

Moncrieff, J. (2009) "A critique of the dopamine hypothesis of schizophrenia and psychosis", *Harvard Review of Psychiatry*, 17(3): 214–25.

Moncrieff, J. (2010) "Psychiatric diagnosis as a political device", Social Theory and Health, 8: 370–82.

Moore, A., Hope, T. and Fulford, K.W.M. (1994) "Mild mania and well-being", *Philosophy, Psychiatry, & Psychology*, 1(3): 165–78.

Morgan, A. and Felton, A. (2013) "From constructive engagement to coerced recovery" in Coles, S., Keenan, S. and Diamond, B. (eds) *Madness Contested: Power and Practice*. Ross on Wye: PCCS Books.

Morgan, C., Dazzan, P., Morgan, K., Jones, P., Harrison, G., Leff, J., Murray, R. and Fearon, P. (2006) "First episode psychosis and ethnicity: Initial findings from the AESOP study", *World Psychiatry*, 5(1): 40–6.

Morgan, J. (2007) *Giving Up Culture of Blame, Risk Assessment and Risk Management in Psychiatric Practice*. London: Royal College of Psychiatrists.

Morgan, S. (2000) *Clinical Risk Management: A Clinical Tool and Practitioner Manual*. London: Sainsbury Centre for Mental Health.

Morrall, P. and Hazleton, M. (2000) "Architecture signifying social control: The restoration of asylumdom in mental health care?", *International Journal of Mental Health Nursing*, 9(2): 89–96.

Mountain, D. and Shah, P. (2008) "Recovery and the medical model", *Advances in Psychiatric Treatment*, 14: 241–4.

Mozley, C.G., Huxley, P., Sutcliffe, C., Bagley, H., Burns, A., Challis, D. and Cordingley, L. (1999) "'Not knowing where I am doesn't mean I don't know what I like': Cognitive impairment and quality of life responses in elderly people", *International Journal of Geriatric Psychiatry*, 14: 776–83.

Muir-Cochrane, E. (2006) "Medical co-morbidity risk factors and barriers to care for people with schizophrenia", *Journal of Psychiatric and Mental Health Nursing*, 13: 447–52.

Munro, E. and Rumgay, J. (2000) "Role of risk assessment in reducing homicides by people with mental illness", *British Journal of Psychiatry*, 176: 116–20.

Musalek, M. (2010) "Social aesthetics and the management of addiction", *Current Opinion in Psychiatry*, 23: 530–5.

Nagai-Jacobson, M.G. and Burkhardt, M.A. (1996) "Viewing persons as stories: A perspective for holistic care", *Alternative Therapies*, 2, 54–8.

National Institute for Mental Health England (2004) "The National Framework of Values for Mental Health". Originally published on the NIMHE website at www.nimhe.org.uk/ValuesBasedPractise. Now available online at the Values-based Practice website (accessed 29 May 2015) or in Woodbridge, K. and Fulford, K.W.M. (2004) *"Whose Values?" A Workbook for Values-based Practice in Mental Health Care*. London: Sainsbury Centre for Mental Health.

National Institute for Mental Health in England (NIMHE) and the Care Services Improvement Partnership (2008) *3 Keys to a Shared Approach in Mental Health Assessment*. London: Department of Health.

NEF (New Economics Foundation) – Slay, J. and Stephens, L. (2013) *Co-production in Mental Health A Literature Review*. Available at: http://s.bsd.net/nefoundation/default/page/fi le/ca0975b7cd88125 c3e_ywm6bp3l1.pdf (accessed 10 April 2014).

Newman, F. (2000) "Does a story need a theory? Understanding the methodology of narrative therapy" in Fee, D. (ed.) *Pathology and the Postmodern: Mental Illness as Discourse and Experience*. London and New York: Sage.

NICE (National Institute for Health Care Excellence) (2012) *Service User Experience in Adult Mental Health – NICE Guidance on Improving the Experience of Care for People using Adult NHS Mental Health Services*. British Psychological Society and Royal College of Psychiatrists, National Collaborating Centre for Mental Health.

NIMHE (2003) *Inside Outside. Improving Mental Health Services for Black and Minority Ethnic Communities in England*. Available at: http://webarchive.nationalarchives.gov.uk/20130107105354/http://www.dh. gov.uk/prod_consum_dh/groups/dh_digitalassets/@dh/@en/documents/digitalasset/dh_4019452. pdf (accessed 29 May 2015).

Noddings, N. (2012) "The language of care ethics", *Knowledge Quest*, 40(5): 52–6.

Nolan, M., Davies, S. and Grant, G. (2001) "Integrating perspectives" in *Working with Older People and Their Families: Key Issues in Policy and Practice*, Nolan, M., Davies, S. and Grant, G. (eds). Buckingham: Open University Press.

Nolan, M.R., Davis, S. and Grant, G. (eds) (2003) *Working with Older People and Their Families: Key Issues in Policy and Practice*. Buckingham: Open University Press.

Norfolk, Suffolk and Cambridgeshire Strategic Health Authority (2003) "Independent Inquiry into the death of David Bennett". Norfolk, Suffolk and Cambridgeshire Strategic Health Authority.

Nozick, R. (1969) "Coercion" in *Philosophy, Science and Method: Essays in Honour of Ernest Nagel*, Morgenbesser, S., Suppes, P. and White, M. (eds). New York: St Martin's Press.

Nussbaum, M. (2003) "Capabilities as fundamental entitlements: Sen and social justice", *Feminist Economics*, 9 (2–3): 33–59.

O'Brien, A.J. and Golding, C.G. (2003) "Coercion in mental healthcare: The principle of least restrictive", *Journal of Psychiatric and Mental Health Nursing*, 10: 167–73.

O'Brien, A.J., McKenna, B. and Kydd, R. (2009) "Compulsory community mental health treatment: Literature review", *International Journal of Nursing Studies*, 46: 1245–55.

O'Byrne, P. and Holmes, D. (2007) "The micro-fascism of Plato's good citizen: Producing dis(order) through the construction of risk", *Nursing Philosophy*, 8(2): 92–101.

O'Hagan, M. (1996) "Two accounts of mental distress" in Read, J. and Reynolds, J, (eds) *Speaking Our Minds: An Anthology*. Basingstoke: Palgrave Macmillan.

O'Keefe, M., Hills, A., Doyle, M., McCreadie, C., Scholes, S., Constantine, R., Tinker, A., Manthorpe, J., Biggs, S. and Erens, B. (2007) *UK Study of Abuse and Neglect of Older People. Prevalence Survey Report*. King's College, London: National Centre for Social Research.

O'Neill, O. (1994) "Kantian ethics", in Singer, P. (ed.) *A Companion to Ethics*. Oxford: Blackwell.

Office for National Statistics (2013) *Personal Well-being across the UK, 2012–13*. Available at: http://www.ons.gov.uk/ons/dcp171778_328486.pdf (accessed 10 December 2013).

Olsen, D.P. (2003) "Influence and coercion: Relational and rights-based ethical approaches to forced psychiatric treatment", *Journal of Psychiatric and Mental Health Nursing*, 10(6): 705–12.

Packard, E.P.W (1874) *Modern Persecutions, or Insane Asylums Unveiled, As Demonstrated by the Report of the Investigating Committee of the Legislature of Illinois, Volumes I and II*. Hartford, CT: Case, Lockwood & Brainard.

Packard, E.P.W. (1866) *Marital Power Exemplified in Mrs. Packard's Trial and Self-Defense from the Charge of Insanity; or, Three Years Imprisonment for Religious Belief, by the Arbitrary Will of a Husband, with an Appeal to the Government to so Change the Laws as to Afford Legal Protection to Married Women*. Hartford, CT: Case, Lockwood.

Parker, C. (2001) "Review of mental health legislation in the UK", *Updates*, Volume 4(5). London: Mental Health Foundation.

Parker, I., Georgaca, E., Harper, D., McLaughlin, T. and Stowell-Smith, M. (eds) (1995) *Deconstructing Psychopathology*. London: SAGE.

Patel, V., Boardman, J., Prince, M. and Bhugra, D. (2006) "Returning the debt: How rich countries can invest in mental health capacity in developing countries", World Psychiatry, 5(2): 67–70.

Paterson, B. and Stark, C. (2001) "Social policy and mental illness in England in the 1990s: Violence, moral panic and critical discourse", *Journal of Psychiatric and Mental Health Nursing*, 8: 257–67.

Pattoni, L. (2012) "Strengths-based approaches for working with individuals", *Insights* No. 16. London: Institute for Research and Innovation in Social Services.

Paulsen, J. (2011) "A narrative ethics of care", *Health Care Analysis*, 19(1): 28–40.

Pembroke, L. (2007) "Recovery and arts as activism", *Journal of Psychiatric and Mental Health Nursing*, 14: 768–70.

Pembroke, L. (ed.) (1994) *Self-harm: Perspectives from Personal Experience*. London: Survivors Speak Out.

Perry, E., Barber, J., and England, E. (2013) *A Review of Values-based Commissioning in Mental Health*. London and Birmingham. National Service User Network (NSUN) and NHS East Midlands.

Peterson, D. (ed.) (1982) *A Mad People's History of Madness*. Pittsburgh: University of Pittsburgh.

Pickersgill, M. (2014) "Debating DSM-5: Diagnosis and the sociology of critique", *Journal of Medical Ethics*, 40(8): 521–5.

Pierre, M.P. (2008) "Deconstructing schizophrenia for DSM-V: Challenges for clinical and research agendas", *Clinical Schizophrenia and Related Psychoses*, 2(2): 166–74.

Pilgrim, D. (2005) "Protest and Co-option: The Voice of Mental Health Service Users" in Bell, A. and Lindley, P. (eds) *Beyond the Water Towers: The Unfinished Revolution in Mental Health Services 1985–2005*. London: Sainsbury Centre for Mental Health.

Pilgrim, D. (2007) "New 'mental health' legislation for England and Wales: Some aspects of consensus and conflict", *Journal of Social Policy*, 36(1): 79–95.

Pilgrim, D. (2008) "Recovery and mental health policy", *Chronic Illness*, 4: 295–304.

Pilgrim, D., Tomasini, F. and Vassilev, I. (2010) *Examining Trust in Health Care: A Multi-disciplinary Perspective*. Basingstoke: Palgrave Macmillan.

Plant, N. and Narayanasamy, A. (2013) "Ethical theories", in Stickley, T. and Wright, N. (eds) (2013) *Theories for Mental Health Nursing*. London: Sage.

Porter, R. (2002) *Madness: A Brief History*. Oxford: Oxford University Press.

Post, S.G. (1995) *The Moral Challenge of Alzheimer's Disease*. Baltimore, MD: John Hopkins University Press.

Post, S.G. (2006) "Respectare: Moral respect for the lives of the deeply forgetful" in *Dementia: Mind Meaning and the Person*, Hughes, J.C., Louw, S.J. and Sabat, S.R. (eds). Oxford: Oxford University Press.

Priebe, S., Burton, A., Asby, D., Ashcroft, R., Burns, T., David, A., Eldridge, S., Firn, M., Knapp, M. and McCabe, R. (2009) "Financial incentives to improve adherence to anti-psychotic maintenance medication and non-adherent patients: A cluster randomised controlled trial (PACT)", *BMC Psychiatry*, 9: 61.

Quinton, A. (1973) *The Nature of Things*. London: Routledge.

Radden, J. (ed.) (2004) *The Philosophy of Psychiatry. A Companion*. Oxford: Oxford University Press.

Raphael, D.D. (1981) *Moral Philosophy*. Oxford: Oxford University Press.

Rapp, C. and Goscha, R. (2012) *The Strengths Model: A Recovery Oriented Approach to Mental Health Services* (3rd edn). New York: Oxford University Press.

Rappaport, J. (2000) "1999 Seymour B. Sarason Award. Community narratives: Tales of terror and joy", *American Journal of Community Psychology*, 28: 1–24.

Raptopoulos, A. (2012) "Becoming an Expert by Experience" in Weinstein, J. (ed.) *Mental Health Service User Involvement and Recovery*. London: Jessica Kingsley.

Read, J., Dillon, J. and Lampshire, D. (2014) "How much evidence is required for a paradigm shift in mental health?", *Acta Psychiatrica Scandinavica*, 129: 477–81.

Recovery in the Bin (2015) "18 key principles". Available at: http://studymore.org.uk/binrec.htm (accessed 29 May 2015).

Redman, R. (2005) "The power of narratives", *Research and Theory for Nursing Practice: An International Journal*, 19: 5–7.

Reed, J. and Ground, I. (1997) *Philosophy for Nursing*. London: Arnold.

Repper, J. and Carter, T. (2011) "A review of the literature on peer support in mental health services", *Journal of Mental Health*, 20(4): 392–411.

Repper, J. and Perkins, R. (2003) *Social Inclusion and Recovery: A Model for Mental Health Practice*. Edinburgh: Balliere Tindall.

Repper, J. and Perkins, R. (2003) *Social Inclusion and Recovery*. Edinburgh: Balliere Tindhall.

Repper, J. and Perkins, R. (2009) "Recovery and social inclusion: Changing the mental health agenda" in Brooker, C. and Repper, J. (eds) *Mental Health From Policy to Practice*. Edinburgh: Churchill Livingstone.

Richardson, G. (2008) "Coercion and human rights: A European perspective", *Journal of Mental Health*, 17(3): 245–54.

Ricoeur, P. (1992) *Oneself as Another*, translated by Kathleen Blamey. Chicago: University of Chicago Press.

Roberts, M. (2004) "Psychiatric Ethics: A critical introduction for mental health nurses", *Journal of Psychiatric and Mental health Nursing*, 11(5): 583–8.

Roberts, M. (2008) "Facilitating recovery by making sense of suffering: A Nietzschean perspective", *Journal of Psychiatric and Mental Health Nursing*, 15: 743–8.

Robinson, S., Murrells, T., Hickey G., Clinton, M. and Tingle, A. (2005) *A Tale of Two Courses: Comparing Careers and Competencies of Nurses Prepared via Three-year Degree and Three-year Diploma Courses*. Kings College London Nursing Research Unit, Careers and Working Lives Research. Available at: http://www.kcl.ac.uk/nursing/nru/nru_res_rep.html (accessed 20 September 2005).

Rogers, C. (1980) *A Way of Being*. New York, NY: Houghton Mifflin.

Romme, M. and Escher, S. (1993) *Accepting Voices*. London: MIND.

Romme, M. and Escher, S. (2000) *Making Sense of Voices*. London: MIND.

Romme, M., Escher, S., Dillon, J., Corstens, D. and Morris, M. (2009) *Living with Voices: 50 Stories of Recovery*. Ross on Wye: PCCS Books.

Rose, N. (1999) *Powers of Freedom*. Cambridge: Cambridge University Press.

Rose, N. (2006) *The Politics of Life Itself: Biomedicine, Power and Subjectivity in the 21st Century*. Princeton: Princeton University Press.

Rose, N. (2007) "Beyond medicalisation", *Lancet*, 369(9562): 700–2.

Rose, N. and Abi-Rached, J.M. (2013) *Neuro. The New Brain Sciences and the Management of the Mind*. Princeton: Princeton University Press.

Russo, J. (2012) "'Give me your story and I will take care of the rest?' *The case of Agnes's jacket: A psychologist's search for the meaning of madness*", *Asylum*, winter: 28–30.

Sabat, S.R. (2001) *The Experience of Alzheimer's Disease – Life Through a Tangled Veil*. Oxford: Blackwell.

Sabat, S.R., and Harré, R. (1997) "The Alzheimer's disease sufferer as semiotic subject", *Philosophy, Psychiatry, & Psychology*, 4(2): 145–60.

Sackett, D.L., Straus, S.E., Scott Richardson, W., Rosenberg, W. and Haynes, R.B. (2000) *Evidence-Based Medicine: How to Practice and Teach EBM* (2nd edn). Edinburgh and London: Churchill Livingstone.

Sadler, J.Z. (2005) *Values and Psychiatric Diagnosis*. Oxford: Oxford University Press.

Sadler, J.Z., van Staden, W. and Fulford, K.W.M. (eds) (2015) *The Oxford Handbook of Psychiatric Ethics*. Oxford: Oxford University Press.

Sainsbury Centre for Mental Health (2001) *The Capable Practitioner – A Framework and List of the Practitioner Capabilities required to implement The National Service Framework for Mental Health*. Available at: http://www.centreformentalhealth.org.uk/pdfs/the_capable_practitioner.pdf (accessed 12 December 2013).

Sandel, M. (2012) *What Money Can't Buy: The Moral Limits of Markets*. London: Allen Lane.

Sartorius, N., Chiu, H., Heok, K., Lee, M.-S., Ouyang, W.-C., Sato, M., Yang, Y. and Yu, X. (2014) "Name change for schizophrenia", *Schizophrenia Bulletin*, first published online January 2014.

Sato (2006) "Renaming schizophrenia: A Japanese perspective", *World Psychiatry*, 5(1): 53–5.

Schafer, R. (1981) "Narration in the psychoanalytic dialogue" in Mitchell, W.J.T. (ed.) *On Narrative*. Chicago: Chicago University Press.

Schauer, C., Everett, A., del Vecchio, P. and Anderson, L. (2007) "Promoting the value and practice of shared decision-making in mental health care", *Psychiatric Rehabilitation Journal*, 31(1): 54–61.

Schizophrenia Commission/ Rethink (2012) "Schizophrenia the abandoned illness", Available at: http://www.rethink.org/media/514093/TSC_main_report_14_nov.pdf (accessed 29 May 2015).

SCIE (Social Care Institute for Excellence) (2007) *A Common Purpose: Recovery in Future Mental Health Services*. Available at: http://www.scie.org.uk/publications/positionpapers/pp08.pdf (accessed 29 May 2015).

Scott, A. and Wilson, L. (2011) "Valued identities and deficit identities: Wellness recovery action planning and self-management in mental health", *Nursing Inquiry*, 18(1): 40–9.

Scott, J. (2001) *Power*. Cambridge: Polity Press.

Sedgwick, P. (1982) *Psycho Politics*. London: Pluto Press.

Segal, S. and Burgess, P. (2008) "Use of community treatment orders to prevent psychiatric hospitalisation", *Australian and New Zealand Journal of Psychiatry*, 42: 732–9.

Seltan, J. and Cantor-Graee, E. (2007) "Hypothesis: Social defeat a risk factor for schizophrenia?", *British Journal of Psychiatry*, 191: s9–s12.

Sen, A. (2001) *Development as Freedom*. Oxford: Oxford University Press.

Shah, A., Heginbotham, C., Fulford, K.W.M., Banner, N. and Newbiggin, K. (2009) "The early experience of old age psychiatrists in application of the Mental Capacity Act: Issues for black and minority individuals", *Ethnicity and Inequalities in Health and Social Care*, 2(2): 4–10.

Shah, A.K., Banner, N., Heginbotham, C. and Fulford, K.W.M. (2009) "The application of the Mental Capacity Act 2005 among geriatric psychiatry patients: A pilot study", *International Psychogeriatrics*, 21(5): 922–30.

Shaw, I. and Taplin, S. (2007) "Happiness and mental health policy: A sociological critique", *Journal of Mental Health*, 16(3): 359–73.

Shaw, R., Atkin, K., Becares, L., Albor, C., Stafford, M., Kiernan, K., Nazroo, J., Wilkinson, R. and Pickett, K. (2012) "Impact of ethnic density on adult mental disorders: Narrative review", *British Journal of Psychiatry*, 201: 11–19.

Shepard, J., Boardman, G. and Slade, M. (2008) *Making Recovery a Reality*. London: Centre for Mental Health.

Shingler, A. (2008) *One in a Hundred*. Oregon: Thorntree Press.

Shingler, A. (2008) *One in a Hundred*. Derbyshire: Thorntree Press.

Showalter, E. (1987) *The Female Malady: Women, Madness and English Culture, 1830–1980*. London: Virago Press.

Singer, P. (ed.) (1994) *Ethics*. Oxford: Oxford University Press.

Singh, S. (2007) "Institutional racism in psychiatry: lessons from inquiries", *Psychiatric Bulletin*, 31: 363–5.

Skills for Health (2013) *Revised National Occupational Standards for Mental Health*. Bristol: Skills for Health. Also available at: https://tools.skillsforhealth.org.uk/competence_search/

Slay, J. and Stephens, L. (2013) *Co-production in Mental Health: A Literature Review*. London:New Economics Foundation.

Snow, N. and Austin, W. (2009) "Community treatment orders: the ethical balancing act in community mental health", *Journal of Psychiatric and Mental Health Nursing*, 16: 177–86.

Social Perspectives Network (2007) *Whose Recovery Is It Anyway?* London: SPN.

Spandler, H., Secker, J., Kent, L., Hacking, S. and Shenton, J. (2007) "Catching life: The contribution of arts initiatives to recovery approaches in mental health", *Journal of Psychiatric and Mental Health Nursing*, 14(8): 791–9.

Stacey, G. and Hardy, P. (2011) "Challenging the shock of reality through digital storytelling", *Nurse Education in Practice*, 11(2): 159–64.

Stacey, G., Johnson, K., Stickley, T. and Diamond, B. (2011) "How do nurses cope when values and practice conflict?", *Nursing Times*, 107(5): 20–4.

Stalker, K. (2003) "Managing risk and uncertainty in social work: A literature review", *Journal of Social Work*, 3(2): 211–33.

Stickley, T. and Bonney, S. (2008) "Recovery and mental health: A review of the British literature", *Journal of Psychiatric and Mental Health Nursing*, 15(2): 140–53.

Stickley, T. and Wright, N. (2011) "The British research evidence for recovery. Papers published between 2006 and 2009 (inclusive). Part One: A review of the peer-reviewed literature using a systematic approach", *Journal of Psychiatric and Mental Health Nursing*, 18: 247–56.

Summerfield, D. (2012) "Afterword: Against 'global mental health'", *Transcultural Psychiatry*, 49 (3): 1–12.

Sweeting, H. and Gilhooly, M. (1997) "Dementia and the social phenomenon of social death", *Sociology of Health and Illness*, 19(1): 93–117.

Symonds, B. (1998) "The philosophical and sociological context of mental health care legislation", *Journal of Advanced Nursing*, 27(5): 946–54.

Szasz, T. (1963) *Law, Liberty, and Psychiatry: An Inquiry into the Social Uses of Mental Health Practices*. New York: Macmillan.

Szasz, T. (1972) *The Myth of Mental Illness: Foundations of a Theory of Personal Conduct*. St Albans: Paladin.

Szasz, T. (1976) *Schizophrenia: The Sacred Symbol of Psychiatry*. New York: Basic Books.

Szasz, T. (2010) "Psychiatry, anti-psychiatry, critical psychiatry: What do these terms mean?", *Philosophy, Psychiatry, & Psychology*, 17: 229–32.

Szmukler, G. (2014) "When psychiatric diagnosis becomes an overworked tool", *Journal of Medical Ethics*, 40(8): 517–20.

Szmukler, G. and Appelbaum, P. (2008) "Treatment pressures, leverage, coercion and compulsion in mental health care", *Journal of Mental Health*, 17(3): 233–44.

Szmukler, G. and Holloway, F. (1998) "Mental health legislation is now a harmful anachronism", *Psychiatric Bulletin*, 22: 662–5.

Szmukler, G. and Holloway, F. (2000) "Reform of the Mental Health Act. Health or safety?", *British Journal of Psychiatry*, 177: 196–200.

Tam, L. (2013) "Whither indigenizing the mad movement? Theorising the social relations of race and madness through conviviality" in LeFrançois, B., Menzies, R. and Reumme, G. (eds) *Mad Matters: A Critical Reader in Canadian Mad Studies*. Toronto: Canadian Scholars' Press Inc.

Tenney, L. (2006) "Who fancies a revolution here? The Opal revisited", *Radical Psychology*, vol 5.

Tew, J. (2013) "Recovery capital: What enables a sustainable recovery from mental health difficulties?", *European Journal of Social Work*, 16(3): 360–74.

Thistlethwaite, J. (2012) *Values-based Interprofessional Collaborative Practice*. Cambridge: Cambridge University Press.

Thomas, P. (2008) "Towards a critical perspective on 'narrative loss' in schizophrenia", in Morgan, A. (ed.) *Being Human. Reflections on Mental Distress in Society*. Ross-on-Wye: PCCS Books.

Thomas, P., Seebohm, P., Wallcraft, J., Kalathil, J. and Fernando, S. (2013) "Personal consequences of the diagnosis of schizophrenia: A preliminary report from the Inquiry into the 'schizophrenia' label", *Mental Health and Social Inclusion*, 17(3): 135–9.

Thompson, D. (ed.) (1996) *Oxford English Dictionary*. .Oxford: Oxford University Press.

Thornicroft, G., Brohan, E., Rose, D., Sartorius, N. and Leese, M. (2009) "Global pattern of experienced and anticipated discrimination against people with schizophrenia: A cross-sectional survey", *Lancet*, 373: 408–15.

Thornton, T. (2006) "Tacit knowledge as the unifying factor in EBM and clinical judgement", *Philosophy, Ethics, and Humanities of Medicine*, 1:2doi:10.1186/1747-5341-1-2. Available at http://www.peh-med.com/content/1/1/2. BioMed Central Ltd (accessed 29 May 2015).

Thornton, T. (2007) *Essential Philosophy of Psychiatry*. Oxford: Oxford University Press.

Timimi, S. (2013) "No more psychiatric labels: Campaign to abolish psychiatric diagnostic systems such as ICD and DSM (CAPSID)", *Self and Society*, 40(4): 6–14.

Torrey, E. and Yolken, R. (2010) "Psychiatric genocide: Nazi attempts to eradicate schizophrenia", *Schizophrenia Bulletin*, January, 36(10): 26–32.

Tournier, P. (1978) *Meaning of Persons*. London: SCM Press.

Treffert, D.A. (1973) "Dying with their rights on", *American Journal of Psychiatry*, 130: 1041.

Tucker, B.P. (1998) "Deaf culture, cochlear implants, and elective disability", Hastings Center Report, 28(4): 6–14.

United Nations (2006) *Convention on the Rights of Persons with Disabilities*. Available at http://www.un.org/disabilities/default.asp?id=259 (accessed 21 February).

Van Os, J., Kenis, G. and Rutten, B. (2010) "The environment and schizophrenia", *Nature*, 468: 203–12.

Vassilev, I. and Pilgrim, D. (2007) "Risk, trust and the myth of mental health services", *Journal of Mental Health*, 16(3): 347–57.

Von Wright, G.H. (1963) *The Varieties of Goodness*. London: Routledge & Kegan Paul.

Voren, R. van (2002) "Editorial: The WPA World Congress in Yokohama and the Issue of Political Abuse of Psychiatry in China", *Mental Health Reforms*-1, vol. 7.

Wall, S., Churchill, R., Hotopf, M., Buchanan, A. and Wesseley, S. (1999) *A Systematic Review of Research Relating to the Mental Health Act (1983)*. London: Department of Health.

Wallcraft, J., Schrank, B. and Amering, M. (eds) (2009) *Handbook of Service User Involvement in Mental Health Research*. London: Wiley.

Walsh, J., Stevenson, C., Cutcliffe, J. and Zinck, K. (2008) "Creating a space for recovery focused psychiatric nursing care", *Nursing Inquiry*, 15(3): 251–9.

Watters E (2010). *Crazy Like Us: The Globalization of the American Psyche*. New York: Free Press.

Whitaker, R. (2010) *Anatomy of an Epidemic – Magic Bullets, Psychiatric Drugs and the Astonishing Rise of Mental Illness in America*. New York: Broadway Paperbacks.

WHO (World Health Organization) (2010) *mhGAP Intervention Guide for mental, neurological and substance use disorders in non-specialised health settings*. World Health Organization.

Wilks, T. (2005) "Social work and narrative ethics", *British Journal of Social Work*, 35(8): 1249–64.

Winslow, F. (1854) 'Spiritual pathology; or, the autobiography of the insane', *Journal of Psychological Medicine and Mental Pathology*, 7, July 1: 356–385.

Winslow, F. (1855) 'Autobiography of the insane', *Journal of Psychological Medicine and Mental Pathology*, 1, July 1: 338–353.

Wisdom, J., Bruce, K., Saedi, G., Weis, T. and Green, A. (2008) "'Stealing me from myself': Identity and recovery in personal accounts of mental illness", *Australian and New Zealand Journal of Psychiatry*, 42(6): 489–95.

Woodbridge, K. and Fulford, K.W.M. (2004) *"Whose Values?" A Workbook for Values-based Practice in Mental Health Care*. London: Sainsbury Centre for Mental Health.

Woodbridge, K., Williamson, T., Allott, P., Fleming, B. and Fulford, K.W.M. (2005) "Values, mental health and mental capacity: Debates in cyberspace", *Mental Health Review*, 10(4): 25–9.

Woods, A. (2013) "Rethinking 'patient testimony' in the medical humanities: The case of Schizophrenia Bulletin's first person accounts", *Journal of Literature and Science*, 6(1): 38–54.

Woods, A. (2013) "The Voice Hearer", *Journal of Mental Health*, 22(3): 263–70.

Woods, R.T. (2001) "Discovering the person with Alzheimer's disease: Cognitive, emotional and behavioural aspects", *Ageing and Mental Health*, 5(Suppl. 1): S7–S16.

Woodson, M. (1994 [1932]) *Behind the Door of Delusion*. New York: Macmillan.

Worthington, A. and Hannan, R. (2013) *The Triangle of Care - Carers Included: A Guide to Best Practice in Mental Health Care in England* (2nd edn). London: Carers Trust (www.carers.org).

Worthington, A., and Hannan, R. (2013) *The Triangle of Care – Carers Included: A Guide to Best Practice in Mental Health Care in England* (2nd edn). London: Carers Trust.

Yates, I., Holmes, G. and Priest, H. (2012) "Recovery, place and community mental health services", *Journal of Mental Health*, 21(2): 104–13.

Zerubavel, N. and Wright, M. (2012) "The dilemma of the wounded healer", *Psychotherapy*, 49(4): 482–91.

Index